MW00532208

THE VALUE OF THE HUMANITIES

The Value of the Humanities provides a critical account of the principal arguments used to defend the value of the Humanities. Engaging closely with contemporary literary and philosophical work in the field, Helen Small distinguishes between arguments that retain strong Victorian roots and those that have developed or been substantially altered since. Unlike many works in this field, Small does not offer a polemic or manifesto, her purpose is to explore the grounds for each argument, and to test its validity for the present day. Tough-minded, alert to changing historical conditions for argument and changing styles of rhetoric, it promises to sharpen the terms of the public debate.

Helen Small is Professor of English at Oxford University and Jonathan and Julia Aisbitt Fellow of English at Pembroke College, Oxford. She is the author of *The Long Life* (OUP, 2007) (awarded the Truman Capote Award for Literary Criticism 2008) and the editor of *The Public Intellectual* (2002).

THE VALUE
OF THE
HUMANITIES

HELEN SMALL

OXFORD
UNIVERSITY PRESS

OXFORD
UNIVERSITY PRESS

Great Clarendon Street, Oxford, OX2 6DP,
United Kingdom

Oxford University Press is a department of the University of Oxford.
It furthers the University's objective of excellence in research, scholarship,
and education by publishing worldwide. Oxford is a registered trade mark of
Oxford University Press in the UK and in certain other countries

© Helen Small 2013

The moral rights of the author have been asserted

First published 2013
First published in paperback 2016

Published in the United States of America by Oxford University Press
198 Madison Avenue, New York, NY 10016, United States of America

British Library Cataloguing in Publication Data
Data available

Library of Congress Cataloging in Publication Data
Data available

ISBN 978-0-19-968386-4 (Hbk.)
ISBN 978-0-19-872805-4 (Pbk.)

Contents

Acknowledgements

I acknowledge with gratitude the support received in writing this book from Pembroke College, Oxford, and the University of Oxford in the form of sabbatical leave. Its completion was enabled, sooner than would otherwise have been possible, by a nine-month Research Fellowship grant from the Arts and Humanities Research Council (UK). I am grateful to Vicky Drew, in the University of Oxford Humanities Division, for guiding me through the complexities of the applications process.

My greatest debt is to the people who have read the typescript in whole or in very large part and commented in detail: Isobel Armstrong, Stefan Collini, John Kerrigan, Michael Levenson, Bruce Robbins, and Sally Shuttleworth. I owe special thanks to Roger Crisp for casting a clear philosophical eye on the Introduction, Chapters 3 and 5, and the Conclusion; to Nicholas Shrimpton for giving me the benefit of his knowledge of Arnold for Chapter 2; and to Peter Robinson for a very close reading of Chapter 5; also to Peter Riviere for reading Chapter 1 with the experience of an anthropologist who chaired his department through the reorganization of Oxford University into a divisional arrangement placing his department (disputedly) in the Social Sciences rather than the Humanities. I am grateful to Wilfred Beckerman and Ken Mayhew for guiding my reading in the economic literature covered in Chapter 3; also to Richard Pring for help with the education literature. Chapter 4 was assisted by thought-provoking discussion in the early stages with Frances Cairncross and Hamish McRae, and Chapter 3 by detailed comments from David Keen on the penultimate draft. Individual chapters have benefited greatly from exposure to intelligent audiences in the following places: Cambridge University, the University of Charlottesville (Virginia), University of Chicago, Columbia University, Oxford University (Humanities Division,

Balliol MCR, and Jesus College English Society), Rutgers University, and the University of Delhi. Special thanks are due to my hosts on these occasions: Helen Cooper, Michael Levenson, Jim Chandler, Bruce Robbins, Sally Shuttleworth, Sumudu Watugala, Olivia Hanson, Kate Flint, Brinda Bose and Prasanta Chakravorty. I owe a particular debt to Michael Levenson as the inaugurating spirit of the 'Global Humanities' initiative—an ongoing series of conferences that aims to broaden perspectives on advocacy for the humanities beyond the immediate pressures of their national situations, and enable better-informed comparisons between them. If the imprint of those discussions on this book is not as visible as it might be, this is primarily because my focus is on the rhetorical and philosophical analysis of arguments rather than on institutional and political settings, which are subject to constant and sometimes rapid change. I have, nevertheless, learned much from exposure to different national conditions of debate, and very different kinds and degrees of pressure on the humanities to account for themselves.

Tim Gardam spotted the politically pressing nature of this subject early on, urged me to write about it, and continued to ask me the hard questions throughout. Such as it is, this book is for him, with love.

A small portion of the material in Chapter 3 (on Mill crying) appeared in ' "Letting Oneself Go": John Stuart Mill and Helmuth Plessner on Tears', *Litteraria Pragensia* 22/43 *Towards a Lachrimology: Tears in Literature and Cultural History*, ed., Timothy Webb (July 2012), 112–27. The rest of this book is published here for the first time.

Introduction

The humanities might ideally find justification simply in our doing them. The act of justification has seemed to many humanities scholars to beg more than one question: that the value of their subject area is in question, and that the value is capable of being expressed in the mode of justification. The particular form of justification that involves articulating reasons why we should consider the higher study of the humanities (university teaching and research) a public good is a modern undertaking, driven by institutional, political, and economic pressures. Its practitioners can look for inspiration to two related genres with a distinguished history: 'the defence of poetry' and advocacy for 'the idea of the university'. The second of those genres is often now seen as imperilled, discredited, or (in its liberal forms at least) entirely defunct; the first is in rather better shape, but its concern is with only one aspect of the broad range of practices that have come to be grouped, since the 1940s, under the term 'humanities'. The value of the humanities certainly includes qualities associated with poetry and with liberal education, but the dual comparison highlights a problem of scale: any claims made for 'the humanities' must be rather less specific than in the case of poetry, rather more specific than in the case of the university. Given the difficulties, there is a serious temptation to insist that ongoing practical commitment is enough. And yet, there remain situations in which it is, obviously, necessary to respond to demands from government, and from university administrators who have to answer to government, that those who study and teach the humanities should be able to articulate the public value of their work: giving reasons why their subject area matters comparatively with other subject areas, and why it matters in its own right.

The hardest of those situations involves justifying the humanities' claim to a share of the public budget for research. This book was written against

a background of intense public debate about successive British governments' incremental retreat from the idea that the state should bear most of
the economic cost of higher education. The state still pays, however, for
research in the humanities, as it pays also for research in the social sciences
and sciences; it underwrites the cost of every undergraduate's education,
and it subsidizes graduate education for many. The most politically pressing question, at the point of writing, is what the state thinks it is paying
for, in the case of the humanities, and whether the people who make
decisions about public spending can be helped to recognize the distinctive
nature of humanities scholarship (a more accurate word than research[1]),
and distinctive contributions to the public good.[2]

The primary aim of the following pages is to examine the most
commonly proffered reasons why the study of the humanities has
distinctive purpose and value for us as individuals and as a society. My
hope is that, insofar as the approach here is taxonomic, it may assist
those tasked with making decisions about the respective claims on the
public purse of incommensurable, but not incomparable, goods. (The
Conclusion to this book explains in greater detail what I understand to
be involved in the problem of comparing incommensurables.) In such
practical decision-making circumstances, it is desirable, for the sake of
accuracy and clarity, to understand that there are multiple distinct ways
in which the humanities can be said to have public value, to be cognizant of the different senses of the term 'value' involved, the different
contexts in which they hold good, and the quite different kinds of contribution made to the public good. The dual ambition of *The Value of
the Humanities* is that it may, to borrow a phrase from the American
critic Amanda Anderson (in turn reworking a title of Trollope), improve
'the way we argue now'—as academics, debating among ourselves, and
as representatives of our universities or our disciplines facing outwards
to the general public; also that it may improve the way 'we' as a society
debate the public good of the humanities. However public the book's
external prompts and hoped-for effects, I would not have written it had
the subject not seemed attractively difficult. The taxonomic approach is,
at base, a sign of someone trying to get her thoughts in order on a sub-

---

[1] See Stefan Collini, 'Against Prodspeak: "Research" in the Humanities', in his *English
Pasts: Essays in History and Culture* (Oxford: Oxford University Press, 1999), 233–51.
[2] See esp. the essays collected in Jonathan Bate (ed.), *The Public Value of the Humanities*
(London: Bloomsbury, 2011).

ject no less tricky for being very well worn, and no less personally involving for having to do with the public good.

The following chapters identify five arguments for the value of the humanities that have been influential historically and that still have persuasive power. Each of them can yield more specific arguments, which I treat here as logically 'subordinate' or attendant, but which others might want to treat as distinctive and deserving of more notice in their own right. Together they offer a pluralistic account of value. One of my assumptions, throughout, has been that any persuasive account of the humanities' contribution to the public good has to be so plural, and that pluralism (at this level) does not entail incoherence. It is an understandable consequence of the political pressure to produce compelling justifications that many advocates for the public value of the humanities have sought to locate a single claim that will over-power all imagined resistance. Hence, in part, the popularity in recent years of the 'Democracy Needs Us' defence. There is no such all-silencing justification to be had: rather a number of distinct defences, each arising out of particular ways of thinking about value, purpose, and the nature of the implied opposition. A defence is, after all, a defence against a perceived threat, which may be a defined set of alter-native needs and values (economic utility, for example; or an exclusive empiricism; or a narrowly quantitative estimation of human happi-ness), or it may be the more impersonal threat posed by an inhospita-ble economic climate in which all public goods are subject to much tougher demands for justification. In all these contexts, not just the last, the threat to the humanities will be one facet of a threat to the good working of the university as a whole. A defence that pits one area of intellectual activity against the others risks becoming 'a raft of Medusa', as the historian John Burrow once animatedly observed: 'a boat-load of castaways cannibalizing each other to survive.'[3] 'Ironic high comedy', he suggested, may be preferable, under really unfavour-able conditions, to the default temptation towards 'lament', or the 'tragic dignity' of defending 'a last bastion': 'the prospect of death by starvation', he added with comic exaggeration (and more optimisti-cally than not), 'concentrates the mind'.

---

[3] 'The English Tradition of Liberal Education' (review of Sheldon Rothblatt, *Tradition and Change in English Liberal Education* (1976)), *History of Education Quarterly* 20/2 (1980), 247–53 (252, 248, 247, 252–3).

The main claims for the value of the humanities are:

1. that they study the meaning-making practices of the culture, focusing on interpretation and evaluation with an indispensable element of subjectivity. Strictly speaking this is not a claim for value: it is a justification for the humanities based on perceptions of their distinctive disciplinary character and their distinctive understanding of what constitutes knowledge—differentiating them from the social sciences and the sciences where the emphasis on subjectivity is less strong, though not nil. Any assertions of value attached will be secondary to that description of purpose. I place this claim first because it has a kind of logical priority; also because it commands widespread conviction, and it is, I think, right. It has, however, accrued supporting, often incorrect assumptions about the disciplinary differences between the humanities, the sciences, and the social sciences. The traditional point of comparison (and sometimes opposition) for the humanities has been the sciences. More recently, there has been a shift to casting the social sciences in that role, given the influence they are seen as exerting on government through schools of economics and business and management. I argue that it is vital to preserve a core description of the distinctiveness of humanistic interpretation (there are clear and definitive differences between the kinds of work pursued in the different faculties of universities), but there are good reasons to be wary of reinventing the two cultures debate with the social sciences now mis-described as the antagonist.

2. the claim that the humanities are useful to society in ways that put pressure on how governments commonly understand use, especially the prioritization of economic usefulness and the means of measuring it. There is an old line of argument that the humanities are necessarily (some will say laudably) useless, or at a remove from accounts of practical ends and economic utility. This has been a common line of resistance to political economists from Adam Smith onwards who have stressed usefulness as a desirable aim of publicly funded education. More recent advocates for the humanities have worked hard to invert the long-standing defence, arguing (with good evidence) that they make a significant contribution to the knowledge economy and to the economy proper—measurable in terms of the benefits to GDP, footfalls in bookshops, museums, theatres, heritage sites, and so forth. Though some who hang on to the old claim defend it absolutely (deeming the value of the humanities to be deformed or betrayed as soon as questions of utility or application are brought into consideration), a more plausible interpretation

treats usefulness as a legitimate but only minor or secondary, and often accidental, aspect of humanities scholarship's public value. I am particularly interested in the version of this moderate claim that sees the practical utility of the humanities as pertinent to the evaluation of a basic or primary education, but diminishing in importance as one goes up the scale into higher education, where one is, almost by definition, dealing with forms of enquiry whose value is more intangible or not yet known. This tapering away of usefulness will be less true for some other disciplines (notably medicine, and the applied sciences and social sciences), but there will be a strong measure of truth in the description wherever new and unfettered intellectual enquiry is involved.

3. the claim that the humanities have a contribution to make to our individual and collective happiness. This may be the least trusted line of defence now, but it has a distinguished history and renewed topicality within government at the time of writing. Efforts to understand gains to the public good in ways that go deeper than economic benefits have received serious attention in recent years, and there have been warm encouragements to think of the emotions and passions as, themselves, goods. Chapter 3 ('Socrates Dissatisfied') explores the grounds for a qualitative hedonistic argument for the humanities, testing its weight as a means of rebalancing arguments that stress too exclusively the humanities' critical function. The core assertion here is not the (overpitched) one that 'the humanities will make you happy'; rather, that the humanities can help us to understand better what happiness is, how we may better put ourselves in the way of it, and how education may improve the kind and quality of some of our pleasures. For Mill the impediment in the way of securing the larger claim (that they can improve the quality of the society's happiness) was the difficulty of persuading individuals interested in their own happiness, and presumed to be egoistically motivated, why they should care also for the collective or general well-being. That problem can still detain politicians; it is less likely to worry utilitarian philosophers, for whom the goal can just consist in individual psychological improvements.

4. 'Democracy Needs Us'. This fourth claim is the most politically ambitious argument now regularly heard for the humanities in Britain. It is clearly a claim one would want to have on one's side, if it can be made secure. It has a proximate source in the American liberal arts tradition and prominent recent exponents in Martha Nussbaum, Geoffrey Harpham,

and (in the UK) Francis Mulhern. Its longer roots lie in Socrates' claim to be 'a sort of gadfly, given to the *Polis*'. Chapter 4 examines the strengths and potential weaknesses of the classical model, making a case for adapting and modernizing what was, in its origins, a description of the philosopher as isolated agitant (not, as it now needs to be, a description befitting institutionally based professionals). I suggest that we should treat with caution any version that lends unduly narrowed and exclusive importance to the humanities on the basis of their (serious, but not *definitive*) role in assisting informed and properly critical perspectives on social and political life. Proponents of the 'democracy needs us' argument also need to work harder if they are to explain satisfactorily how and why, when adopted by higher education professors and students, it does not commit us to a guardianship model of the democracy that many would instinctively resist. Should we not rather trust the intelligence of the majority of sufficiently but not 'highly' educated people? With those caveats in place, the claim stands that the humanities, centrally concerned as they are with the cultural practices of reflection, argument, criticism, and speculative testing of ideas, have a substantial contribution to make to the good working of democracy.

5. The final claim explored here is that the humanities matter for their own sake. A common feature of all the other justifications treated is that they are consequentialist, resting on a conviction that the humanities have good effects in the world by their impact on our cultural life, our happiness, our politics. That consequentialism will be attractive to anyone tasked with demonstrating the humanities' public benefit, but it neglects what has often been thought of as the 'intrinsic value' of the objects studied. With good reason. Intrinsic value has been something of an embarrassment as a criterion for aesthetic and other modes of judgement. It runs counter to many modern critics' understanding of how pervasively valuations are coloured by the perceiver's interests. It is also frequently hampered by being drawn into a mistaken opposition with instrumental value. I consider the most influential efforts to secure the claim to intrinsic value, but conclude that this is not, finally, the ground humanities scholars want to be on. We shall do better to argue for the value of the objects and practices that matter to us by calling on long-standing intuitions of value (often taken as self-evident by the wider public), and, relatedly, on the ground of long-standing cultural settlements, and evolving agreements, about how and why the humanities have value 'for their own sake'—a value that is neither purely intrinsic nor merely subjective.

It will be apparent from this initial outline of the terrain that my approach to the subject is political and driven in part by topical concerns. It is also however more fundamentally or, for want of a better word, abstractly philosophical. My aim has been to avoid, as far as possible, immersion only in the current state of institutional debate, which will quickly date, and to try rather to ascertain what the grounds for argument are with each of the conventional claims: where they work, what they imply, under what conditions they will cease to have credibility or must acknowledge limits on their credibility. To an extent I have also been interested in genealogies of argument (though a fully historical account of genealogies is clearly beyond my scope here). No one trained in the literature and history of the nineteenth century can fail to perceive that the arguments going on today about the value of the humanities have deep roots in the efforts of many of the best-remembered Victorian writers to articulate, for their period, the value of a 'liberal' education and culture that included extensive attention to 'humane letters'. The grounds of argument are, in many cases, much older than that, but the Victorian period retains explanatory importance because it is then that one sees emerging the now familiar pressure to justify expenditure on educating students in the humanities in the face of resistance from many political economists. It is also then that one starts to see a critical distinction, within the wide remit of a liberal education, between the work of the humanities and the work of the sciences and social sciences. And it is then that there emerges a conscious division of approach between those thinkers (often identified in the period as utilitarian) who approach questions of public value by prioritizing the desired end for society (an increase in prosperity and/or general well-being) and those who understand the proper focus of attention to be the cultivation of the individual mind.[4] Finally, it is in this period that there takes hold the idea that the extension of education is a democratic good: that it is, indeed, a prerequisite for a properly functioning democracy. The understanding that this extension should include *higher* education is not obviously implied, but it has put down gradually strengthening roots over recent decades in America and (relatively recently) in Britain.

[4] See Sheldon Rothblatt, 'The Limbs of Osiris: Liberal Education in the English-Speaking World', in Rothblatt and Björn Wittrock (eds.), *The European and American University since 1800: Historical and Sociological Essays* (Cambridge: Cambridge University Press, 1993), 19–73 (esp. 59–66).

I have, therefore, tried to write a book that may attract two different kinds of audience (or appeal to two kinds of interest in the same reader). For the reader primarily concerned with the immediate political purchase now of arguments for the value of the humanities, this book may be read selectively for its taxonomic description of the relevant arguments, and its conclusions about their strengths and (when mishandled, or overpitched) their potential weaknesses. For the more scholarly reader interested in the defence of the humanities as a philosophical activity with a long political and literary history (by 'literary history' I mean to isolate questions of style and rhetorical effectiveness, as well as content), there may be more interest in the book's close consideration of past attempts to argue for the value of education and culture that can, secondarily, help us to construct a persuasive defence of the humanities now, and to avoid some known pitfalls.

I am far from the first to argue that many of today's debates about the value of the university, of education, and of the arts and humanities specifically, bear the traces of earlier imprints.[5] Many of the best contributions to discussion of each of these overlapping subjects in recent years have made the same observation: all Sheldon Rothblatt's writing about the history of the university stresses the critical importance of the nineteenth century in shaping subsequent developments;[6] Bill Readings structures his painfully disenchanted (and still compelling) analysis of the state of today's universities around the contrast between the Humboldtian university of culture and today's internationally marketized 'university of excellence';[7] Stefan Collini's *What Are Universities For?* (2012) constructs its opening arguments against ongoing marketization in the form of critical 'dialogue' with Victorian idealism.[8] By way

---

[5] See esp. Alan Ryan, *Liberal Anxieties and Liberal Education* (New York: Hill and Wang, 1998), and Dinah Birch, *Our Victorian Education* (Oxford: Blackwell, 2008).

[6] See esp. *The Modern University and its Discontents: The Fate of Newman's Legacies in Britain and America* (Cambridge: Cambridge University Press, 1997); *Tradition and Change in English Liberal Education: An Essay in History and Culture* (London: Faber and Faber, 1976); *The Revolution of the Dons: Cambridge and Society in Victorian England* (Cambridge: Cambridge University Press, 1968); and, co-edited with Björn Wittrock, *The European and American University since 1800* (see n. 1).

[7] See *The University in Ruins* (Cambridge, Mass.: Harvard University Press, 1996).

[8] (London: Penguin Books), xi. Though its focus is on the German situation, it is important also to acknowledge the influence of Fritz Ringer's classic study of the process by which the culture of Bildung declined in Germany, as the reactionary educational elite of Germany was at last diminished (if not entirely overcome) by modernization. See *The Decline of the German Mandarins: The German Academic Community, 1890–1933* (1969; rpt Hanover, NH: University Press of New England, 1990).

of justification for this historical emphasis it would be difficult to improve on Dinah Birch's *Our Victorian Education* (2008). Though Birch focuses on primary and secondary rather than on higher education, her clear-eyed description of why we should keep the Victorian origins of our current educational arguments in view is equally applicable to the condition of our universities. As she observes, our society has inherited from the Victorians a driving belief in the value of education that shaped and continues to shape our society for the better; but we also owe to them patterns of joined debate, and often bitter disputation, over what education should be about, what it should be for, who should pay for it, and how we can best be sure of its worth. She rightly concludes that 'we have not yet resolved [these] disputes'. 'Simply recalling [earlier] thinking will not get us far'—but a sound 'understanding of the origins of our present problems' may show us ways in which 'we can begin to extricate ourselves'.[9]

This is evidently more the case with some arguments than with others. In two of the chapters that follow, the Victorian imprint, though palpable, is plainly much less salient than later transformations of the grounds of defence for the humanities. So: Chapter 1's examination of two and three cultures arguments as they have helped (and hindered) definition of the distinctive work of the humanities acknowledges the formative role played by T. H. Huxley's long-running public argument with Matthew Arnold about the relative priority of literature and science within a liberal education curriculum. Their influence on contemporary ways of articulating the distinctive purpose of the humanities is, however, less relevant and less remembered now than C. P. Snow and F. R. Leavis's antagonistic working of the same terrain in the late 1950s and early 1960s, or, indeed, Alan Sokal's in the 1990s. Changes in the political and institutional contexts within which the humanities function have substantially altered the framework for such claims—though, as I argue, the dead hand of convention has been especially oppressive in this sphere of argument.

The 'Democracy Needs Us' chapter, similarly, has to be cognizant of marked differences between Victorian political contexts and those of today. This claim is the most fervently adopted argument for the humanities now, and it is, for obvious historical reasons, all but absent from English traditions of defence until very recently. It is missing even from the Victorian educational and political literature where one might

[9] (Oxford: Basil Blackwell), viii, 144.

most expect to find it—for example in the writing of William
Morris. Most of the leading defenders of humane letters in that
century—John Stuart Mill, Ruskin, Newman, Arnold, Pattison—
would have agreed in seeing the Socratic model as the origin of modern forms of dialectical argument and, in its accent on the character
and ethos of the teacher's influence on the pupil, the ideal educational
model. Some (not all) of them held that the objectives of education
should include the formation of good citizens. None of them thought
that the arts and humanities had a privileged, let alone primary, role to
play in training people for civic responsibility. Politically most of us
have long ago evolved past most of their reservations about democracy
(where there are reservations now they tend to be more about func-
tionality than desirability), but the sense that the political good of
higher education depended on its breadth, not on any narrow claims
on behalf of the humanities, still requires a response. We can also ask
whether our circumstances now are so different as to legitimize the
argument on different grounds: for example, do we now inhabit a
public sphere so distortively geared to thinking in terms of economic
profitability that we need a corrective input from the humanities to
redirect our attention to human goods more variously described?
I think we do, though it seems to me too narrowly territorial a claim
that such corrective thinking is exclusively the task of the humanities.

One recent institutional development (contemporary with the time of
writing this book) offers to significantly alter the weighting given to the
democratic claim. The potential of higher education to encourage the
evolution of democratic structures and to assist democratic practices has
been very greatly enhanced by the arrival of massive open online courses
(MOOCs). The economic model for those courses is still in the early
stages of development in the UK.[10] If their popularity continues, as
current patterns suggest it will, they are likely to present a deep challenge
to the Socratic model of teaching as the mode of assisting individual
education, but they are also likely to boost the credibility of arguments
that seek to harness the humanities' training in language use, the evidences
of history, varieties of culture, and philosophical enquiry, to the good

---

[10] An initial consortium of eleven UK universities announced in December 2012 the
launch of free, non-credit-bearing internet courses to be available to internet users globally,
and expected (as in the US model) to prove particularly attractive to emerging economies.
See Rebecca Ratcliffe, 'Top Universities Launch Free Online Courses', *Guardian* 14
December 2012, <http://www.guardian.co.uk/education/2012/dec/14/top-uk-universi-
ties-launch-free-online-courses> (accessed 20 December 2012).

working of democracy. Not least, they may offer the first opportunity for serious sociological testing of those claims.

For the 'Distinctions' argument, then, the import of historical comparison is monitory (if we follow closely the history of these arguments to date we shall continue to argue badly). In the case of the 'Democracy Needs Us' argument, it is a reminder that our argumentative needs are (in the UK at least) relatively new, our problems not especially well defined by our history. But there are two conventional modes of arguing for the value of the humanities that warrant rather closer attention to earlier historical modes of defence: the argument with 'use value', and the argument for a contribution to happiness. It seems to me that in both these instances we are in danger of forgetting what earlier advocates for the humanities knew well: the power and the limitations of these particular lines of reasoning, even granting major differences in the contexts and audiences of debate. Accordingly, I have asked my reader to go fairly deeply into Mill on happiness, and Arnold on graduated usefulness. The reader should expect a cranking up of the scholarly apparatus in keeping with the shift to historical reclamation as well as philosophical scrutiny.

Chapter 2's exploration of 'instrumental value' examines one route out of the familiar structural opposition between use and uselessness— a focus prompted by a comparative reading of *Culture and Anarchy* (1869) with reports Arnold wrote during the same period as an Education Department inspector of schools and universities. This is, clearly, not the Marxist definition of use value as pure non-economic consent to a lived need, as against economic exchange value. 'Use value' for Arnold meant something much closer to the common currency of today's government policy directives to enhance practical use as an end of education. 'Culture and its Enemies' (the lecture that formed the kernel of *Culture and Anarchy*) was written in the immediate aftermath of two years' work reporting on *Schools and Universities on the Continent* (1868), in the course of which Arnold had ample cause to reflect on the validity but also the limits of use value in education. To read Arnold on primary schools is to find an author fully prepared to talk in terms of practical use value, especially when standards of attainment are low for historically or politically contingent reasons. But even in such circumstances, Arnold hardly ever talks solely in such terms. Usefulness is important at the beginning of any individual's schooling, but 'higher' and longer-term ways of thinking about the good of education quickly come into play. They include the power to employ one's intelligence freely, or non-mechanically—not least in maintaining scepticism towards any self-serving claims about the greater importance of one area of study over another. For Arnold, this controlled appeal to 'use' entails a point about public values, but also a point about the language in which we debate and uphold such values. One of the reasons why *Culture and Anarchy* has continued to hold such a prominent place in the critical literature on the meaning and value of culture (heavily contested, but no less strong for being so) is that, though it was written by a man one could (without stretching the term too far) call a bureaucrat, it concedes almost nothing to the formulaic language of bureaucracy that standardly places a high value on practical usefulness and economic utility. Arnold's alternative terms of validation did not last, but he knew that this fate will befall any language that attempts to fix the value of culture. I am interested in the reverberations of that strategy for today's defences of culture and education, arguing that Arnold's conclusion retains validity, and need not bring in its train his high-cultural assumptions.

The most famous formulation of the 'improvement in happiness' argument for the humanities, even now, is John Stuart Mill's description of how reading Wordsworth rescued him from the mental aridity of an unsentimental education. Mill's claims for poetry have clear continuities with the Romantic valuation of feeling over reason, but they also show him going back to the roots of utilitarianism in Epicurean hedonism. So, Chapter 3 rereads Mill in order to test the weight of qualitative hedonistic arguments as a means of rebalancing claims that place all the emphasis on the humanities' critical function. Mill gave us some widely respected reasons for saying that poetry, specifically—but, by implication, all writing that assists the cultivation of feeling—can help us to understand better what happiness is, and how we may better put ourselves in the way of it (though doing so will never be entirely within our control). In *Utilitarianism* and other writings on politics and education he also gave some good reasons to support a claim that a liberal higher education with literature, languages, and history in its remit may, for that relatively small proportion of the population that pursues it, increase the kind and quality of our individual intellectual pleasures. (In this vein he has been an acknowledged influence on some recent writing in behavioural economics—though the majority of writers in that field seem oddly unaware that their subject has a philosophical history.) In his role as Rector of St Andrews University, in the 1870s, Mill argued more directly for the importance of the humanities as one element in a liberal education, on the grounds that they help to preserve the cultural inheritance for following generations in ways that are not merely custodial but assist ongoing human intellectual and cultural achievements. All these things said, he put a check on any too ambitious claim for the humanities' role in promoting the happiness of society, identifying some serious problems in the way of connecting gains in individual happiness to that great utilitarian goal, quantifiable improvements in 'the general happiness'.

The final chapter ('For its Own Sake') necessitates some close attention to philosophy of value, but its conclusions encourage greater movement away from historical precedent than we have yet seen. The idea that the humanities have value in their own right, in ways that are not primarily consequentialist or to be accounted for by evidence of their instrumental effects in the world, has had strong advocates during the last two and a half centuries, among them Ruskin, in the Victorian period, and Geoffrey Hill, rereading Ruskin (and others) at the end of the twentieth century. Both attempted to secure the ground for valuation by reference to 'intrinsic value'. Readers of Hill have often detected a declining level of conviction in his writings on this subject over recent years: awareness that such an argument now must be knowingly 'failed', though it is not to be absolutely abandoned. Chapter 5 explores these efforts to redeem intrinsic value, briefly contrasting Hill's astringency with the more optimistic defence of contextual valuation offered by John Dewey. It then develops in its place the more readily defensible claim that the areas of study we now call 'the humanities' have value 'for their own sake'. Though the 'for its own sake' claim is not without its own philosophical difficulties it is relatively free of the fetishistic quality often attached to belief in 'intrinsic value' and, as described in Chapter 5, it does not require the 'value isolationism' that has derailed many attempts to define and defend 'intrinsic value' over the years.

We look to past educational debates 'not ... for the sake of analogy', Sheldon Rothblatt warns, 'for analogy is limiting'; rather 'for the sake of recognition'.[11] This is right, but there are evident points at which continuities are imperfect, and some at which recognition must be

---

[11] *Revolution of the Dons*, 17.

quite baffled. Most obviously, the term 'humanities' has no very close equivalent in earlier periods beyond the relatively vague 'language and letters'. It arose out of American efforts to define the special qualities of the study of literature, language, history, and the arts in response to 'an aggressive form of positivism' that, in the 1940s and 1950s, promoted the supposed methods of the natural sciences as the basis for all true knowledge.[12] 'The Humanities' remains, even now, arguably a more American than English term, given the extent to which the single honours system still dominates in England. For well over a century the predominant model of university education here has been deep study of one discipline during the undergraduate years, with still more specialized study following at graduate level. Few English universities offer the liberal (in the sense of 'broad') educational base favoured in America, Canada, Australia, New Zealand, and many other national systems with which I have less familiarity. Given a university system where most students specialize from the start, the term 'humanities' will tend to operate mainly as an administrative grouping of departments on the basis of fairly loosely observed similarities in subject matter or approach.

The kinds of subject matter studied within 'the humanities' have, moreover, evolved a very long way indeed from Victorian philological, historical, and critical practices. My own field, English literature, was not widely studied at university level until the start of the twentieth century[13] and has since been substantially reshaped in its content and its methods of enquiry many times over. Fundamental changes in what is comprehended by the term 'culture', and continuing disagreements about the relative claims of aesthetics, politics, and sociological considerations in defining the terrain and the purpose of literary study—indeed, not even disagreements: often just a right recognition of the mixed nature of the subject—have taken us a long way from Arnold's 'the best that has been thought and said' (which was in any case never intended as a description of literature to the exclusion of history, philosophy, art history, and—when Arnold was pressed by

[12] Collini, *What Are Universities For*, 63.

[13] See Franklin E. Court, *Institutionalizing English Literature: The Culture and Politics of Literary Study, 1750–1900* (Stanford, Calif.: Stanford University Press, 1992), 12–15 and *passim*; Andrew Milner, *Literature, Culture and Society* (London: UCL Press, 1996), 4–5; Chris Baldick, *The Social Mission of English Criticism, 1848–1932* (Oxford: Clarendon Press, 1983), 60–82.

Huxley—science). Faced with the very diverse kinds of study grouped under 'the humanities' one might easily despair of generalizing. (I am put in mind of Derek Parfit's observation, with respect to that similarly vague designation 'the arts', that 'music is the lost battlefield and graveyard of most aesthetic theories'.[14]) As an administrative term, however, 'the humanities' is clearly here to stay for the foreseeable future.

The continuing contribution of ideas about liberalism to debates about the content and value of a higher education in the humanities presents another kind of difficulty. It is conventional to identify most, though not all, of the Victorian writers I've invoked with 'liberal' thought. The semantic confusions set running by that term have been well summarized by Rothblatt:

> The history of liberal education does not evolve or descend: it dissolves. It is the narrative of a series of departures from a [classical] conception of wholeness or integration which appears to be a 'natural' way of viewing the human condition, beginning with the balance presumed essential to the mental and bodily health and extending to the necessary and palpable interdependence of people.

This irregular historical 'descent' continues even now to put serious difficulties in the way of thinking about what the aims of education should be:

> Appeals to an idea of roundedness rarely fall on deaf ears. But the deeper assumptions upon which ancient ideas of liberal education rest are actually incomprehensible from the standpoint of present-day conceptions of personality. They are not compatible with [the other meaning of 'liberal':] the idea of an autonomous self in competition with other selves for status, income, position, and influence, or with our belief in the importance of skills, proficiencies, and specialities.[15]

Given the splintering effect of the term 'liberal', its ability to stand for quite disconnected and even contradictory ideals—wholeness and specialism; interdependence and freedom—it might well be preferable to avoid it altogether. It is, moreover, a word that now carries in many quarters strongly pejorative connotations of nostalgia and (worse than nostalgia) 'denial' of the actual economic circumstances of modern

---

[14] *On What Matters*, ed. and introd. Samuel Scheffler, 2 vols. (Oxford: Oxford University Press, 2011), i. 54.
[15] 'Limbs of Osiris', 66–7.

education. For those who hold that we are now in the midst of a thoroughgoing economic neoliberalism, 'liberalism' is often little more than a cover for conservatism. I have restricted the word's use here to occasions when the contextualization of a particular mode of defence in the history of thinking about particular ethical and/or political aims for education warrants it. I have tried also to indicate when the designation of a 'liberal' (broad) basis for curricula ought to be clearly detached from any assumption that political liberalism is implied or entailed (in other words, when that slippage seems most likely to occur and to mislead). The increasing number of university courses requiring a liberal arts component at the introductory level is some evidence of a growing conviction in recent years that UK higher education would benefit from some liberalization of content. That conviction is also evidenced in the wide popularity of interdisciplinary work (and ever growing government incentives to pursue it). Nevertheless, as I point out in Chapter 1, interdisciplinary work is, with rare exceptions, work pursued from one primary disciplinary base (the literary thesis, for example, pursued with a substantial component of history of ideas, or history of science; the musicology thesis that draws closely on the methods and findings of anthropology).

It may be worth recording here that, though my own work has often been 'interdisciplinary' (this book included), I am sceptical of the word's value, and indeed its usefulness, as employed by research funding bodies. The primary function of the term 'interdisciplinary' in UK higher education policy-making at present is to assist funding bodies in meeting the government-imposed requirements that public money should promote 'knowledge transfer', 'economic relevance', and 'impact' or social benefit. The word 'interdisciplinarity' has been effectively harnessed so as to encourage applications that will be self-evidently collaborative (because they involve skills and, often, personnel from more than one area of expertise), self-evidently innovative (because not confined by the intellectual and methodological parameters of existing disciplines), and will self-evidently involve the transfer of knowledge beyond old disciplinary boundaries. 'Interdisciplinarity' in such contexts is always deemed to be a good, but is problematically underdefined. It designates not a subject or a method but at most a framework. I am especially suspicious of its value when it is invoked as an answer to the question of what the future of our separate fields of enquiry should be.

One of the ways in which this book has changed significantly in the course of researching and writing has been with the growing realization that the American and English traditions of defence for the humanities are much less readily compatible than I expected to find them.[16] Many of the most high-profile recent defences of the humanities coming out of America, including Martha Nussbaum's *Not for Profit* (2010),[17] Louis Menand's *The Marketplace of Ideas* (2010),[18] and Geoffrey Harpham's *The Humanities and the Dream of America* (2011), have found a ready and sympathetic audience in the UK. Much of the critical literature that I have found most helpful (the work of John Guillory and Amanda Anderson, for example) comes from that section of the American literary profession, principally in English and 'theory', which has concerned itself more broadly with the political responsibilities of 'the academy' and 'the profession'. Thought provoking though these writers are, they are often distinctively American in their concerns, responding to greater pressures to redirect funding from the humanities towards vocational and business studies than have yet operated in Britain, and more worrying drops in the overall numbers and relative proportion of students studying the humanities at undergraduate level. Their core concern is often with faltering commitments on the part of state governments and individual institutions to liberal arts education, from primary school upwards. Their responses can seem (to the external viewer) perhaps excessively preoccupied with the question of whether and how to reduce numbers of doctoral students, given the reduced opportunities for entry into the academic profession, and how to reverse a process (not true, though it may become true, in the UK) by which graduate teaching has come to be valued at the expense of undergraduate teaching. They have also been more preoccupied with threats to academic freedom (necessarily, given the extent of budget control by state legislatures, and the degree of interference in the content of education

---

[16] This is not to deny the growing convergence of national systems in the globalized landscape of higher education. See Tony Becher and Paul R. Trowler, *Academic Tribes and Territories: Intellectual Enquiry and the Culture of Disciplines*, 2nd edn. (Buckingham: The Society for Research into Higher Education & Open University Press, 2001), 2–4.

[17] *Not for Profit: Why Democracy Needs the Humanities* (Princeton: Princeton University Press).

[18] *The Marketplace of Ideas: Reform and Resistance in the American University* (New York: W. W. Norton).

in many universities). The case in England is not the same. It would be difficult to say whether it is 'better' or 'worse' other than on a case-by-case basis—the major difference being the greater centralization of the economic framework for higher education and of research funding and assessment policy.[19] The relative rarity of elective courses removes the major source of demand for the humanities found in the US liberal arts system—but removes also their most immediate vulnerability to changes in any given institution's commitment to that system.

In part because the liberal arts model has been so important historically and ideologically in the United States, in part also because of the much greater number of privately funded institutions of education in the higher education system and the more entrenched resistance to the idea that the state (in the British sense) should provide ('public good' does not automatically register a government-funded good in the USA, as it does in the UK), the kinds of claim investigated here will inevitably look different to transatlantic eyes. To take only the most obvious example: my reservations about the extent to which one can push the 'democracy needs us' argument will be weighed differently by readers within a liberal arts system. (I suspect they will be read as excessively or unhelpfully sceptical.) Even within such a system, there seems to me a need to ensure that the corrective function often ascribed to a broadly informed 'liberal' intelligence does not become a claim for a specific humanities advantage without explaining how and why the humanities should be thought to have a special purchase on critical intelligence (or even historical critique, or rhetorical analysis).

A large question for anyone trying to assess the force of historic justifications now, in almost any national context, is whether talk of non-market values, of whatever political cast, where the goals of higher education are concerned, still has purchase in an economic context that many commentators would describe, after the American example, as 'neoliberal'—that is, thoroughly under the sway of market forces. More strenuously described: neoliberalism is the name given to a mode of government, understood to be globally in the ascendant, in which 'all dimensions of human life are cast in terms of

---

[19] A clear account of the increasing externalist pressures on academic cultures in Britain is given by Becher and Trowler, *Academic Tribes and Territories*. See esp. preface to the 2nd edn.

a market rationality' and under which, in England, 'the role of the
state is to deploy a variety of strategies (including privatization,
deregulation, reregulation, commercialization, and marketization)' to
quell resistance to that market rationality—preferably, indeed, to
make us enthusiastic adherents to it.[20]

There is a variety of hard-headed realism (as it presents itself) that
would have us believe, in such a situation, that the non-market-
directed arguments have all been made well enough before and that
the time for making them has passed. The best we can hope for now
is that we can persuade governments that the humanities are important
to the marketplace,[21] and (more ambitiously) that university administrations might be able to exploit the logic of commerce on our behalf.
They might, for example, look to abduct rhetorically, and perhaps
more than rhetorically, the figure of the financial derivative, applying
it to the ways in which research grants, league tables, university
strategic plans seek to leverage the value of higher education before it
is realized.[22] This seems to me a mistake on several levels. First, neither
our students, nor the parents or benefactors who increasingly fund
those students' higher education, have ceased to possess higher ideas
about what an education in the humanities should be for; nor
do most of them set much store by inflated promissory notes, as
against the visible content of curricula, the scholarly achievement of
academics, and the reported experience of current or recent students.
Nor have most academics entirely parted company with idealism—

---

[20] Sarah Amsler, 'Beyond All Reason: Spaces of Hope in the Struggle for England's
Universities', *Representations* 116 (Fall 2011), 62–87 (64)—summarizing a now very large
literature on the subject, including Wendy Brown, 'Neoliberalism and the End of Liberal
Democracy', in *Edgework* (Princeton: Princeton University Press, 2005), 37–60; Noel Cas-
tree, 'Neoliberal Environments: A Framework for Analysis', *Manchester Papers in Political
Economy*, Working Paper no. 04/07, 10 December 2007; Les Levidow, 'Marketizing Higher
Education: Neoliberal Strategies and Counter-Strategies', in Kevin Robins and Frank
Webster (eds.), *The Virtual University? Knowledge, Markets, and Management* (Oxford: Oxford
University Press, 2002), 227–48.

[21] See esp. *'That Full Complement of Riches': The Contributions of the Arts, Humanities and
Social Sciences to the Nation's Wealth* (London: The British Academy, 2004).

[22] See Randy Martin, 'Taking an Administrative Turn: Derivative Logics for a Recharged
Humanities', *Representations* 116/1, Special issue on The Humanities and the Crisis of the
Public University (2011), 156–76; and Regenia Gagnier, 'Operationalizing Hope: The
Neoliberalization of British Universities in Historico-Philosophical Perspective', forth-
coming in *Occasion: Interdisciplinary Studies in the Humanities* 5 (2013) <http://arcade.stan-
ford.edu/journals/occasion/>.

not least because most of us have been greatly the beneficiaries of earlier generations' idealism. Secondly, though the arguments for considering higher education in the humanities a public good have been well made, many times over, they have not been made in ways that clearly distinguish different kinds of justification from one another. In particular, there seems to me some virtue and some use value to a taxonomic defence of the humanities based on the assumption of value pluralism.

The further error in the 'hard-headed' view that the time for non-market-led value claims is over is an error in the description of neoliberalism. Public culture and higher education certainly inhabit a market, but that market is not free in the UK. It remains in important ways constrained politically, legally, ethically. Not the least of the constraints upon it is what the informed public will bear in the way of marketization. Regulation is often cynically perceived as a means by which 'neoliberal governmentality' produces a distorted market in which thinly described standards of performance mask the loss, or the active dismantling, of humanistic aspirations for education (or broadcasting, or healthcare—one can substitute other kinds of public good here). The cynicism is partly, but only partly, justified. As long ago as 1996, in what remains one of the best modern books on the idea of the university, Bill Readings diagnosed a major threat to the humanities and to the university as a whole, understood as a place of serious, rational, and imaginative intellectual culture. He saw the threat as arising from the imposition by administrations and government agencies of a distorted simulacrum of the marketplace, according to which what matters is the ostensibly quantifiable but increasingly contentless 'excellence' of its teaching and research 'outputs'.[23] Turning back the tide of ill-thought-through, grossly expensive, and time-wasting systems of accounting for the receipt of public money is, indeed, one of the major problems facing universities and other public institutions today (Readings was right). But there is reason to resist taking his argument, as some have been tempted to do, all the way toward cynicism. Cynicism can be alluring. It speaks, historically and stylistically,

---

[23] I update Readings's terminology slightly to reflect changes in the idiom of university administration since he wrote, but the core description is his. See *The University in Ruins*, esp. chs. 2 and 4. For a lucid account of the ways in which the current UK market in higher education (at 2012) is not 'a true market', see Peter Scott, 'What Kind of University?', *Oxford Magazine* 320 (2nd week, Hilary Term, 2012), 5–7 (6).

of critical independence, scepticism of the default moral currency, a willingness to debase 'the ideal stamp' (and thereby renew the possibility of a credible idealism) that will sometimes be a better representation of the values we attach to intellectual life than more measured argument. But the cynic position, in this context, tends to ignore the extent to which the value of a higher education, not only in the humanities, continues to be understood by students, teachers, parents, alumni, but also in my experience by many politicians and civil servants, in ways that resist market valuation and economic quantification.

I do not underestimate the extent of the damage that has been done to university education in Britain by saying that our institutional deformation is not complete and that protesting it (as Readings did in writing *The University in Ruins*) has produced demonstrable victories. But the fact that the humanities continue to receive substantial sums of public investment, that our students are still publicly (and in some privileged instances, institutionally) subsidized, that regulation in the form of assessment of scholarship is a matter of peer review, conducted by respected members of the profession, and (most saliently) that students, parents, teachers, and many politicians perceive the marketization of higher education to be distortive of its true value, are all signs that we are operating under something other than full-blown neoliberalism—and reasons to keep cynicism in check. One of the most damaging effects of a sense of embattlement, periodically evident in our cultures of debate, is that it can prevent advocates for the humanities from doing one of the things they may legitimately claim to do best—submitting claims of value to proper scrutiny: rhetorical, historical, philosophical.[24] If the effect of the requirement for the humanities to justify their public value, or the terms in which they are permitted to do so, is to stifle their ability to ask the hard questions of their own intuitions of purpose and value then they really will be in trouble.

To be competent to offer a pluralist account of the value of the humanities is, as I have observed, politically obligatory, from time to time; to do so using the techniques of literary criticism and philosophy of value, and with an eye on the historical evolution of ways of arguing, has

---

[24] I am echoing here Jonathan Bate's claim, in the introduction to *The Public Value of the Humanities*, that there is 'a simple answer to the question "what is the value of research in the humanities?" It is that the humanities is the only activity that can establish the meaning of such a question' (3)—though it will be clear from the summary of Ch. 4 that I am less persuaded that the humanities have exclusive rights or powers here.

been my own intellectual choice. If the value of the humanities is a topic one can quickly grow tired of in the professionally self-justifying ways in which it is most often encountered, it seems to me nevertheless a topic to attract anyone curious about intellectual history, rhetorical persuasion, philosophy of value, deliberative reasoning. The question of how and why large numbers of people agree to value the higher study of the humanities is, at its core, a question about the ideas that guide thinking about education, about culture, and about certain versions of a happy private life and a good public life. It is conventional, and intellectually mandatory, to treat high Victorian idealism on these matters with a pinch of latter-day salt. And yet the really significant part of any remaining Victorian legacy for us now may be less the content of their ideals than the fact of engaging seriously with the task of public valuation. The lastingly relevant endowment they have given us culturally and politically may be the written record of a serious effort to find a proper level for one's values, to make them persuasive to others, and to find a language in which we can advance claims about public values and their relation to private values without that language becoming quickly co-opted to other ends, and as quickly losing its appeal.

I

Distinction from Other Disciplines

Definition of the Humanities

The humanities study the meaning-making practices of human culture, past and present, focusing on interpretation and critical evaluation, primarily in terms of the individual response and with an ineliminable element of subjectivity. It may be only at this level of generalization that a positive description of their work can command complete assent—and the well-trained reader will quickly turn a critical eye on the words 'meaning', 'culture', 'individual', 'subjectivity', and probably 'interpretation' and 'evaluation' too. Anodyne and somewhat ungainly though the claim may be, it says something about a distinctive content (cultural practices, including but not limited to the arts) and about a distinctive understanding of what is involved in being truthful (an acceptance that truth claims will not, and cannot, be founded only on positivistic appeals to evidence; rather that they will necessarily entail the exercise of judgement). This initial description does not provide a valuation, rather a basic specification of the objects of study, and modes of scholarship, on the basis of which claims of valuation might be made. That it says nothing about further acquirements often associated with the humanities—historical interpretation, rhetorical analysis, the cultivation of style, creativity, imagination—is because I take these things to be, though vital elements in much of the practice of the humanities, not absolutely generalizable across them.

Even the basic claim is not entirely uncontentious. One potential objection arises out of its implicit joining of the word 'humanities' to the word 'human'. Jonathan Culler notes that 'our language proposes a strong link not just between the humanities and the human being but between humanistic thinking and even humane behavior'. That proposition, he thinks, 'risks leading us astray' (38): 'much of the most interesting work in the humanities' in recent years has been concerned with teaching us that human intentions and purposes are 'not a reliable guide to what is actually happening in history, in discourse, in the psyche' (39).[1] But to question the force of the etymological connection between 'human', 'humane', 'humanities' and insist upon the non-transparency of human experience—its historical contingency, its at least partial psychological inscrutability, its linguistic conditioning—is not to render the link invalid. The humanities concern themselves with human culture, not in the first instance with animal behaviour, or the physical world, or financial systems, or laws, or mathematic models, or the operations of businesses (though any of these things may come within their remit as they are represented in culture). Their students take the philosophical and psychological difficulty of knowing and appraising human intentions as a condition for their work. One can grant Culler's caveat without reaching his conclusion: that it is time the humanities found themselves a more appropriate name. The fact that few of us working within humanities departments seem to identify closely with the term 'humanist' is more a sign of its inevitable looseness than its objectionable authority. Changing the name would require a greater political momentum than has yet made itself evident.

A more substantive question concerns the extent of the claim for the humanities that can be built on the technical training and ethical commitments comprehended in critical reflection or 'critique'. It is a tempting idea that the critical reflex which prevents 'the well-trained reader' from passing over the terms 'meaning', 'culture' and so forth as unproblematic itself belongs distinctively to the humanities.[2] This educated response may come into play at the level of the language (probing the definition, the etymology, the cultural resonance and stylistic disposition of the words), at the level of history (assessing the origins of the claim, its changing significance or its durability over

---

[1] 'In Need of a Name: A Response to Geoffrey Harpham', *New Literary History* 36/1 (2005), 37–42 (38–9).

[2] See, for example, Edward W. Said, *Humanism and Democratic Criticism* (New York: Columbia University Press, 2004), 21–2.

time), at the level of philosophy (testing the argumentative premisses). The more philosophically strenuous term 'critique' covers a wide range of practices from the 'high Kantian enterprise' to what Foucault quaintly termed the 'little polemico-professional activities' ('les petites activités polémico-professionnelles'[3]), and across an ethical gamut from narrowly focused 'fault finding',[4] through the normative exercise of judgement as defined in various philosophical schools (e.g. Kantian, Marxian, Habermasian), to the non-judgemental, non-prescriptive forms of moral enquiry associated with scepticisms old and new (linking writers as remote as, say, Foucault and Montaigne).

Recognizing the extent of the humanities' involvement in such trained modes of engagement with culture, some contributors to the condition of the humanities debate in recent years have sought to avert or subvert claims that the field is 'in crisis' with the cheerfully perverse defence that, given their orientation towards critical reflection and critique, crisis is their ideal element.[5] Culler grants something to this self-conception, but he is wary of granting too much. One reason, likely to weigh more heavily if the field is under threat of diminishing financial support, is that justifying the humanities by way of their commitment to critical scrutiny (of language and other expressive media, of history, of modes of reasoning) may not seem to afford them enough by way of a positive public function. Too much critical reflexivity may suggest 'possibilities of paralysis through excess of self-consciousness and infinite regress' (39). To which one can add that other people can easily become exasperated (one may oneself become bored) with critique as a default mode of operation.

If yoking the humanities to the work of criticism is insufficient by way of distinctive justification, however, it does not follow that these

---

[3] 'Qu'est ce que la critique? Critique et *Aufklärung*', *Bulletin de la Société française de philosophie* 84/2 (1990), 35–63 (36).

[4] See Michel Foucault. 'What is Critique?' and Judith Butler, 'What is Critique? An Essay on Foucault's Virtue', both in David Ingram (ed.), *The Political*, Blackwell Readings in Continental Philosophy (Oxford: Blackwell Publishers Ltd, 2002), 191–211, 212–26. Butler contrasts the meaning of critique in the work of Foucault with its interpretation by Raymond Williams, Adorno, Habermas. The first two quotations are from Foucault (191), the second from Williams, as cited by Butler (212).

[5] See esp. Geoffrey Galt Harpham, *The Humanities and the Dream of America* (Chicago: University of Chicago Press, 2011); Culler (cited at the start of this chapter) was responding to an earlier articulation of this argument, 'Beneath and Beyond the "Crisis in the Humanities"', *New Literary History* 36/1 (2005), 21–36.

are self-descriptions the humanities should be giving away. A defensible version of the 'critical thinking' claim can be reasonably modest but tenacious: though critical self-reflection is not unique to the humanities, and not all they do, it is indispensable. It is sufficiently characteristic of much of their work to be one basis among others for the ascription of distinctive purpose, and will often be more prominent in their self-descriptions than in an equivalently general account of the sciences or social sciences. As with many defences for the humanities, the problems arise when one part of the characterization is made to stand for the whole.

Both criticism and 'critique', whatever their particular valency, omit a great deal. The work of the humanities is frequently descriptive, or appreciative, or imaginative, or provocative, or speculative, more than it is critical. It includes ways of attending to objects of study that are, variously, technical, aesthetically evaluative, curatorial. Its public purposes can include maintaining and reanimating knowledge of the cultural heritage, explication of the products and processes of culture, the stimulation of public curiosity in new subjects—again, not primarily critical activities. In the main the humanities are as concentrated on the character of an individual response as on any generalizable knowledge claims, and they typically have an interest in the colour and temper of that response that goes well beyond conveying knowledge or pursuing a critical interpretation of it.[6] Not least, the humanities are rightly most admired when their practice rises to an art: a writing, or speaking or creative performance, that bears the stylistic and temperamental imprint of the individual voice. Their work is not always conducted from a position of high seriousness; some of its best expressions will seem trivial, silly, even frankly irresponsible judged from the position of the philosophically or politically committed critic. (Which is not to assume that philosophically and politically committed criticism is always humourless, or conducted in its highest mode.)

A number of recent writers have accordingly asked whether it is time to direct critique towards itself ('the critique of critique') in order

---

[6] Michael Warner, 'Uncritical Reading', in Jane Gallop (ed.), *Polemic: Critical or Uncritical* (London: Routledge, 2004), 13–38; also (an important early reflection on modern professionalized criticism's privileging of 'paranoid suspicion' over 'naive' sympathy), Eve Kosofsky Sedgwick, 'Paranoid Reading and Reparative Reading; or, You're So Paranoid, You Probably Think this Introduction Is about You', in Sedgwick and Adam Frank, *Touching Feeling: Affect, Pedagogy, Performativity* (Durham, NC: Duke University Press, 2003), 123–52 (126).

to contest the normative effects of critique's professionalization in recent decades and to ask what other forms of engagement with culture it is precluding or forgetting.[7] The peculiarity of the 'critique of critique', as the label suggests, is that it continues to take its warrant from critique. Work that expels critique altogether in favour of testimony to an emotional response or the practice of style, or any of the other forms of subjective or performative response open to it, may find it harder to justify itself and will earn its keep only insofar as it produces an alternative form of authority or charisma. If it fails to do so it can expect to be dismissed as no more than the exhibition of an ego (as Hayden White once put it, after Lacan, 'a demand for love'[8]).

The recent popularity of 'the critique of critique' notwithstanding, claims that the special purpose of the humanities is (more and less stringently) 'critical thinking' tend to find wide approval within the field. The unexamined intellectual life is not worth defending. But as a core element in a justification for the humanities it has one more objection to answer: a questionable assumption of privilege over other fields. Philosophers will no doubt sense a special interest in the Socratic injunction to think hard about one's thinking,[9] but there is a limit to how far even philosophy can claim special ownership of critique, and to how far the humanities can, as the home of philosophy, assert their difference on that basis from the sciences and social sciences. The knowledge base and critical tools of historicism, rhetorical analysis, philosophical enquiry, etc., are developed to the highest level within their particular disciplines but critical and philosophical reflection are indispensable to intellectual work everywhere. A scientist or social scientist who just gets on unreflectingly with the current method will be functioning as a competent technician, not someone who can advance deeper understanding of the

---

[7] See Butler, 'Critique, Dissent, Disciplinarity', *Critical Inquiry* 35 (2009), 773–95; Warner, 'Uncritical Reading', Sedgwick, 'Paranoid Reading', and, on reading as act of piety, Saba Mahmood, *Politics of Piety* (Princeton: Princeton University Press, 2004) (discussed by Warner, p. 18).

[8] He was amending the silencing effect of a particularly long and difficult question he had posed to a seminar speaker in Bristol, *c.*1995.

[9] I am following the majority, though not quite ubiquitous, practice of locating philosophy within the humanities. On philosophy at once belonging to and problematizing the category of 'the humanities', especially the presumed universalism of the 'human', see Jacques Derrida, 'The Right to Philosophy from the Cosmopolitan Point of View (the Example an International Institution)', in *Negotiations: Interventions and Interviews, 1971–2001*, ed., trans., and with an introduction by Elizabeth Rottenberg (Stanford, Calif.: Stanford University Press, 2002), 329–42.

field. A number of writers have accordingly found themselves wrestling in recent years with the disciplinary self-interest bound up in the Kantian view that philosophy alone concerns itself purely with the exercise of the critical function, and must therefore be free from the state requirement that it directly serve the public good. Critique, Judith Butler asserts, 'belongs not just to the discipline of philosophy but throughout the university'.[10] She is glossing Derrida. In fact Derrida's own formulation carefully preserves the priority of philosophy at the same time that it dislodges it: 'The freedom of philosophy is *absolute*, but it is a freedom of judgment and intra-university speech'—and it will always find itself in conflict with the desire of the 'higher faculties' (theology, law, and medicine, for Kant) to govern or dominate. Philosophy must be 'permanently armed' to defend it.[11]

A common line of argument from those advocates for the humanities who have wished to retain a *distinctive* claim to be concerned with critical enquiry is therefore to say that other fields are behaving 'humanistically' (as opposed to 'empirically' or 'positivistically') when they respond to a proposition by the impulse to test its assumptions. They are, in short, borrowing qualities more commonly associated with the humanities, and especially with philosophy. At this point the description may look somewhat imperialistic, but in practice any proactive effort at dominance over other disciplines is bound to prove self-limiting. As the sociologist Andrew Abbott describes them, such attempts at expansion of the domain

give an aggressive discipline its most extensive cross-section. (...English [for example] claiming control of everything written in texts because English thinks of itself as the master discipline of the interpretation of texts.) For each discipline, there is some dimension of definition along which its projection is greater than that of the other disciplines. In moments of aggression, it will emphasize this dimension, although doing so may expose it to insufferable competition.[12]

---

[10] Butler, 'Critique, Dissent, Disciplinarity', 780.

[11] 'Mochlos, or The Conflict of the Faculties', in Derrida, *Eyes of the University: Right to Philosophy 2*, trans. Jan Plug et al. (Stanford, Calif.: Stanford University Press, 2004), 83–112 (108–9, 108). I am leaving aside for the moment the closely related question of how far, and in what sense, academic enquiry can ever be construed as entirely free.

[12] *Chaos of Disciplines* (Chicago: University of Chicago Press, 2001), 139. See also Tony Becher and Paul R. Trowler, *Academic Tribes and Territories: Intellectual Enquiry and the Culture of Disciplines*, 2nd edn. (Buckingham: The Society for Research into Higher Education & Open University Press, 2001).

So, History may claim mastery in moments of buoyant self-assertion, because everything has a history; Linguistics may claim mastery because nothing enters representation except through the structures of language; Philosophy (as we have seen) may claim priority over all intellectual operations as the discipline that thinks about thinking.[13]

If advancing strong claims for a discipline, or a grouping of disciplines, can be a gesture of imperial advancement that meets with resistance, it can also, with better justification, be a protective gesture with regard to particular kinds of enquiry and forms of knowledge. Cross-faculty appropriations of the name of the humanities have particular force at present in contexts where certain kinds of work find themselves without a strong defence internal to the current conduct of the field: economic study that neglects economic history, for example; cognitive psychology that reserves no scepticism about the explanatory reach of brain imaging; rational choice modelling that fails to consider the uneven possession of agency; theorizing about science that forgets to allow for the perspective of the theorist. In all these cases the term 'humanistic' operates polemically on the front that most clearly distinguishes a neglected edge of those other fields from their 'aggressive edge'. One can perceive the marginal prestige of the term 'humanistic' within the fields of social science and science, and yet know its value in bringing back to notice currently undervalued ways of thinking about the subject, rebalancing the claims of the other disciplines, helping to retain a broader view and sometimes to restore public conviction.

It is in such circumstances (offensive and defensive) that the qualities by which the humanities claim distinctive purpose become most sharply apparent: their tendency to value qualitative above quantitative reasoning; their distrust of proceduralism; their greater faith in interpretative than in positivistic thinking; their orientation as much toward historical analysis as toward synchronic structural analysis; and their attention to the role of the perceiver in ascertaining even the most philosophically secure of knowledge claims; (relatedly) their interest in the specificity of the individual response (its content and its style) over and above the generalized or collective response, and their concern with what can be

---

[13] For a sharp critique of the idea of disciplinary self-interest and, relatedly, the conflict of the faculties, see Bruce Robbins, 'Less Disciplinary than Thou: Criticism and the Conflict of the Faculties', *Minnesota Review* NS 45–6 (1995–6), <www.theminnesotareview. org/journal/ns45/robbins.htm>. Accessed 18 June 2012.

known or understood even though it is incapable of empirical verification.[14] On these occasions the humanities project their most forceful self-image outside the discipline, albeit at the price of temporarily losing sight of the other kinds of activity that they also foster.

The forceful self-image (considerably stronger than the initial claim) draws to the surface the underlying structural assumption of all efforts to account for distinction, and the source of the real difficulties here— the nature and logic of the contrast with other fields.

Cultural Differentiation on the Two Culture Model

Distinctiveness in the way of intellectual cultures is surprisingly hard to describe, given that we recognize it all the time as, at a minimum, the social and technical expression of patterns of intellectual specialization that start early on in modern education, and especially early in the UK. External comparisons are logically necessary to capture the particular qualities of an intellectual field: what makes it unlike other intellectual fields. Explicit characterizations of how the humanities differ from the sciences and/or social sciences are therefore, in principle, only articulating in more detail differences in the objects and nature of attention that are no less structurally important for being, in the main, underarticulated or not articulated at all. It would, however, be difficult to look at the efforts made over the past two centuries to render the comparative features and virtues of work in the different university faculties at the most general level and sense that this is promising argumentative terrain. Unlike the later arguments explored in this book, 'distinctive cultures' arguments have had an unhappy tendency to convince almost no one, even as they have been subject to a powerful compulsion to repeat. To date the most famous contributions to the genre have proven at once profoundly unhelpful for the work of advocacy (as distortive for the sciences and social sciences as for the humanities) and yet perversely, as if ineluctably, captivating.

My intention here is not to rerun in detail the history of 'two' and, latterly, 'three cultures' debates for its own sake, but (with an eye on that

---

[14] See Gayatri Chakravorty Spivak, 'Speaking for the Humanities', *Occasion: Interdisciplinary Studies in the Humanities* 1/1 (15 October 2009), <http://occasion.stanford.edu/node/19>.

history) to try to fathom what kinds of reasoning are involved in claims by way of comparison between different intellectual fields, and what positive contribution such claims can hope to make to public justification of the humanities now. I assume that readers of this book have some familiarity with C. P. Snow's charge, in 1959, that the representatives of the 'traditional culture', 'literary intellectuals', were no longer the 'true' intellectuals of their day and that the future belonged, or should belong, to the scientists, who have remade our reality in ways the literary intellectuals were (he thought) at once culpably ignorant of, and intuitively hostile to.[15] I also assume some familiarity with F. R. Leavis's (still startlingly vituperative) counter-claims, in 1962, for the importance of the best literature, which has its 'immediate and crucial relevance' because it asks, and makes us ask, 'What, ultimately, do men live by?'[16]

Many will know that Snow/Leavis was a reworking of a famous but less sharply antagonistic series of encounters between Thomas Huxley and Matthew Arnold during the early 1880s (remembered as another confrontation between science and literature, though Arnold and Huxley spoke more broadly of a contrast between scientists and 'humanists' or 'humane letters'[17]). The Snow/Leavis argument has found numerous subsequent repetitions.[18] The most striking in recent decades was the Sokal Affair of 1996, when the physicist Alan Sokal placed a hoax article with the cultural studies journal *Social Text* purporting to demonstrate the social constructedness of gravity—and

[15] C. P. Snow, *The Two Cultures*, introduction by Stefan Collini (Cambridge: Cambridge University Press, 1993), esp. 4–11.

[16] F. R. Leavis, 'Two Cultures? The Significance of C. P. Snow', *Spectator* (9 March 1962), rpt as 'Two Cultures? The Significance of Lord Snow', in his *Nor Shall my Sword: Discourses on Pluralism, Compassion and Social Hope* (London: Chatto and Windus, 1972), 41–74 (55–6).

[17] *OED* (3rd edn. 2009) dates the term 'humanities' (meaning Literary learning or scholarship; secular letters as opposed to theology; esp. the study of ancient Latin and Greek language, literature, and intellectual culture (as grammar, rhetoric, history, and philosophy)) to the later fifteenth century, the first attribution being to Caxton; 'humane letters' (an import from the French 'lettres humaines') is dated to the early seventeenth century. Accessed 22 June 2012.

[18] See esp. Miroslav Holub, 'Rampage, or Science in Poetry', in Robert Crawford (ed.), *Contemporary Poetry and Contemporary Science* (Oxford: Oxford University Press, 2006), 11–24; and Peter McDonald v. Peter Atkins, 'Poetry is Beautiful, but Science is What Matters?' <http://www.ox.ac.uk/oxford_debates/past_debates/hilary_2009_poetry_and_science/>. Accessed 18 June 2012. Holub's revival of the two cultures conflict is discussed in Helen Small, 'The Function of Antagonism: Miroslav Holub and Roald Hoffmann', in John Holmes (ed.), *Science in Modern Poetry: New Directions* (Liverpool: Liverpool University Press, 2012), 19–37.

prompting a great deal of soul searching within the humanities about comparative understandings of 'fact' and 'truth' in the disciplines, the ethics of professionalism, the function of scepticism, the nature and limits of social construction arguments in particular, and, perhaps most revealingly, the implicit battle for the future of the social sciences.[19]

Two culture arguments are, by their nature, polemical and take what credibility they have from walking a thin line between plain statement and overstatement. As others have noted, their conventional locus has until recently been the lecture, the public speech, the polemical essay; in more recent years also the blog and the web posting.[20] They have often, though not always, been occasioned by an external incitement, sometimes a prescriptive requirement, to stage a debate. In very recent decades a number of writers have attempted to improve the terrain of argument by filling out Snow's hint that 'two' might have better been 'three', and allowing for characterizing distinctions not only between the work of the humanities and the sciences, but between the humanities, the sciences, and the social sciences. Snow conceded that he might have allowed a distinctive role for social historians; later writers have adopted as standard the larger institutional grouping 'the social sciences', though the internal 'humanistic/empiricist' qualification tends to make this newer triad look like something of an overlay on an original binary. Typically, attempts to flesh out the concept of a third culture have tried to avoid the model of cultural antagonism, and to correct its excesses and misrepresentations. In the main they have taken

[19] For Sokal's original article, the responses by the editors of *Social Text* (Bruce Robbins and Andrew Ross), and the principal contributions to the immediately subsequent debate see John Brenkman, Elizabeth Lloyd, and David Albert (eds.), *The Sokal Hoax: The Sham that Shook the Academy* (Lincoln, Nebr.: University of Nebraska Press, 2000). The best of the subsequent contributions to that literature, in my own view, is John Guillory, 'The Sokal Affair and the History of Criticism', *Critical Inquiry* 28/2 (2002), 470–508. See also his two-stage exchange of views with Christopher Newfield: 'Critical Response I: The Value of Nonscience', *Critical Inquiry* 29/3 (2003), 508–25; Guillory, 'Critical Response II: The Name of Science, the Name of Politics', *Critical Inquiry* 29/3 (2003), 526–41. Guillory argues that the revival of the old puppet war between literature and social sciences conceals and makes manageable a less readily confronted conflict 'in the social sciences themselves, as they both embrace and resist the extension of natural scientific methodologies to the domain of the social'—the primary cost of that conflict being that the middle ground of 'an interpretative human science...remains underdeveloped to this day' (482–3, 507).

[20] On the importance of the lecture form, see Collini, introduction to Snow, *The Two Cultures*, xxviii–xxix. For examples of more recent forms see McDonald v. Atkins, 'Poetry is Beautiful, but Science is What Matters?'; and (among the more influential blogs) <www.michaelberube.com/index.php/weblog> and <http://crookedtimber.org/>.

the form of the scholarly monograph or article. Among the most extensive to date are Wolf Lepenies's *Die Drei Kulturen: Soziologie zwischen Literatur und Wissenschaft* (1985) and Jerome Kagan's *The Three Cultures: Natural Sciences, Social Sciences, and the Humanities in the 21st Century* (2009).[21]

Two and three culture arguments alike have, in the past thirty years especially, coincided with efforts to replace the concept of opposing cultures by a 'one culture' model: that is, by work that consciously rejects the imprisoning power of specialization and seeks to establish the depth of cultural overlap and productive interaction between different spheres of knowledge.[22] If I do not say more about that kind of work here it is because, with more than a quarter century of history and intellectual achievement behind it now, it is nevertheless the case that most interdisciplinary work continues to be undertaken from the position of authority afforded by primary training in one field—in rare cases, by the breadth achieved through a move from one discipline to another. 'One culture' criticism has made a strong mark on 'literature and science' studies, especially, since the 1980s, but, as Abbott points out, interdisciplinarity more broadly conceived is not the late reaction against the constraints of disciplinary specialization that it is often taken to be. 'The emphasis on interdisciplinarity emerged [in the 1920s and 1930s] contemporaneously with, not after, the disciplines. There was no long period of ossification; the one bred the other almost immediately.'[23]

The moment there is specialization, in other words, there is also the impulse to reach out across the specialisms in order to correct for their narrowness. New specialisms emerge on a regular basis, often out of

[21] (Cambridge: Cambridge University Press). See also Wolf Lepenies, *Die Drei Kulturen: Soziologie zwischen Literatur und Wissenschaft* (1985), trans. R. J. Hollingdale, *Between Literature and Science: The Rise of Sociology* (Cambridge: Cambridge University Press, 1988); Bruce Mazlish (citing Jacob Bronowski as an inspiration) in 'The Three and a Half Cultures', *Leonardo* 18/4 (1985), 233–6; and Bent Flyvbjerg, *Making Social Science Matter: Why Social Inquiry Fails and How it Can Succeed Again* (Cambridge: Cambridge University Press, 2001).
[22] Among the most influential early contributions to the field were Robert M. Young, *Darwin's Metaphor: Does Nature Select?* (San Jose, Calif.: San Jose College, 1971); Gillian Beer, *Darwin's Plots: Evolutionary Narrative in Darwin, George Eliot and Nineteenth-Century Fiction* (London: Routledge and Kegan Paul, 1983); L. J. Jordanova (ed.), *Languages of Nature: Critical Essays on Science and Literature* (New Brunswick, NJ: Rutgers University Press, 1986); George Levine (ed.), *One Culture: Essays in Science and Literature* (Madison: University of Wisconsin Press, 1987); John Christie and Sally Shuttleworth (eds.), *Nature Transfigured: Science and Literature, 1700–1900* (Manchester: Manchester University Press, 1989).
[23] *Chaos of Disciplines*, 132.

cross-disciplinary collaborations (history of science, sciences studies, postcolonial studies, area studies, women's studies), but this process of structural and curricular evolution is sustained by forms of training that are recognized as discipline-particular (historical interpretation, literary criticism, political analysis, language study, musicology, and so forth). As Abbott observes, the most striking feature of our modern disciplines is not their structural fertility but the cohesion and core immobility of their social and cultural arrangements: they permit a great deal of flux at the perimeters (Abbott develops a detailed technical account of what he calls their 'fractal lineages' (149 and *passim*)) but the 'overall structure... seems virtually unbreakable' (149). Just what would be needed to break it is the subject of his concluding chapter: briefly, a cultural revolution affecting the central symbolic system of a discipline that would unmoor its authority and unbalance the system as a whole (an explanatory shift as fundamental as those presented by the Copernican or Darwinian theories) (150); more conceivably, a reorientation in the system of professional rewards to value teaching above the command of abstract knowledge via research, or 'a systemwide switch in the importance of audience' (150). The ongoing change from a structure in which 'academics control each others' rewards' to one in which they are far more answerable to 'students, administrators, and others [who] control them' (central government, in the UK) seems to Abbott potentially a shift of that order (150).

Of the many reiterations of the two cultures conflict, the rewriting of the Huxley and Arnold 'science and literature' debate in the Snow/ Leavis 'two cultures' conflict has most relevance for this book's examination of established defences for the humanities. In retrospect, those two moments mark out (first) a high point of optimism in Britain about the possibilities for a liberal secular model of education in which the sciences and the humanities each have a protected place, and (secondly) a low point for the expression of relations between the 'traditional culture' of literary intellectuals, specifically, and the modern culture of natural scientists—an announcement of an absolute failure in understanding. With Snow/Leavis what had been a friendly contest of priorities within a context of more important shared commitments (to a non-sectarian, secular model of modern education and to the increasing democratization of that education) became a far more rivalrous exhibition of distinct commitments (opposing politics, conflicting attitudes to history and modernity). Snow was not interested, as Huxley had been, in ensuring the place of science in a more holistic educational culture; he wanted to act decisively to counter a bias against science institutionalized, as he thought, with the help of politically too-influential literary men; also to enable future governments to employ new scientific technologies effectively in the war against world poverty. In short, he raised (if 'raised' is the word) a debate about respective strengths to a struggle for political dominance.

It is a standard, and correct, observation on the most famous and fractious of two culture encounters that it tells us very little about the kinds of work the participants' university colleagues were doing at the time but a great deal about the wider social, cultural, institutional, and political factors that had a bearing on the argument. Successive historical rereadings have pointed to the influence on both men of early 1960s debates over social class, culture, meritocracy, university expansionism, democracy, and the relation between technological progress and political progress.[24] Recent commentators have stressed, especially, Snow's occlusion of the strength and political importance of the contemporary drive for technocratic modernization behind a largely fictitious argument about scientism—keeping alive (as did Leavis's reply) a notion of culture as the foundation of judgement, but at the cost of misrepresenting his historical moment and his own role in it.[25]

Looking at the progression of two cultures antagonisms across the nineteenth and twentieth centuries, it is clear that the social contexts, not least the class contexts, that contained them in the high Victorian period could no longer be relied upon by the 1960s, even if the predominant response to Leavis was dismay at his abandonment of politeness ('an impermissible tone', in Lionel Trilling's much repeated

---

[24] See Collini, 'Introduction'; and for a review of the literature up to 2008, Guy Ortolano, 'The Literature and the Science of "Two Cultures" Historiography', *Studies in History and Philosophy of Science* 39 (2008), 143–50.

[25] See esp. David Edgerton, 'C. P. Snow as Anti-Historian of British Science: Revisiting the Technocratic Moment, 1959–1964', *History of Science* 43 (2005), 187–208; David A. Hollinger, 'Science as a Weapon in *Kulturkämpfe* in the United States during and after World War II', *Isis* 86 (1995), 440–54. Equivalently contextualizing arguments can and have been made about the influence on the Arnold/Huxley conflict of utilitarian and sectarian religious pressures on government education policy in the 1880s (the literature/science conflict being a means by which they differently asserted a shared commitment to secular, liberal education)—but they are less germane, in proportion as the conflict they inspired was less sharply oppositional.

phrase[26]). But it is equally clear that when the two cultures conflict
came back to prominence in the 1990s it was to a degree contained by
an alternative ethos that had (and has) some of the same constraining
features as Victorian 'gentlemanly' debate—namely, the ethos of professionalism. Much the most striking differences between the Snow/
Leavis exchanges and the Sokal/*Social Text* editorship exchanges occur
on the side of the humanities: Andrew Ross and Bruce Robbins's
defence of their board's actions, and of cultural studies by association,
was not rooted, as Leavis's advocacy for literature had been, in the vital-
ity of the individual response to great literature but in the subscription
of humanities academics, *along with all academics*, to professional values
that include 'intellectual integrity', proper training, and credentialling
within a specialist field (in Sokal's case physics rather than cultural studies),
and (not definitively but desirably) a willingness to engage in outward-
looking discussion about politics in ways shaped by 'the public interest'
not the narrow interests of the discipline as it sees itself in competition
with others.[27] It is critical to the evolving history of 'distinct cultures'
reasoning that the case for the humanities was made, in the Sokal
Affair, by several of the same individuals who took the lead, during the
1980s and 1990s, in reorienting the humanities from their earlier anti-
professionalism towards a positive endorsement of professionalism as a
social and ethical structure within which advanced knowledge is now
pursued and mediated to a wider public.[28]

Amidst shifting historical conditions the dominant note of 'two
cultures' conflicts has always been a temporary breaching of social
constraints, whether the old codes of gentlemanliness or the newer

[26] Lionel Trilling, 'Science, Literature, and Culture: A Comment on the Leavis–Snow
Controversy', *Commentary* (1962), reprinted in his *Beyond Culture: Essays on Literature and Learning* (New York: Viking Press, 1965), 133–58 (152). Cf. the response of *The World* to Arnold's
Royal Academy toast on behalf of 'Literature' in 1882: 'There is, perhaps, no other man
alive who would have had the intrepidity to make such a speech... in returning thanks.'
Quoted in David A. Roos, 'Matthew Arnold and Thomas Henry Huxley: Two Speeches
at the Royal Academy, 1881 and 1883', *Modern Philology* 74/3 (1977), 316–24 (320).

[27] Robbins and Ross, 'Mystery Science Theatre', *Lingua Franca*, <http://linguafranca.mor-
ror.theinfo.org/9607/mst.html>. Rpt in Brenkman et al. (eds.), *The Sokal Hoax*, 54–8 (58).

[28] There is a large literature on this subject. Particularly influential have been the essays
on professionalism collected in Stanley Fish, *Doing What Comes Naturally: Change, Rhetoric
and the Practice of Theory in Literary and Legal Studies* (Oxford: Clarendon Press, 1989); Richard Rorty, 'Reply to Andrew Ross', *Dissent* (Spring 1992), 263–7; Bruce Robbins, *Secular
Vocations: Intellectuals, Professionalism, Culture* (London: Verso, 1993); Michael Bérubé,
Employment of English: Theory, Jobs, and the Future of Literary Studies (New York: New York
University Press, 1996).

ones of professionalism. The attraction to these conflicts, within and outside the academy, has much to do with the Swiftian lure of a suspicion that something truthful, as well as something distortively extreme, is being said when politeness goes to the winds. *In irae veritas*? Strikingly, the university tends to emerge from these staged rivalries at the border between the institution and the wider public life little if at all altered in its behaviour. The Sokal Affair is the exception insofar as it can be credited with effecting 'the virtual disappearance of the term "social construction" from serious venues of [cultural] criticism'; the 'hypothesis' remains current, and it has not departed from anthropology and sociology, but the language of cultural studies has shifted—a change attributable (I am agreeing with John Guillory here) to the accuracy with which Sokal captured not just the shorthand idiom of that field at a certain moment, but the 'dubious correlation of epistemology with politics' (social constructionism with left-wing commitments).[29] For the participants, of course, the attention generated by these high-profile contests can be reputationally transformative. Snow seems likely to be remembered as the author of 'The Two Cultures' long after he is forgotten as a novelist. Sokal would probably not have been heard of by most people in the humanities had he not authored the hoax and its exposure. But quite what the element of suspected truth is that attracts the wider intellectual community, even as its collective judgement repeatedly condemns these conflicts as mistaken, is a question worth pondering. Why the compulsion to repeat?

A small part of the answer has to do with the imaginative grip of historically entrenched genres. That a form of argument has a strong genealogy can, in itself, give it a measure of validity, providing a reason to recall it, play it out again in each new generation, pay homage, or attempt to dispel the shadow. Sokal was a repetition of Snow/Leavis; Snow/Leavis of Huxley/Arnold; but the deeper historical roots go back into classical antiquity. Arnold and Huxley's encounters were closely related to Carlyle and Coleridge's opposition to Bentham and (James) Mill earlier in the nineteenth century; those conflicts were in part repetitions of the 'Ancients v. Moderns' debate of the previous century; the Ancients and Moderns debate was in its turn a revisiting of the Humanism/Scholasticism confrontations of the Early Modern period; and one can find a kind of origin for all these oppositions in

---

[29] See Guillory, 'Sokal Affair', 484, 494.

the classical distinction between *ars* and *scientia*, perhaps also that between metaphysics and physics. All these repetitions are impure in various ways, but they share two positive features: a recognition of the rhetorical power of binary oppositions; and a provisional commitment to their utility as diagrammatic accounts of the educational field as it encounters the political field. They crudify matters, but they also clarify them, and when faced with complexity we may be persuaded to put up with quite a lot of crudeness in the service of getting a basic outline from which refinements can start.

The proximate hosts in all these conflicts can fairly be said to have benefited more than they lost by the association. The attention attracted on each occasion was intense and, on the whole, enjoyed. These were intellectually engaging events. They demonstrated that large matters of educational principle and political priority were getting a hearing where they ought to be getting a hearing, at the interface of the educational institution with the wider public and political life. But to construe the act of playing institutional host more aggressively (to see Cambridge, the Royal Academy of Arts, *Lingua Franca*, Duke University[30] as having a vested interest in promoting two cultures arguments) would overestimate how coherent universities and learned societies were, in the past, in their work of self-description, how exclusively they owned the debate,[31] and how much control they exercise, even now, over their members.

The institutional investment that matters in construing the cultural impact of these arguments, then, is not the immediate host so much as 'the academy' in the inclusive sense, the profession of higher education as it encounters other parts of public intellectual life (schools, the media, government policy-making, in earlier periods also the church) and as it recognizes itself, or declines to recognize itself, in rivalrous statements about the distinctive contributions of its major faculties to

[30] Cambridge University and the Royal Academy of Arts, London, hosted the major parts of the Arnold/Huxley exchanges. See Roos, 'Matthew Arnold and Thomas Henry Huxley'. Snow's 'The Two Cultures and the Scientific Revolution' was the Rede Lecture for 1859; Leavis's reply was delivered as the Richmond lecture, at Downing College, Cambridge, in 1962. See Collini, introduction to Snow, *The Two Cultures*. The 'hosts' of the Sokal Affair were, in a narrow sense, Duke University as the publishers of *Social Text* and *Lingua Franca* (published independently). It had, however, something of a New York flavour in that the principal disputants happened all to be geographically based in that city.

[31] The Arnold/Huxley debate, for example, occupied a variety of venues: speeches to schools and colleges, public lecture tours, newspaper articles, private letters.

public life. If the initiating provocation is (usually) an effort by a representative of one of the faculties to advance the public standing of that field, or resist the perceived imperialism of the other, the role of the institution on the whole is to contain the rivalry and display a proper valuation of both.

Ethos and Character on the Two Culture Model

The question for the advocate of the humanities, now, is whether the complexity of modern disciplines (their fragmentation into more sharply defined specialisms, and yet also the multiple connections between them, under the aegis of interdisciplinarity) can admit of any more credible articulation of a 'distinctive cultures' argument than has been achieved in the past. Generalizations are generally unsatisfactory, and in the case of the 'humanities', 'sciences', 'social sciences' the level of generalization is uncomfortably high. An institutional grouping that puts together formal logic, biblical scholarship, the study of imaginative literature, Middle High German, Sufi mysticism, and the archaeology of the ancient world creates serious problems for any attempt to characterize it cohesively. But is the problem of focal length insuperable?

A distinguishing feature of cultural antagonism arguments is that the descriptions they have yielded have always been recognized as stereotyping—if strictly believed, then certainly misleading, but useful as a broad guideline to behaviour. Much like Aristotle's accounts of the rhetorical features of certain social groups (the well born, the wealthy, the powerful, the young, the old, those in the prime of life) the conflict of intellectual fields draws on recognizable, repeatable features of how social groups speak and act, and what kinds of speech and action they find persuasive. If any one representative of the group possessed all those features, he or she would be a gross caricature, but the behavioural observation is not the less serviceable for being reductive.[32] John Guillory captures an essential feature of all such antagonisms when he observes that caricatures of disciplinary group formation are effective to the extent that they accurately capture the current shorthand by which intellectual fields mark out their own common ground. They

---

[32] See Helen Small, *The Long Life* (Oxford: Oxford University Press, 2007), 62–6.

identify 'tokens of verbal exchange' that make visible the 'imagined community of the discipline'.[33] These tokens are less articles of faith than provisional currencies, their value contingent on internal and external factors, including (however grudgingly) the perception of their credibility in the eyes of the educated general public.

The choice to focus, as Guillory does, on rhetoric has always been the hallmark of humanities readings of 'two cultures' conflicts. It is, in part, a predictable orientation towards one's own discipline-specific skills: the cynic will say an assertion of discipline-specific interests. (If one turns to the sociological literature on disciplinarity one finds an equally selective emphasis on the role of social structures in shaping epistemology.[34]) But when C. P. Snow put the phrase 'two cultures' into general circulation he explicitly attempted to gloss it as something other and more than a rhetorical gesture. Not far into 'The Two Cultures' he confesses his unease about whether 'down to earth' non-scientific acquaintances were right to warn him that he is over-simplifying:

> The number two is a very dangerous number: that is why the dialectic is a dangerous process. Attempts to divide anything into two ought to be regarded with much suspicion. I have thought for a long time about going in for further refinements: but in the end I have decided against. I was searching for something a little more than a dashing metaphor, a good deal less than a cultural map, and subtilizing any more would bring more disadvantages than it's worth. (8)

What exactly is it that might qualify as more than a metaphor but 'a good deal less than a cultural map'? The attraction of the word 'culture' to Snow was, as he elaborated in 'The Two Cultures: A Second Look' (1963), that it combined two senses: the personal sense of 'intellectual development, development of the mind' (62), and 'the anthropologists' sense' (64). One could not deny that scientists, as highly educated men, possessed culture in the developmental sense, so the first usage was unproblematic. For Snow there was a 'very strong additional attraction'

---

[33] Guillory, 'Sokal Affair', 500.
[34] Becher and Trowler, *Academic Tribes*, 37 and *passim*. See also an influential early work in this field: Clifford Geertz, 'Towards an Enthnography of the Disciplines', mimeo (Princeton: Princeton Institute of Advanced Study, 1976); and D. A. Kolb, 'Learning Styles and Disciplinary Differences', in A. Chickering (ed.), *The Modern American College* (San Francisco: Jossey-Bass, 1981).

in the anthropological denotation of 'a group of persons living in the same environment, linked by common habits, common assumptions, a common way of life' (64). What he intended was a kind of anthropological sketch from his own perspective as someone with a claim to have inhabited both cultures—'science' by higher education and profession, 'literature' by early education, life-long familiarity, and in recent years also by profession. He wanted, that is, a mode of description more substantive than the rhetorical performance (the dashing metaphor) but less exacting than an empirically grounded and observationally verifiable analysis (the anthropologist's detailed 'map').

The argument by way of 'cultural' differentiation is, then, a quasi-anthropological argument: claiming a relation to anthropological observation but not empirically grounded and necessarily having as much to do with rhetoric. (I am, in effect, restating what was, for Leavis, a matter of strenuous objection: 'there is no evidence...' (47).) But an anthropological-cum-rhetorical sketch leaves quite a lot of opacity about how the two senses of 'culture', personal development and collective behaviour, are related other than through the magic performed by the word 'culture'. The vagueness of the claim to cultural distinctiveness infects the argument at both its levels of operation: as an account of the effects of educational specialization on the psychological development of individuals, evidenced in their speech and actions, and as an anthropological description of the effect of educational patterns of specialization on professional and public life, evidenced in 'common habits, common assumptions, a common way of life'. From both perspectives, 'two cultures' claims are typically and problematically inexplicit about the presumed relation between education and ethos: between trained habits of intellection and individual behaviour; and between trained habits of intellection and group behaviour.

The problem is not much better illuminated if one turns to the more recent sociological literature for help. The proper scope of any claim that disciplinary structures in education have effects that go beyond epistemology to ethics has been an area of difficulty for the social sciences in recent years (though, as indicated above, rather less so than for the humanities in the wake of Sokal). Tony Becher and Paul Trowler carve a fairly representative path through the difficulties in *Academic Tribes and Territories: Intellectual Enquiry and the Culture of Disciplines* (2001), when they observe that the constructivist view sees a training in the academic disciplines as an induction into 'a particular "way of being"', a personal and professional identity, a set of values, attitudes, taken-for-granted knowledge, and recurrent practices. Some room, they caution, should be allowed for the 'creative power of individuals' but it should not be 'overstressed'.[35] As they see it, initiation into academic communities today is an efficient process, particularly so at the postgraduate level.

There are in short 'social facts', as Durkheim put it: the effects of education, like other social facts, are not rigid and unchanging but they are observably constraining. Insofar as educational patterns of specialization shape our language, the ways in which we identify objects worthy of study, and the ways in which we deal with them, they have sociological force. Observing how a humanities professor, a social scientist, and a scientist speak and act at a cross-disciplinary seminar may or may not tell you anything about the inner psychological states of the individuals concerned but will certainly tell you something about their understandings of conventions of intellectual behaviour and something about their values. The more difficult question is how *much* it tells you about their values.

The names conventionally given, in philosophy and in common parlance, to the internalization of values along with habituated behaviour are 'character' and 'ethos'. That there is a connection between education and character at the level of individual development is obvious. This is what we mean by education: the 'leading out' and guiding of the qualities of a person and the group. Where two cultures arguments in the past have repeatedly gone wrong is in raising the quasi-sociological description of behaviour to a too firm ascription of characterology. At their strongest these ascriptions ask us to believe that patterns of specialization in higher education, overseen by the institutional structures of the university, produce deeply entrenched characterological types, as if a collective 'ethos' were formed as directly and observably as an individual character.

I am maintaining a distinction here between character and ethos that not all writers on the subject would observe (and that the dictionary does not legislate for): retaining the former term for the individual expression of qualities (including virtues) and the latter term for the

---

[35] *Academic Tribes*, 48.

communal expression of qualities (including educational and professional values).[36] As *OED* puts it, after Aristotle (*Rhetoric* II. ii–xiv), ethos
is 'The characteristic spirit, prevalent tone of sentiment, of a people or
community; the "genius" of an institution or system'.[37] The extent of
the shaping influence of education is, I am suggesting, less clear in the
case of the collective ethos than in that of an individual character,
though even in the case of the individual far from absolute. Individuals
will respond to the same educational programme quite variously, but it
is at least relatively plain what we mean in talking about the effect of
education on character: the installation of certain guiding ideas about
action and conduct, certain values rather than others. In the case of the
larger group the claim cannot but be weaker. The more one aggregates
the experience the more one also abstracts from it and in abstracting
mutes the force of the description. 'Characterology' is a reductive
enough instrument applied to individual behaviour, but it can in that
case at least appeal to the integrity of the life; applied to large groups
characterology risks seeming not much more than a metaphorical
transfer to the idea of a community (a discipline, a profession, a
nation).

Scholars of education nevertheless standardly observe that there is
such a thing as a 'national character' of education: 'Humboldtian, Napo-
leonic, Anglo-American, Soviet', and so forth.[38] In the case of the collective ethos of large groups of disciplines, we are talking about aggregative
effects across a range of scales: different individual experiences of education, different kinds of institution, different local relations to national
policy-making. To describe them well, anthropologically, would require
a lot of observational data. But characterology as it has been applied
at this level historically as a tool of anthropological-cum-rhetorical

---

[36] See, for example, Amanda Anderson, 'Character and Ideology: The Case of Cold War
Liberalism', *New Literary History* 42/2 (2011), 209–29 (212), defending their use not
'interchangeabl[y]' but in constant association so as to assist thinking about 'the significance of the existential and ethical dimensions of intellectual and political positions, in
part because terms we associate with character (particularly adjectival ascriptions) often
signal moments where the existential or lived elements of theory are making their force
felt'. I am more concerned here to isolate moments in which that ascription typically goes
wrong, being prejudicial and not confirmed by common observation.

[37] Accessed 24 July 2012. Entry last revised 1989.

[38] Donghui Zhang, '*Tongshi* Education Reform in a Chinese University: Knowledge, Values, and Organizational Changes', *Comparative Education Review* 56/3 (2012),
394–420 (for the discussion of cultures and subcultures of education as they bear on
national 'character' see 399–400).

analysis, has made very little use of data and has tended to be a very reductive instrument. Indeed, the most dispiriting aspect of the history of 'distinct culture' arguments, as it runs from Arnold and Huxley, through Snow and Leavis, to the Sokal Affair, is the extent to which the characterological interpretation of differences between 'the two cultures' has developed in force and antagonism even as the rationale for reading ethos as so strong a collective characterology has remained almost entirely unexamined.

So: in the course of defending their respective priorities within a liberal approach to education, Arnold and Huxley elaborated opposing accounts of the intellectual and moral benefits conferred by an education in humane letters and an education in the sciences, but science was still in search of respectability and the characterology was relatively mild and corrected for by the assumption of a liberal educational structure. The 'scientific "criticism of life"' was admirable, for Huxley, because it 'appeals not to authority, nor to what anybody may have thought or said, but to nature. It admits that all our interpretations of natural fact are more or less imperfect and symbolic, and bids the learner seek for truth not among words but among things',[39] the hardest thing Huxley has to say about humanists is that they illegitimately arrogate for themselves 'the monopoly of culture' ignoring 'the vast and constantly increasing part which is played by natural knowledge'.[40] For Arnold, in reaction, the scientist gives us knowledge, yes, but *only* knowledge—'not put for us into relation with our sense of conduct, our sense of beauty, and touched with emotion by being so put'. It is the great power of 'humane letters' to create that relation, and thereby to 'make [one] live more'.[41] Both Huxley and Arnold assumed that human beings are to an extent divided from birth in their aptitudes: they have a natural bent of mind. That assumption, along with the liberal generalism, dilutes the degree to which education can be deemed responsible for cultural distinction in the personal and the collective senses (there is something like a natural distribution of aptitude in the population, which would be apparent

[39] Huxley, 'Science and Culture', in *Science and Education: Essays* (London: Macmillan and Co., 1893), 134–59 (150).
[40] Huxley, 'Science and Culture', 152, 149.
[41] Arnold, 'Literature and Science', in R. H. Super (ed.), *Philistinism in England and America, The Complete Prose Works of Matthew Arnold* , vol. x (hereafter *CPW*) (Ann Arbor: University of Michigan Press, 1974), 53–73 (65, 70).

even without advanced education, and something like a natural difference of priorities, for which the Arnold/Huxley encounters are themselves evidence[42]).

To turn from this strong but not intolerant articulation of cultural and 'natural dispositional' differences in the 1880s to the aggravated antagonism of Leavis v. Snow is to find the theatre of character far more exaggerated. For Snow the scientific culture is, distinctively, 'intensive, rigorous, . . . constantly in action' (12), 'exacting' in its requirements for objectivity and reasoned argument. It is also 'optimistic' about 'progress', however pessimistic the scientist in his individual character may be (6). Literary men are complacent in their no longer earned cultural authority; they tend to pessimism, and to conservatism, in certain prominent cases even to fascism. (Snow has in view 'Yeats, Pound, Wyndham Lewis, nine out of ten of those who have dominated literary sensibility in our time—weren't they not only politically silly, but politically wicked?' (7).) For Leavis, again in reaction, Snow's view of the modern world is deadening, vulgar, and dangerously self-aggrandizing. If we want an understanding of what it would mean for individual lives to be 'filled with satisfaction and significance' in anything beyond the basic material sense of 'satisfaction' we must turn to 'the great novelists and poets' to enliven our individual sensibilities (54–5).

For Snow, in pursuit of his cultural sketch, individual character is irrelevant (he correctly states that the character of the particular scientist may or may not be congruent with the collective ethos of scientists, acting on the basis of shared technical expertise and professional affiliation); Leavis, on the other hand, is battling to preserve the idea of an individual sensibility at work and an individual character in action. Much of what offends him in Snow's view of intellectual development is that in order to assert the superiority of the scientists' collective

---

[42] In Huxley's words: 'The native capacities of mankind vary no less than their opportunities; and while culture is one, the road by which one man may best reach it is widely different from that which is most advantageous to another.' 'Science and Culture', 153. In Arnold's: there is such a thing as a 'born naturalist', and born naturalists are relatively rare. They are those with 'exceptional and overpowering aptitudes for the study of nature', which might seem to justify an educational concentration on 'collecting natural knowledge and reasoning on it'—though in Arnold's view it is all the more important that such minds be educated in the humanities, which 'will call out their being at more points, will make them live more'. 'Literature and Science', 70.

ethos he so entirely overrides specificity of individual outlook (which, for Leavis, should be legible as an individualized style of utterance).

In Sokal's handling, the base characterology of the scientist, as indicated above, remains strikingly unchanged from Snow's account—unchanged, even, from Huxley's. The humanistic side of the description, however, has become more aggressively delineated. The scientist is, still, 'modest', 'meticulous', 'progressive', wedded to 'intellectual rigor' and to 'truth', opposed to 'dogma', and, where circumstances require, 'pragmatic'; the humanist (qua cultural studies professor) is 'arrogant', 'lazy', historically regressive as ever, a slave to dogma, and therefore one has to assume incapable of pragmatism.[43] The ethical claims were in this case fuelled by Sokal's conviction that 'the American academic humanities' in the mid-1990s were betraying what was once the common political cause of many in the academy, Enlightenment commitment to 'evidence and logic' underpinning progressivist left-wing politics. That project, as he understood it, could now only look to the sciences for support. If the content of the *Social Text* editors' defence of professionalism sounded, in earlier summary, short on characterological description of the humanities, character was nonetheless strongly there in the writing performance. Probably the most frequently cited line in Andrew Ross and Bruce Robbins's response to Sokal is the line that most vividly enacts the defence of professionalism as something more and other than an appeal to technocratic proceduralism: 'From the first, we considered Sokal's unsolicited article to be a little hokey'... (55).

The easy explanation for the hardening and sharpening of characterology over the years would be the growing institutional power of science. But the easy explanation is inadequate. It is far from obvious that the enhanced institutional standing of the sciences should produce greater animus against the humanities. Benign condescension, perhaps? Obliviousness? Why not mutual respect? The assumption that any of the faculties aims at domination of the university requires one to forget both the extent to which these conflicts have, rightly, been limited in credibility within the institution, and (in the case of Sokal especially) widely perceived as backward steps within a developing public conversation that assumed, and should still assume,

---

[43] All these terms are drawn from Sokal's *Lingua Franca* self-exposé, and the subsequent exchange with the editors of *Social Text*.

friendly and mutually respectful relations between the disciplines and a common commitment to the pursuit of ideas.[44]

Enter a Third Culture

There is now a substantial literature within the social sciences seeking to advance the argument from the position it had reached at the time of the Sokal Affair. Several of them flirt, more or less seriously, with a 'three cultures' description, inclusive of the social sciences, that might better reflect the institutional and cultural arrangements of today's university. Among the most recent and most openly polemical (explicitly presenting itself as a reworking of the terrain of Snow/Leavis) is Jerome Kagan's *The Three Cultures* (2009). Unlike Snow and Leavis, Kagan (emeritus professor of psychology at Harvard and a specialist in developmental psychology) does not, in the first instance, do much in the way of sketching distinct characterologies. He concentrates instead on the differences in vocabulary, mental tools, and internal 'hierarchy of motives' which support a delineation of three cultures.

Culture is defined by Kagan as 'a community of persons who share the same symbolic meanings' for various domains of experience, including 'actions and beliefs classed as right and wrong' (107). Human beings participate in an overarching culture whose symbolic meanings they have in common, but they also participate in more specific locations of culture: educational setting and professional situation are two such locations (potentially one and the same); others are ecological setting, family, class, nation, and so forth. This is, I take it, the classic Tylorian definition of culture,[45] somewhat modified through Durkheim.[46] Culture as Kagan describes it, after Durkheim, is explicitly pluralistic (in principle Snow made this allowance, but the characterology and the

[44] See esp. the *Social Text* editors' response to Sokal, and Stanley Fish, 'Professor Sokal's Bad Joke', *The New York Times* 21 May 1996; rpt in *The Sokal Hoax*, 81–4. The subsequent political collaboration between Sokal and Bruce Robbins is a much better reflection of the mutually respectful ethos I take to be dominant.

[45] 'That complex whole which includes knowledge, belief, arts, morals, law, custom, and any other capabilities and habits acquired by man as a member of society.' E. B. T. Tylor, *Primitive Culture: Researches into the Development of Mythology, Philosophy, Religion, Art and Custom* (London: J. Murray, 1871), 1.

[46] See esp. *De la division du travail social* (1893), trans. Lewis A. Coser (New York: The Free Press, 1984).

descriptions of culture were so strongly drawn as to make the concession seem unimportant). Revealingly, it is also an account assisted by
historical reflection on how thinking about culture has evolved within
the social scientific field—away (Kagan argues) from a late Victorian
suspicion that the group was only an artefactual construction on top
of what we know about individuals, towards acceptance of group
phenomena as 'natural phenomena with features that are not deriva-
tives of the features of individuals'. For as long as the social sciences
tacitly assumed that the individual was the fundamental unit of
enquiry, they remained 'blind' to the fact that 'each person assumes
novel properties when studied as part of a collective, even though
personal properties are preserved when the individual is a member of
a group' (114).

I am less interested in challenging Kagan's definition of culture
(though it seems to me challengeable in its appeal to the natural) than
in ascertaining the grounds on which it endeavours to speak authoritatively about the distinctions between the three cultures. There is
no more generally accepted definition of culture now within the social
sciences than one can find in the humanities or, for that matter, in
the sciences. The 'magic' of the word is, here again, its spectacular
capaciousness—its ability to accommodate (in this case) two meanings,
one of them conventionally associated with the humanities (the definition by way of access to shared symbolic meanings), the other explicitly shared with the natural sciences (the definition by way of analogy
between the observation of natural 'kinds' (that is, classes or groups,
generating new properties in the individual)) (114).[47] Its merit, for
Kagan's purposes, is not very different from what Snow's ambiguated
account of culture permitted him to do: to appear to speak with the
doubled authority of the man with a foot in both camps, or (more
accurately in this case) the man with a view of both sides of his own
field—the humanistic and the scientistic.[48]

---

[47] 'Although water retains its arrangement of two hydrogen and one oxygen atom in
all contexts, a collection of water molecules can assume unique properties in different
settings. Water contains haemoglobin when in the bloodstream, dust pollutants in the
clouds over a large city, and pesticides in a river near a farm' (114).
[48] As Kagan (repeatedly) describes the social sciences, they can attempt to limit or at
least be explicit about the cultural constraints that accompany the act of observation but
cannot eliminate them altogether (4); here again, he looks to draw on both the scientistic
and the humanistic qualities of his own discipline.

For Kagan there are three primary 'dimensions' and six secondary ones (2) through which the 'three cultures' generate distinct properties in their inhabitants. Those dimensions are:

1. Their primary concerns (the questions asked, and the relative emphasis on prediction, explanation, and description).

2. Their sources of evidence.

3. Their vocabulary.

4. The degree to which social and historical conditions influence the questions asked.

5. The degree to which ethical values penetrate questions and conclusions.

6. The degree of dependency on financial support from beyond the institution.

7. The probability of the scholar working alone or with one or two others, or as a member of a large team.

8. The contribution to the national economy.

9. The criteria members of the group use in judging work produced as elegant or beautiful.

(abbreviated version of Kagan, *The Three Cultures*, 2–3)

At the core of the behavioural description is a series of claims (see his Table, pp. 4–5) filling out the most important dimensions: 1 to 3. Kagan tends to work from the sciences across to the social sciences and then to the humanities, but I shall keep the primary focus on the relevant claims for the humanities. They are: that in the main the humanities are interested in 'understanding human reactions to events and the meanings humans impose on experience as a function of culture, historical era, and life history', where the natural sciences are interested in prediction and explanation of natural phenomena, the social sciences in prediction and explanation of human behaviours and psychological states. The evidential base for the humanities is written texts and other records of human behaviour 'gathered under conditions of minimal control'; for the natural sciences it is experimentally controlled observations of material entities; for the social sciences behaviour, verbal statements, and (less often) biological measures, 'gathered under conditions in which the context cannot always be controlled'. Each of the cultures uses vocabulary in ways special to its own historically evolved network of ideas, and not always congruent with usage in the other cultures. The humanities are distinguished by heavy reliance on semantic and (to a lesser extent) schematic forms, little if any on mathematical forms (30–9); they have a high tolerance for ambiguity (the social sciences a moderate tolerance, the natural sciences very little) (39–40); and they conceive of the truth value of their claims in terms of 'coherence' and 'rightness' rather than 'correctness' and 'validity' ('most natural scientists' trust only 'correctness' and 'validity'; social scientists, 'coherence' and 'validity' (40–2)).

One can add to this. Perhaps most obviously, one can incorporate different levels of tolerance for truth claims that do not go by way of normative rationalism, and a very different degree of emphasis on style and performativity as not just vehicles of ideas but integral aspects of them. (In both cases the humanities would have a high investment, the social sciences less, and the sciences very little.) Similar attempts at a sociological taxonomy of disciplinary characteristics in recent years have stressed also the 'reiterative' and 'holistic' character of the humanities and (non-pejoratively) the existence of 'dispute over criteria for knowledge verification and obsolescence; [and the] lack of consensus over significant questions to address'.[49] But as a behavioural description Kagan's opening schematic account of the three cultures seems thorough enough, and a recognizably accurate description of much of the behaviour of the three fields.

The general claims advanced in the opening section of *The Three Cultures* barely venture on the kind of characterological claim that was so problematic, and so alluring, in the two culture models of the past. There are hints in the direction of characterology—to say that a field is more 'tolerant of ambiguity' or less 'controlled' is a claim whose epistemological neutrality shades easily into characterology—but no more than hints. Then something goes wrong. Characterology makes a bold and very dubious appearance when Kagan comes to delineating each of the cultures in its own right. In the case of the humanists it does not take long for one to sense that the overpowering determinant in the character sketch is his sense of the field's enforced, and historically recent, institutional humility.

[49] Becher and Trowler, *Academic Tribes*, 36 (revised from Tony Becher, 'The Significance of Disciplinary Differences', *Studies in Higher Education* 19/2 (1994), 151–61 (154)).

Many contemporary humanists would answer the question, 'What are the functions of humanistic scholarship?' with 'To provide divergent perspectives on the human condition and to create objects of beauty'. These praiseworthy goals are far less ambitious than those of Plato, Dante, Bacon, Montaigne, Hume, Kant, or Toynbee who thought they were communicating profound insights about human nature that should be incorporated into ethical positions, political actions, or daily rituals. (231)

This observation is followed by a quotation from Anthony Kronman,[50] calling for humanists to throw off their (post-modern) qualms and take up their ethical role lest they become 'a laughingstock, both within the academy and outside it' (an intervention much discussed in the United States, though it has been little noticed in the UK).

Though he does not gloss the quotation, Kagan clearly shares Kronman's desire to rescue for the humanities some kind of authenticating relation to human 'emotional states', and cultural and historical predicaments, but he wants to do so in ways that prioritize their descriptive over their critical function, or that wrap their critical function up in their descriptive function and to that degree limit it. Humanists 'remind society of its contradictions, articulate salient emotional states, detect changing cultural premises, confront their culture's deepest moral dilemmas, and document the unpredictable events that punctuate a life or historical era' (231). Their 'rich descriptions of emotional blends that are not yet amenable to scientific study should motivate scientists to invent procedures that might assess these states more accurately' (234). It is not a small problem with this model that the 'humanists' doing all the exemplary work are creative writers, life writers, and artists—rather than those who study them. Kagan is not in fact describing modern scholarship, but an area of practice adjacent to it. We are back in the old terrain of expectation, familiar from Arnold and from Leavis, that the study of the humanities, ostensibly best represented by literature, should deliver something 'more' than the scientific pursuit of *knowledge* can ever give us: something that matters for *life*. The slip, from the description of the professional field to description of the work it studies, recalls Stanley Fish's observation that one of the most flattering but stubbornly unhelpful legacies of Romanticism for advocates of higher education in the humanities

[50] *Education's End: Why our Colleges and Universities Have Given Up on the Meaning of Life* (New Haven: Yale University Press, 2004), 139.

is the perception that the humanities matter because they study 'life itself: once you identify the proper object of...study with something so general...it is hard to see why there would be any need for an army of specialists'.[51]

The fullest consequences of the characterological turn in Kagan's argument are heard late on, but they are arresting:

The uncertainty and cynicism that characterize the current historical moment cry out to the next cohort of humanists to initiate a crusade.... The current confusion over which moral standards deserve a resolute commitment, combined with a skeptical view of the utility of honouring the traditional standards for honesty, justice, and loyalty, have created an ethical vacuum.... The lack of consensus among contemporary Americans and Europeans has forced humanists to adopt a more timid posture and to suppress the impulse to rouse the public to demand change, whether a serious reduction in class privilege, the gap in academic achievement between the children of the poor and the privileged, or less violence on television. Only the economists feel confident in their recommendation that a guilt-free self-interest is the only rational way to conduct a life. (243)

It is tempting to pass over this in silence, but the wishes expressed are often enough heard to need comment. It is not the move to characterology per se that is objectionable but the unwarranted ascription of very strong characterological consequences to an (in itself) strong reading of the comparative economic status of disciplines within the institution. Economic size is not, of course, the same thing as economic independence; the income earning potential of the sciences is in some respects a strength, but in others a constraint (the physical sciences especially are dependent upon a much larger revenue stream than the humanities and social sciences[52]). Much of the jostling for position within the social sciences depends on the perceived disciplinary imperialism of economics, which itself depends on the financial system that supports and is supported by it. Moreover the economic balance within the university has a habit of changing very quickly

---

[51] 'Profession Despise Thyself', in *Doing What Comes Naturally*, 197–214 (200). Fish's concern is more specifically with the professional standing of English literary studies, but this particular observation seems to me to go to the heart of a more general problem for the humanities.

[52] On the disproportionate financial support given to the natural sciences in the USA, see Christopher Newfield, *Unmaking the Public University: The Forty Year Assault on the Middle Class* (Cambridge, Mass.: Harvard University Press, 2008), ch. 13.

with alterations in government funding policy (the bolstering of the economic position of the humanities by the new student fees regime in the UK is the immediate example at the time of writing[53]). The attitudinal stance ascribed to the modern humanist by Kagan is feeble in the extreme: possessed of impulses towards the public good that are perforce beaten down and can go nowhere, he or she can only adopt a posture of helpless timidity. That timidity is reinforced by the lack of any receptive social consensus about the legitimacy of the humanists' once distinctive ethical concerns. (It is some measure of relief for the humanist that the lack of consensus appears a general social affliction rather than something the humanities are guilty of contributing to, though other versions of this argument in recent years have been quick to take the further step.[54])

To a non-US reader, there is something recognizably American, though not exclusively so, about such rebukes to the Humanities for having dropped the torch of moral encouragement to the world, requiring the launching of a new moral 'crusade'. (I find it hard to believe, reflecting on the recent history of that metaphor, that Kagan can rest content with it.) The Humanities are hardly short on strongly conceived ethical and political work at present (it is well represented in the Humanities departments of his own university) but listing counter-examples is not quite the point. The characterology offered here rests on a tendentious attribution of symbolic meaning to the relative economic size of the university faculties alone. Characterology is, properly and by etymological development, read off from behaviour and, in the case of the individual, from physiognomy. It has to command agreement from other observers, and this particular characterological reading is eminently contestable by other observations.

But if something has gone wrong here, to the detriment of an initially credible account of intellectual distinction, was the derailing inevitable? Could the characterization have been got right?

[53] On the vulnerability of the physical sciences, also, to falling enrolments, see Michael Bérubé, *Rhetorical Occasions: Essays on Humans and the Humanities* (Chapel Hill, NC: University of North Carolina Press, 2006), 158, and (more polemically) his 'Breaking News: Humanities in Decline! Film at 11', <http://crookedtimber.org/2010/11/16/breaking-news-humanities-in-decline-film-at-11/>. Accessed 30 July 2012.

[54] See, for example, Kronman, *Education's End*, esp. ch. 4.

Characterizing the Humanities now

Many philosophers have thought that we are obliged to say no: that the rendering of a tendency of mind produced by education as a distinctive temperament and a distinctive ethical and political response to the world has no justification in logic. There can be no interpretation of habits and techniques of thought, especially when drawn as broadly as they must be to distinguish just two or three kinds of intellectual endeavour— humanistic, scientific, social scientific—that follow naturally or inevitably from the habits and techniques themselves. All that happens when one moves from a description of epistemological arrangements to an ascription of character is that one illegitimately 'props the epistemological on the psychological'.[55] On this view, arguments by way of a characterological elaboration of distinctions between the main intellectual departments of the university are in error from the start.

The force of the objection and a defence of characterology against it have been very intelligently explored in recent years by Amanda Anderson, who treats the subject historically (examining how various Victorian writers attempted to imagine the methods of science and critical reason in terms of exemplary or heroic characterology) and as a matter of contemporary moment for cultural criticism.[56] In a discussion of pragmatism that has implications for my reading of distinctive cultures arguments here, she draws attention to A. O. Lovejoy's argument with William James as an early articulation of the disputed legitimacy of characterological claims as they have worked through the history of one area of philosophy. Responding to James's assertion that the pragmatist knows he or she is in the presence of truth partly by the feeling of satisfaction gained from recognizing it, Lovejoy objected (in Anderson's summary):

One cannot tell whether [satisfaction] means an experience of certitude or conviction, a desire for consistency or empirical verification, a charm for the imagination, or a general cheerfulness in the face of whatever is being propounded.

Lovejoy argued that 'clarity, consistency, and evidence' were sufficient criteria for pragmatism's truth claims—and such a description, he

---

[55] Anderson, *The Way We Argue Now: A Study in the Cultures of Theory* (Princeton: Princeton University Press, 2006), 117.
[56] See *The Way We Argue Now* and 'Character and Ideology'.

observed, brings no distinctiveness of character to the pragmatist: we are left with (as he put it) 'simply the old, intellectualist criterion supplemented by the psychologically indisputable, but the logically functionless, remark that, after all, a "theoretic" satisfaction is a kind of satisfaction'.[57]

Anderson traces several later iterations of the 'Jamesian' move to install characterology as a component of pragmatist argument, despite full knowledge on the part of the critics concerned that this introduction of characterology may be deemed 'logically functionless', a loose supplement to the intellectualist criteria (she looks particularly at the work of Barbara Hernstein Smith, Stanley Fish, and Richard Rorty). She then asks what the status can be of these appeals to character. Are they just an 'informal fallacy'? Have the critics in question 'stopped making real arguments' and opted instead for a kind of psychological theatre, as if in demonstration of their own late-pragmatist liberation from traditional epistemology into a relaxed acceptance that all knowledge is evolving and contingent?

This is a tempting way to dispense with things but one I think we should reject. It would leave us with a very pared down intellectualism, when in fact what . . . is most interesting . . . is the incorporation of the dimension of character into the discussion of intellectual practice. The incorporation of the characterological is, I suggest, potentially a deep and important move, reorienting us toward the question of whether and how certain ideas can be expressed as a way of life . . . The merit of an attention to characterology . . . lies in the way it brings theory and practice into relation, vivifying and testing theory through embodiment and enactment. (121–2)

In short, the attempt at characterology marks the point at which epistemological claims declare a relation to the conduct of life. And in any given individual case it will be the point at which a *particular* understood relation between intellectual formation and an ethical mode of living in the world is revealed.

As a first observation on how far this defence of character might work to support the plausibility of a 'distinct cultures' argument it is necessary to confront again the fundamental problem of scale, and to adjust the work of characterization accordingly. In looking for the

---

[57] A. O. Lovejoy, *The Thirteen Pragmatisms and Other Essays* (Baltimore: Johns Hopkins, 1963), 20; quoted and discussed in Anderson, *The Way We Argue Now*, 117.

characterological consequences of a training in the humanities, as distinct from the sciences or social sciences, one is trying to identify something more specific than an orientation towards professionalism, though it has in the past been thought to include that orientation,[58] but rather less specific than a commitment to the particular discipline. The philosophical literature on how different practices of the self emerge from different philosophical trainings is helpful here only up to a point. There is a difference between a practice of the self devolved from a particular philosophy (which is likely to be relatively exacting and highly specified) and a practice of the self devolved from a far looser set of sociological and educative factors which can admit of numerous and potentially conflicting philosophical allegiances, and indeed a considerable amount of vagueness or nonchalance about philosophy—a long way short of allegiance. In the case of a philosophical school we may well be warranted in talking about the expression of ideas as a way of life; in the case of a broad disciplinary area there is no such warrant. To confront the lingering objection in the form of a question: can the many kinds of knowledge and *techne* captured under the umbrella term 'the humanities' possess the coherence requisite to a 'theory' available for 'embodiment and enactment'?

To ask for *philosophical coherence* at this point is to ask for too much. But one can stand some way short of that prescription and find some coherence to the practices and values pursued on a daily basis within the academy. Some of the values that attach characterologically to the intellectual practices of the academy are generalizable across the university. They have to do, for example, with commitment to teaching as an educative endeavour and not just a paid function, with treating one's students and one's colleagues with respect and with fairness, with pursuing intellectual work, of whatever specialist variety, 'at the highest level'. The ethical import of these commitments is only partly summarized with reference to professionalism, though one of the purposes of professionalization is to codify them and give them institutional support. At the level of the discipline, the ethical characterization of academics will look far richer, having to do, for example, with what we think are or are not 'good' readings of texts, legitimate ways of obtaining

---

[58] See Fish, 'Profession Despise Thyself', and Robbins, *Secular Vocations*, on the anti-professionalism often distinctive of literature departments up to the late 1990s.

and employing historical evidence, just ways of treating animals, or intervening in an ecosystem, and so forth.

If one is asked (without aggressive political provocation) to describe the work done under the broad aegis of the humanities the resulting characterization is likely to be much less striking than the descriptions delivered up at moments of conflict between disciplines would have us believe, but still more distinctive than the broad account of educative and professional traits associated with work in the university. The initial description is, indeed, barely a characterization:

The humanities study the meaning-making practices of human culture, past and present, focusing on interpretation and critical evaluation, primarily in terms of the individual response and with an ineliminable element of subjectivity.

But in moments where it is politically necessary to display a more aggressive or defensive 'edge' we can say more:

In the main the humanities value qualitative above quantitative reasoning; they place greater faith in interpretative than in positivistic thinking; unlike the sciences and the scientific wing of the social sciences they do not have a dominant methodology, and many of their truth claims are not verifiable as those of the natural sciences are verifiable; they tend, accordingly, to distrust proceduralism and to value independence of thought. They are orientated as much toward historical analysis as toward synchronic structural analysis, and as much toward the medium of expression as towards its content (tending to see the form/content distinction as itself problematic). They attend to the role of the perceiver in ascertaining even the most philosophically secure of knowledge claims; and they have an interest, often they also take pleasure, in the specificity of the object of study and the specificity of the individual response (its content and its style) over and above the generalized or collective response. Not least, they respect the products of past human endeavours in culture, even when superseded.

These claims relate to trained habits of mind: distinctive intellectual priorities and tools brought to bear on distinctive kinds of object; distinctive relations to truth claims. They entail some basic assertions of value (what objects we think it worth while concentrating much of our time and attention upon, what modes of studying them we think valid and even important). The greater latent characterological force of the more aggressive/defensive claim emerges in, and is a product of, those moments when there is a competition for priority on matters of common interest across the disciplines. At that point the

humanities will need the stronger self-characterization as one element
in the repertoire of advocacy for their own interests. They will need it
whenever other disciplines promote their 'aggressive edge' within the
institution, and need it more when that aggressive edge starts to dominate the wider public conversation on matters of public interest.
At those moments distinction of aims and priorities may even legitimately be raised to the order of distinctive characterological virtues.[59]

The weakness of this way of arguing for the good of the humanities, it will have been clear throughout, is a product of the level of
generalization. In order to say something more characterful about
the comparative and distinctive purposes of different kinds of intellectual training one needs to get much closer to the subject matter
than the term 'humanities' allows. It is desirable to be able to talk
about a specific body of knowledge, and a specific critical purchase on
it—on the working of the language, for example, or on musical forms
and expressions, or on the uses of the historical record. Only at that
closer distance can characterology be developed beyond the broad
and stereotypical outline to the more precise imaginative construction, tightly bound historically and etymologically to the resources
of writing, that make characterology itself of special interest to the
humanities.

As it is, a description of distinctiveness in objects and modes of study
provides a structural basis for assertions of value. The most contentious
of such assertions, now as so often in the past, is the claim that higher
scholarship in the humanities has instrumental value beyond the
immediate usefulness involved in teaching. The terms on which that
demand has most convincingly been met and resisted are the subject
of the next chapter.

---

[59] This claim is further developed in Chapter 4.

2

Use and Usefulness

The spectre of trial by proven utility has accompanied universities in one version or another since they came into existence. A medieval college that emerges out of a need to produce a more literate clergy,[1] and whose fellows are required to pray for the souls of the founders, is implicitly as use-directed, under certain theological lights, as the twenty-first-century institution that claims centrality to 'the knowledge economy'. But for an explicit opposition between economic usefulness and cultured uselessness as a structuring topos of debate about the purpose of the university we are indebted, Robert Young argues, to Adam Smith's elaboration of a 'human capital' theory of education in *The Wealth of Nations* (1776).[2] Smith held that universities should be subject to free market forces because, left to themselves, university teachers had no interest in respecting utility as an educational aim: *vide* the parlous state of teaching in Oxford and Cambridge in the mid-eighteenth century, where tutors, no longer preparing the majority of their students for the ecclesiastical life, taught only 'a few unconnected shreds and parcels of this corrupted course; and even these . . . very negligently and superficially' (V.i.f.33).[3]

The paradox in Smith's free market attack on public educational institutions for the rich, Young observes, is that he nevertheless wanted

---

[1] See R. W. Southern, 'From Schools to University', in T. H. Aston (gen. ed.), *The History of the University of Oxford*, i: *The Early Oxford Schools*, ed. J. I. Catto (Oxford: Clarendon Press, 1984), 1–36.

[2] Robert J. C. Young, 'The Idea of a Chrestomathic University' (1992), in *Torn Halves: Political Conflict in Literary and Cultural Theory* (Manchester: Manchester University Press, 1996), 290–351.

[3] *An Inquiry into the Nature and Causes of the Wealth of Nations*, gen. eds. R. H. Campbell and A. S. Skinner, textual editor W. B. Todd, 2 vols. (Oxford: Clarendon Press, 1976), ii. 772 (hereafter *WN*).

to prescribe a kind of public education for the poor which would be more than simply useful, since a merely instrumental education directed towards meeting the needs of the labour market would (he reasoned) produce moral decline in its recipients.

Smith therefore proposes that such education would involve what he terms 'the necessary introduction to the most sublime as well as to the most useful sciences' (V.i.f.55). But what would be the use of a knowledge that is 'sublime' in a scheme according to which everything must be justified by its usefulness?[4]

And so Smith draws himself into what, in *The Wealth of Nations*, looks like a straight contradiction between a constraining instrumentalism and a space consciously made for uselessness—a contradiction, Young suggests, that might now be made to work for the post-modern university as a kind of Derridean logic of the supplement. The university 'already includes the excessive place of resistance to instrumentality that Derrida advocates… [T]he university must [then] be permanently at variance with itself', with the 'dissension produced by this dislocation… acted out interminably in educational theory and practice' (341).

Young's is an unusually subtle response to the spectre of a bluntly economic instrumentalism brought to bear on education. For reasons I will come to, I am not entirely persuaded by the Derridean turn, but a more immediate problem arises from Young's reading of the term 'sublime'. The preservation of a place, in *Wealth of Nations*, for 'sublime' science does not produce quite the clear distinction between useful-ness and non-usefulness that Young takes from it. Smith's preliminary account (earlier in the same chapter) of the ancient historical divisions of knowledge establishes that by the 'sublime' he means 'metaphysics'. Smith is, as one would expect, disparaging: too much of the attention in education has been given to the department of the 'sublime', espe-cially in the form of theology, too little to 'the more useful science'.[5] When he revisits the word in the passage Young quotes, he deliberately gives it a more specific, and provocatively untheological remit: he pro-

---

[4] Young, 'Chrestomathic University', 333–4; and Smith, *WN* ii. 786.

[5] 'The proper subject of experiment and observation, a subject in which a careful attention is capable of making so many useful discoveries, was almost entirely neglected. The subject in which, after a very few simple and almost obvious truths, the most careful attention can discover nothing but obscurity and uncertainty, and can consequently pro-duce nothing but subtleties and sophisms, was greatly cultivated' (V.i.f.28), ii. 771.

poses to replace the useless 'little smattering in Latin, which the children of the common people are sometimes taught' with the one aspect of the conjectural sciences for which it is feasible to claim usefulness: 'the elementary parts of geometry and mechanicks' for which 'scarce a common trade [will] not afford some opportunities of appl[ication]' (V.i.f.51, *WN* ii. 783–4). So revised, 'the literary education of this rank of people', Smith concludes, 'would perhaps be as complete as it can be' (V.i.f.51, *WN* ii. 783).[6]

A defence of the 'sublime' in education on these grounds offers rather less of an opening to the humanities than Young discerns. Indeed, it might rather reinforce the view that intransigent opposition is the only viable response towards a vein of political economy that, from Smith onwards, has insisted upon usefulness as the main qualifying criterion for public funding of education. The belief that the humanities, almost by definition, must be at odds with such economic instrumentalism has been a potent strand in English thinking about the university, and about culture more broadly, running through Newman, Mill, and Arnold, in the nineteenth century, and continuing, with what sometimes looks like incremental ferocity, through T. S. Eliot's insistence that readers of literature are bound to resist 'Secularism's' assumption that economic explanation should have primacy,[7] to Leavis's fulminations against a 'technologico-Benthamite' age,[8] to Geoffrey Hill much more recently decrying 'technocratic "angelism" ' and 'plutocratic anarchy'.[9]

[6] Smith was happy to acknowledge the importance of a training in civilized 'accomplishments' (including knowledge of literature) for people of rank and fortune routinely. He acknowledged also the covert utility of those acquirements: they have a clear function in fitting out the upper ranks of the professional, business, and trading classes for the intellectual demands as well as the social benefits of distinction (V.i.f.52, *WN* ii. 274). But in terms of what a publicly funded education for the poor should provide, those benefits would be supererogatory.

[7] 'Religion and Literature' (1935), in *Selected Essays*, 3rd enlarged edn. (London: Faber and Faber Ltd, 1951), 388–401 (p. 400).

[8] F. R. Leavis, *Thought, Words and Creativity: Art and Thought in Lawrence* (London: Chatto and Windus, 1976).

[9] The term 'angelism' is taken from Allen Tate. Hill is on record as having thought, until recently, that the second term was his own invention. In fact it is a recasting of William Morris's 'anarchical plutocracy'. See video interview with *The Economist*, <http://www.economist.com/blogs/prospero/2011/12/economist-books-year-festival-geoffrey-hill?fsrc=rss> (accessed 22 December 2012). For Hill, the involvement of the humanities, and of language itself, in the marketplace is something like the stain of original sin in what would otherwise be a purely teleological ethic of literary studies. The term 'technocratic "angelism"' can be found in Geoffrey Hill, 'Confessio Amantis', *The Record* (Keble College Oxford, 2009), 45–52 (51). <http://www.keble.ox.ac.uk/alumni/publications-2/

In, for the most part, more secular tones than Hill's, 'anti-utilitarianism' remains a strong strain in political arguments involving the purpose and the funding of universities today, and not only in the humanities. At the present moment this 'anti-utilitarianism' (a common misnomer for what should, strictly, be called anti-instrumentalism[10]) has its most visible manifestation in the intense hostility generated by the introduction of 'impact', or social benefit, as a category of evaluation in the government's next research assessment exercise—a hostility that risks seeming disproportionate. (Are academics seriously unwilling to concede that activities for which they receive public money should be partly assessed in terms of measurable benefits passed on to society? . . .) What many, I'm guessing most, academics object to is not, however, the idea that they should be socially beneficial; rather, the peculiarly reductive variant of political economy that dictates the terms of assessment, and that fundamentally mistakes the nature and purpose of writing in the humanities, the arts, and the

Record09.pdf> (accessed 11 January 2010). For 'plutocratic anarchy', see 'Strongholds of the Imagination' (interview with Alexandra Bell, Rebecca Rosen, and Edmund White), *The Oxonian Review* 9/4 (8 May 2009) <http://www.oxonianreview.org/wp/geoffrey-hill/> (accessed 11 January 2010), acknowledging a precursor in William Morris's term 'anarchical Plutocracy'. For the wider theological and critical context, see 'Poetry as Menace and Atonement', in *Collected Critical Writings*, ed. Kenneth Haynes (Oxford: Oxford University Press, 2008), 2–20 (16): 'If the socio-political "scene" in recent years has been characterized by an unsuspecting allegiance to "slogans [and] sages", by the worship of charisma, instant wizardry, and all that is "technically sweet", we may ask to what extent literary aesthetics have colluded with such sentimentality and cynicism. In such an epoch, the sense of "empirical guilt" involved with what can be termed "culpably careless proof-reading" has an intrinsic value, for, in such a context (to quote MacKinnon once more), "one can never be quite at ease in the present of the suggestion that . . . a teleological ethic need not have the slightest truck with utilitarianism".' See also p. 118, on T. H. Green as an example of how the 'anti-utilitarian, anti-hedonist, may yet be held in the gravitational field created by those forces'.

[10] Strictly, a utilitarian judgement on the value of the humanities would rest on the question: does it promote the greatest happiness of the greatest number? This is rarely a question that guides government thinking, and when it has done so in recent decades it has been in the field of ethics rather than education or the arts. One such case in recent British history was Roy Jenkins's decriminalization of adult male homosexuality, but not paedophilia, in 1968: who is harmed by sexual acts between consenting adults in private? Nobody. Who is made happy by it? They are. The findings of the 1970s Williams Committee on Obscenity and Film Censorship, significantly in the same period and under a similar liberalizing impulse, is another such case. In neither of these contexts did 'utilitarianism' feature in political arguments as a malign government influence; indeed, the term 'utilitarian' seems scarcely to have been used in general public debate. I am grateful to Nick Shrimpton for the first example.

pure sciences.[11] There is, notwithstanding, a hard core anti-instrumentalist position, not insignificant in the support it commands, that goes further and claims that social benefit is not the brief of universities, and that the pursuit of knowledge and engagement in research must be understood as mattering for its own sake and its own sake alone.

Both these kinds of anti-instrumentalism (soft and hard, as it were) have been part of the common parlance of debate about the idea and function of a university in the late twentieth and twenty-first centuries. Look beyond the context, or the genre, of institutional complaint, however, and the idea that we must oppose the principle of usefulness seems less prominent than it was.[12] Some of the strongest responses to the perceived 'crisis in the humanities' over the last two decades, including John Guillory's *Cultural Capital: The Problem of Literary Canon Formation* (1993), Bill Readings's *The University in Ruins* (1996), and most recently Louis Menand's *The Marketplace of Ideas* (2010), recognize behind the rhetoric of anti-instrumentalism a response to large structural and political changes in the university and in its relationship to the wider public culture. For John Guillory the cause of our current difficulties is 'a decline in the *market* value' of humanities curricula, combined with the emergence of a techno-bureaucratic 'professional-managerial class' in the presence of which humanities departments have come to seem economically and institutionally irrelevant.[13] For Bill Readings, bureaucratization is a part of the explanation, but the

---

[11] See Stefan Collini, 'Impact on the Humanities', *Times Literary Supplement* 13 November 2009, 18–19; and, on the depth of the antagonism to 'impact', Zoë Corbyn, 'Thousands of Academics Call for Impact to Be Axed', *Times Higher Education Supplement* 3 December 2009. <http://www.timeshighereducation.co.uk/story.asp?storycode=409395> (accessed 19 January 2010).

[12] For prominent UK examples of the turn to embrace instrumentalism, while making it compatible with the priorities of the humanities, see Council for Science and Technology, *Imagination and Understanding. A Report on the Arts and Humanities in Relation to Science and Technology* (July 2001) <http://www.bis.gov.uk/assets/cst/docs/files/whatsnew/01-1051-imagination-understanding>. Accessed 31 December 2012. And British Academy, 'That Full Complement of Riches': The Contributions of the Arts, Humanities and Social Sciences to the Nation's Wealth* (London: The British Academy, 2004).

[13] *Cultural Capital*, 46; and see 341–2 on the original expression of this disputed term in the work of Barbara and John Ehrenreich, 'The Professional-Managerial Class', in Pat Walker (ed.), *Between Labour and Capital* (Montreal: Black Rose Press, 1978), 5–48. And for an intelligent prosecution of the argument with respect to UK universities, see Thomas Docherty, *For the University: Democracy and the Future of the Institution* (London: Bloomsbury Academic, 2011).

loss of the university's cultural mission has deeper roots in global capitalism: that is, in the dislodging of the nationalist rationale of the Humboldtian university of culture. Tonally the two books are strikingly divergent—Guillory calm, rational, verging on the austere, where Readings seems with difficulty kept from the Romantic poles of elegy and anarchism.[14] But they are alike in seeing the pressure towards demonstrated economic usefulness as a false description of our problem.

Readings lucidly describes not a hostile instrumentalism so much as a situation in which judgements about usefulness are happening on the basis of an oddly crude understanding of what it means to work in the marketplace of ideas and of language. If he is right (and I have already indicated that I think he is (see Introduction)), the problem is not the market but the distortive simulacrum of a market that forms the theatre of so much debate still about what academics, and universities, and culture are for. As he puts it, universities driven by 'performance indicators', and by dedication to a contentless 'excellence', are not, as the familiar conservative line has it, experiencing 'exposure to market forces'; 'what is occurring is actually the highly artificial creation of a fictional market that presumes exclusive government control of funding....[A] version of the capitalist marketplace is mimed' with the necessary help of a 'virtual accounting mechanism' (37): 'excellence', 'excellence benchmarking', and (Readings would have loved it) 'impact'. That those of us who teach should be useful—above all that we should educate—is unobjectionable; that we should agree to subject ourselves to a form of political economic instrumentalism that deforms the goods it seeks to make use of seems to most people in the humanities a position to be resisted.

Menand's recent contribution to this debate from the combined perspectives of intellectual history and literary criticism is comparatively, if cautiously, optimistic. *The Marketplace of Ideas* (2010) gives a more sharply defined and political genealogy to the changes within institutions of higher education that have produced the current crisis in the humanities (he is writing of America, but the consequences he

[14] *The University in Ruins* was written, he confesses, as 'an attempt to think my way out of an impasse between militant radicalism and cynical despair. I am still inclined to introduce sentences that begin "In a *real* University..." into discussions with my colleagues, even though they know, and I know that they know, that no such institution has ever existed'. Bill Readings, *The University in Ruins* (Cambridge, Mass.: Harvard University Press, 1996), 5.

describes are increasingly true also of Britain). Menand charts a historical process by which American elite universities began in the later nineteenth century to mark out a core element of their curricula as the preserve of a liberal cultivation of knowledge for its own sake. Onto that liberal arts base, the graduate schools grafted an increasingly specialized professional training in the distinct disciplines, the end product of which, he argues, is the modern American and (with differences) also a modern British graduate training whose function is (*prima facie*) almost exclusively to reproduce the profession.[15] The doctorate in English, or History, or Modern Languages, or Philosophy trains students to become university teachers of English, or History, or Modern Languages (etc.). At a time when there are fewer and fewer jobs in academia to be trained *for*, the academics presiding over doctoral education can easily feel in bad faith with their students. Humanities departments should be thinking hard, Menand concludes, about making graduate training 'less exclusionary and more holistic'— enabling the disciplines to engage more openly and purposively with the public culture while preserving their critical function (158). And they should resist, he urges, a temptation to which he thinks the USA peculiarly prone by dint of the grafting of professional specialism onto the broad liberal educational base: the temptation to oppose whatever is 'presentist' or 'instrumental'. Usefulness is not the corruptor of the humanities' intellectual purity: 'Disinterestedness is perfectly consistent with practical ambition, and practical ambitions are perfectly consistent with disinterestedness' (57). More simply: 'Knowledge just *is* instrumental: it puts us in a different relationship with the world' (53).[16]

A blunter conclusion from Menand's analysis would be that, however substantially humanities departments might open themselves out to engagement with the wider public culture, and however worthwhile that change might be, one will not have done enough to secure or even to acknowledge the ways in which graduate education in the

[15] It is not, or not yet, the case that UK universities have seen the decline in student enrolment in the humanities that has affected America, and yet the UK offers from secondary education upwards a narrower specialization in education (more so in England than Scotland). So, the mismatch between the relatively broad liberal arts undergraduate base and the professionally narrowed graduate degree must carry less explanatory weight for any reduction in the perceived instrumental value of a humanities higher education in the UK.

[16] Also p. 57: 'The divorce between liberalism and professionalism as educational missions rests on a superstition: that the practical is the enemy of the true. This is nonsense.'

humanities has practical use value. Some clarification of terms is required at this point. We are, it should be clear, not dealing here with the Marxist definition of use value as pure non-economic consent to a lived need, as against economic exchange value; rather with the earlier, still more standard meaning outside political theory, that is quite the opposite of Marx's handling of the term—literally, the value derived from 'practical use'. Even in its 'unreformed' condition higher education in the humanities evidently possesses such practical value, providing demonstrable benefits to the world. The skills that today's humanities graduates eventually secure are widely transferable in ways Menand underestimates. Humanities students, in the main, take the knowledge and the intellectual training they are given into practical activities: media, businesses, journalism, the civil service, politics, publishing. The link between the training given and how it is used is much less transparent than with vocational subjects such as law and medicine, or in the sciences where the content of the training continues to be used— but there is, demonstrably, a product. Those who elect to spend the additional three to five years in post-graduate study (in America, nine years on average) are doing so (by informal report) because they take pleasure in the intellectual experience despite the poverty of the economic return, because they perceive some remaining cultural value in their studies, and because they can reasonably hope that if they do not stay in academia they will nevertheless not have wasted their time there. They have, after all, become adept at combining realism and optimism towards their own prospects of university employment, cynicism, and confidence about the cultural value of what they teach. Not least, they tend even now to retain an idea that the humanities matter to individuals and to the wider public life. As Nicholas Dames puts it, reviewing Terry Castle's witty examination of the 'neurotic' position of the modern humanities academic in *The Professor* (2011),[17] today's humanities professor

is good… at inhabiting the gap between sincerity and irony, between cultural gatekeeper and cultural rebel, between grandiosity and humility. And she is good at making others feel similarly. [: But o]ne doesn't enter the academy to become a disillusioned professional (although that will happen along the way). One doesn't enter it to equip businesses with flexible analytic intellects

---

[17] *The Professor and Other Writings* (New York: HarperCollins).

(although that will also happen). One enters it...to devote oneself to something greater...[18]

The 'something greater' being, in Dames's warily bold suggestion, 'rescu[ing] lives', giving individuals access to 'salvational or transformational modes of thought'.

This pitches it quite high. It is (consciously) a step up on Menand's recommendation that humanities departments learn to see disinterestedness and practical ambition as compatible qualities within the university. In the context of the long history of anti-instrumentalism in the humanities, what interests me most about Menand's contribution to the debate about the idea of the university, and Dames's attempt to regear it to admit higher ambitions of usefulness (using knowledge and sympathy gained through study of the humanities to change lives for the better), is that they confirm a significant shift in attitudes to utility since Barbara Herrnstein Smith wrote, in 1988, of 'anti-utilitarianism... operat[ing] as a qualifying mark of the contemporary professional humanist and also as his or her perhaps most centrally self-defining ideological stance'.[19] As the description given earlier of everyday anti-instrumentalism in the academy will have shown, it is not that humanities scholars look set to become convinced economic instrumentalists, but usefulness no longer figures quite so plainly as the enemy against which the humanist must characterize him or herself, or as so entirely at odds with 'higher' cultural and political ideals. (Geoffrey Hill is in this respect, as in others, self-consciously conservatively out of step.) The toning down of anti-instrumentalism of which I take Readings, Guillory, Menand, Dames to be a sign has something to do, perhaps, with the fact that the last three at least[20] have involved themselves significantly in the administration of their institutions. Guillory, especially, has been bracing in his recommendations to humanities departments to rethink their traditional and default hostility to the idea that they have social benefit:

the humanistic disciplines need more than anything else right now to legitimize themselves in terms of optimization or, more generously, social

---

[18] Nicholas Dames, 'Why Bother?', *n* + 1, issue 11, *Dual Power* (Spring 2011), <http://nplusonemag.com/why-bother>. Accessed 16 October 2012.

[19] *Contingencies of Value: Alternative Perspectives for Critical Theory* (Cambridge, Mass.: Harvard University Press, 1988), 125–6.

[20] I have no knowledge of Readings's institutional involvements beyond teaching and research.

benefit. The sciences by and large have been very successful in justifying their disciplines by means of a notion such as performativity or optimization; but if it has become evident that the sciences that live by this justification can also die by it, this does not mean that the legitimation narrative is altogether tainted and should be discarded. Social benefit can be defined far more broadly than in terms of technological payoff or market measures and without necessarily excluding these terms. . . . Knowing how to read shrewdly and write well is no small accomplishment and is in fact much more valued in the market than we have begun to acknowledge.[21]

A cynical explanation for the softening of anti-instrumentalism would be that modern universities have become so dominated by their governments' economic instrumentalism that not conceding something to political economy would be institutionally suicidal. But there are reasons, beyond the obvious, for avoiding cynicism, without losing sight of the danger that a defence of the humanities' social impact may quickly degrade into a defence only of its 'exchange value', and that the cultural value of humanities scholarship will have been given away in return for no increase in understanding of what the relationship can be between cultural value and economic value.[22] With that danger in sight, the challenge in assessing the validity of the usefulness claim for the humanities is not to get rid of it again from the argument, but to refine the account of its proper place.

Amidst so much debate about the propriety and acceptability of instrumentalist claims for the humanities in the eyes of those who teach and study them, there has been relatively little sign of an older perception that instrumentalism might have more importance at some stages and in some kinds of education and much less in others; nor about the specific problems the term 'use' raises for a rhetorically cred-ible defence of the humanities. In order to fill out these aspects of the claim, I want now to turn back, and in rather more detail this time, to Matthew Arnold. Arnold's place in the evolution of the humanities' relationship to cultural value is well remembered, and still much con-tested. His views on their relationship with use value, though impor-tant and well known to Arnold scholars, are far less well known—much less likely to be recalled in public debate than John Henry Newman's

---

[21] 'Critical Response II: The Name of Science, the Name of Politics', *Critical Inquiry* 29/3 (2003), 526–4 (541).

[22] I am taking a lead here from Guillory, *Cultural Capital*, esp. ch. 5.

frank opposition to considerations of use (except in a metaphysically directed understanding of use) when defending a liberal 'idea of the university' or John Stuart Mill's defence of poetry as a means to the nurturing of feeling and not just of opinion, the development of culture and not just of reason.

Arnold's contribution on the question of how the university specifically, and culture more generally, should guard against a narrowly instrumental utilitarianism is in some ways harder to assess than Newman's and Mill's—and not, as might be thought, because Arnold, so strongly German Idealist in his thinking about 'the best self', 'right reason', and the wisdom of the state,[23] was uninterested in the practical uses of education. On the contrary, he thought about its uses as closely as any of his contemporaries, and wrote about the subject at more length than perhaps any of them. 'Culture and its Enemies' (1867)—the final lecture delivered during his term as Oxford's Professor of Poetry, and which formed the kernel of *Culture and Anarchy* (1869)—was written in the immediate aftermath of two and a half years spent putting together an extensive survey of secondary and higher education on the Continent, in the form of a report to the Education Office with recommendations for the reform of British school and university education. Much of the content of that report concerns Arnold's assessment of the place afforded to utility as a criterion for education in the European higher academies. When he writes to his mother in early February 1867, then, that the arguments for 'Culture and its Enemies' are forming in his mind,[24] this is the immediate context in which they are back-burnering: 'I shall not write a word of it till my report is fairly done with.'[25]

In what follows, I want to argue that Arnold's defence of culture has a subtler and more complex relationship to the notion of usefulness

---

[23] I am in agreement here with Franklin E. Court's reflection on how 'disconcerting' it is to find literary critics so often 'ignoring the distinctly historical German roots of Arnold's position on the study of the humanities'. See *Institutionalizing English Literature: The Culture and Politics of Literary Study, 1750–1900* (Stanford, Calif.: Stanford University Press, 1992), 7.

[24] Letter to Mary Penrose Arnold, 16 February 1867, in *The Letters of Matthew Arnold*, ed. Cecil Y. Lang, iii: *1866–1870* (Charlottesville, Va.: University Press of Virginia, 1998), 114–15 (114).

[25] Letter to Mary Penrose Arnold, 16 February 1867. 'Also', Arnold continues, 'a letter to the Pall Mall on Compulsory Education' (114).

than its common and casual description as 'anti–utilitarian' allows for:
that it comes out of a strenuous attempt to counter the instrumentalist
tendencies of political economists in the government to which he and
his fellow inspectors were reporting, but that it reflects also a growing
understanding in the course of his work for the Education Department
that opposing usefulness to non-usefulness obscures and distorts much
of what a sound argument about educational values ought to be
concerned with—including breadth of knowledge, recognition of
individual aptitudes, the 'free play of mind', and what, without
embarrassment, he called 'civilizing the nation'. 'Use' and 'utility', for
Arnold, increasingly became terms not incompatible with but barely
relevant to a vision of both education and culture as having to do with
the development of the individual and society—an aim understood as
ongoing, unpredictable, and which must be pursued free of the
pressures of short-term instrumentalism if it was to be genuinely
rational, genuinely intellectual, genuinely beneficial. His prosecution
of that argument has made him of obvious interest to those continuing
the tradition of anti-instrumentalist arguments for the humanities—
but they have tended, as a consequence, greatly to underplay the kind
and extent of the concessions made to 'utility'. Unlike many of his
followers he was not anti-statist. His concern was with persuading the
government of his day to give usefulness an appropriately basic, that is
first-level, place.

   Much of the political terrain mapped out in the report on *Schools
and Universities* will be immediately familiar to any reader of *Culture
and Anarchy*: its description of an educational system which has so far
failed to address, indeed, has actively preserved the rigidities and social
'inconvenience' of class (308); the explicit concern with the middle or
employing class, 'full of complaints of the ignorance and unreasonableness'
of those it employs but not recognizing that its own bad instruction
(or what *Culture and Anarchy* would name its 'Philistinism') is part of
the problem (1868 *Preface*, 28); the case made for centralizing
intervention, and the direct attack on the current English notion of
the state as 'an alien intrusive power in the community, not summing
up and representing the action of individuals, but thwarting it' (1868
Preface, 30). None of this was new ground for Arnold. His view that
the state should take responsibility for primary education, at least, and
his sense of the damaging connection between educational systems
and class structures, had been robustly aired in the earlier report on

The Popular Education of France (1860).[26] The rhetoric of the higher education report is, indeed, markedly less contestatory (and can afford to be since primary education, rather than secondary or tertiary, was the front line of the battle over state schooling), but the shaping significance of Arnold's opposition to economic instrumentalism in higher education was no less strong.

The most striking thing about Arnold's handling of the educational question in the report on *Schools and Universities*, if one considers the political context to which it was addressed, and still more so if one draws a comparison with Mill or Newman, is his consistent refusal to prioritize education's practical value, or even to acknowledge utility as a near pressure. Again, this was hardly because Arnold was unaware of the topicality and force of economic instrumentalism in the political sphere. In the year that he began his work for the schools and universities report (1865), he wrote a letter to the *Pall Mall Gazette*, laying out some of his preliminary thinking about the role of the state in higher education. The letter included an explicit attack on 'the sterile liberalism of the past, with its pedantic application of certain maxims of political economy in the wrong place' (4). The objects of this somewhat oblique one-sentence attack were the supporters of the Revised Code of 1862, which had cut government grants to schools and introduced a system of payment in direct relation to exam results.[27] The principal author of the Code, the Liberal MP Robert Lowe, was, in the Smithian tradition, a free trader, holding that education, like other goods, should be answerable to the principles of supply and demand.[28] The Code imposed what its

[26] 'Democracy' was republished by Arnold as an independent essay in 1879. See Matthew Arnold, *Democratic Education*, ed. R. H. Super, *CPW* ii (Ann Arbor: University of Michigan Press, 1962), 330.

[27] See R. H. Super notes to *Schools and Universities on the Continent*, *CPW* iv, ed. Super (Ann Arbor: University of Michigan Press, 1964), 338–9; Collini, *Arnold* (Oxford: Oxford University Press, 1988), 72–3.

[28] '[Lowe] was an albino, and his eyes were extremely sensitive to light; moreover, he had imperfect vision in both eyes, and one was useless for reading. At Winchester College, which he entered as a commoner in 1825, he was much bullied, and unable to identify his tormentors; later in life, too, he suffered from his inability to recognize people, especially in large groups.' After his marriage, he had to resign his Magdalen fellowship: 'In order to make a living, he had to return to private tutoring. He quickly developed a reputation as the most efficient coach in the university, but the work was hard. His experience of it intensified his contempt for the low general standard of university education and his animosity to the complacency of college fellows, which he thought was caused by the protection given to them by lavish college endowments.' Jonathan Parry, 'Robert Lowe', *New DNB*, online edition. Accessed 27 January 2010.

opponents saw as a grossly blunt instrumentalism, immediately economically damaging to many schools and colleges to the extent that some
were obliged to seek private funding, religiously sectarian in nature.

Arnold's objections had been forcefully elaborated at the time in an
article for *Fraser's Magazine*, 'The Twice-Revised Code' (1862), where,
as Stefan Collini notes, he courageously risked the wrath of his supe-
riors at the Education Department with a swingeing attack on Lowe.[29]
The *Fraser's* article saw the aims of the Code as the coarsest kind of
Benthamite accounting: '"The duty of a State in public education is",
it is said, "when clearly defined, to obtain the greatest possible quantity
of reading, writing, and arithmetic for the greatest number".'[30] Arnold's
trenchant opposition undoubtedly played a part in forming a coherent
opposition to the Code (the article was circulated in pamphlet form
among the conservative opponents of the bill, at the express wish of
James Shuttleworth, who chaired the Anti-Code Committee), giving
Arnold hopes that his centralizing views would triumph: '[the opposition is taking] the very ground I could wish them to take, namely, that
the State has an interest in the primary school as a *civilizing agent*, even
prior to its interest in it as an *instructing agent*.' In the event, his optimism was only partially rewarded, and the wording of the *Pall Mall
Gazette* letter is more polemical than accurate when it refers to 'sterile
liberalism' as a thing 'of the past': Lowe had by then been compelled to
make substantial compromises (had indeed resigned his office in 1864
after his chief civil servant, Arnold's superior at the Education Office,
was censured for overly heavy editing of the inspectors' reports before
publication[31]), but examination of pupils in reading, writing, and arithmetic by Education Department inspectors was retained as one component in deciding the distribution of grants, and '"[p]ayment by
results" remained in the picture of English education until after Arnold's
death'.[32]

The importance of this debate in influencing the particular cast of *Culture and Anarchy's* liberalism has been discussed elsewhere.[33] Among the

[29] Collini, *Arnold*, 73.

[30] Arnold, 'The Twice-Revised Code', in *Democratic Education*, 212–43 (214–15).

[31] See Parry, 'Robert Lowe'.

[32] Arnold, *Democratic Education*, 362.

[33] See Collini, *Arnold*, ch. 5: 'The social critic'; and, esp., W. F. Connell, *The Educational
Thought and Influence of Matthew Arnold* (London: Routledge and Kegan Paul, 1950), reissued
with an introduction by Sir Fred Clarke (1990), chs. 7–9. Connell's work, still the standard
study of Arnold and education, covers the same areas of Arnold's writing as this essay (and

many aspects that deserve more space here is the degree to which Robert Lowe was unfairly depicted by Arnold and others as philistine in his aims, and (equally unfairly) characterized by later critics as a utilitarian.[34] (He was not a Benthamite utilitarian: he was, as Arnold carefully put it, a political economist, but—as Arnold didn't so readily acknowledge—one with a more than usually generous sense of what education should aim to achieve, and considerable sensitivity to how far class controls access to culture.[35]) In this context, however, I am most interested in the *negative* influence of the debate on Arnold: that is, in the way in which his writing about education, culture, and the state after 1862, rather than directly attacking political economists such as Lowe, increasingly sidelines their views, so that the explicitly anti-instrumentalist line of argument one might reasonably expect to issue out of a particular political situation is forestalled or circumvented. This increasing refusal to take the anti-political economy stance, by a man who had already been bravely polemical in his opposition

more). It confines its direct discussion of utilitarianism, however, to a brief examination of the political context behind the setting up of the Education Inspectorate (60–7) and, more obliquely, its account of Lowe and the Revised Code (ch. 9). In effect, Connell approaches the question raised by this essay from the other direction: in what way did Arnold's valuation of culture affect his thinking about education? (rather than, in what way did his experience of utilitarianism in education affect his thinking about culture?). So, p. 167: 'Arnold's man of culture might be regarded as one who showed an educated and responsible approach to social living, shot through with a touch of idealism. But how was education to secure the spread of such men and such attitudes throughout society?'; or, p. 169: 'the practical educational implications of his doctrine were to be found, not in *Culture and Anarchy*, but scattered mainly through his General Reports and Special Reports.' The more general standard study, John William Adamson, *English Education, 1789–1902* (Cambridge: Cambridge University Press, 1930), provides a helpful account of the philosophical origins of utilitarianism in English education (2–6), but makes only occasional reference to Arnold, primarily regarding the detail of specific education reports.

[34] 'The opponents of the code depicted Lowe in an unfairly philistine and anti-clerical light. Its object was not to save money at the expense of standards, since the cost to government was potentially open-ended. The "three Rs" were chosen not because these were deemed to be the only proper components of an elementary education but because they could be examined most easily and provided a good basic test—a test which many schools failed.' Parry, 'Robert Lowe'.

[35] It is an important corrective to any reading that isolates an aggressive utilitarianism as the context for Arnold's writing about education to remember that Mill's *Utilitarianism* was published six years before the report on *Schools and Universities* and 'Culture and its Enemies' (three years before 'The Function of Criticism'), and that its refinement of Benthamite thinking was, by 1867, widely accepted. Even self-described utilitarians were, after 1861, familiar with the idea that pleasure involves quality as well as quantity ('better Socrates dissatisfied than a pig satisfied', in Mill's quickly famous phrase). So, the debate about the utility of education, though it was fierce, was not simple, and certainly not simply dualistic.

to the influence of political economic thinking on education, is not, I think, attributable to any loss of political nerve. Rather, it reflects a perception that the practical uses of education are, genuinely, not the point—not the right ground of engagement regarding educational aims—and that to go on contesting it may be to give it undue prominence.

The utility of education is not denied: it is, indeed, acknowledged, but that value diminishes for Arnold the higher up the educational scale one goes. So, to read Arnold's report on primary schools is to find an author fully prepared to talk in terms of simple utility when standards of education are at their lowest, for local historical or political reasons. He recognizes, for example, that an '*elementary* primary instruction', under the restored French monarchy of the 1830s, necessarily involved a focus on 'the indispensable minimum of knowledge': a child learned 'the elements of grammar; and for the purpose of national convenience, the legal but imperfectly received system of weights and measures'. But even in such circumstances as these, Arnold scarcely ever talks in terms of mere practical use: the clear impression given is that the 1830s was an impoverished period in the history of French education. For Arnold, an education is of value in its deepest civilizing and life-long effects, not primarily for its turning out of functional literates. To read '*fairly*' or '*well*', he writes in 'The Twice-Revised Code', resisting Lowe's accounting terminology, is to attain not a bare measurable 'competence' but a 'considerable... power'—'a power which is a real lasting acquirement for the whole of life' (223).

As one moves higher up the educational ladder, past the point at which basic literacy is involved, utility retreats as a consideration in Arnold's writing, not denied but more completely overtaken by the broader and less readily measured requirement that education should enable a person to use their own intelligence freely, or (as he puts it in *Culture and Anarchy*) non-mechanically, against the default grain of habit. That the two questions, education and the development of culture, were consciously connected in Arnold's mind even before he came to write *Culture and Anarchy* is made plain by the epigraph to the report on *Schools and Universities*, taken from the great Prussian university reformer Wilhelm von Humbolt:

The thing is *not*, to let the schools and universities go on in a drowsy and impotent routine; the thing is, to raise the culture of the nation ever higher and higher by their means.[36]

<hr>

[36] Arnold, *Schools and Universities*, 14.

The body of Arnold's report on *Schools and Universities* thereafter makes few such direct claims about the aims of education, but one can readily gauge the direction in which Arnold's conclusions are tending when he compares the Prussian and Swiss school systems. 'When a nation has got the belief in culture which the Prussian nation has got, and when its schools are worthy of this belief, it will not suffer them to be sacrificed to any other interest' (229). The 'regnant Swiss conception of secondary instruction', by contrast, is 'not a liberal but a commercial one; not culture and training of the mind, but what will be of immediate palpable utility in some practical calling' (253).

Arnold's detailed thinking about the principles that ought to inform secondary higher education, and his consequent recommendations for the reform of the English system, are reserved for the 'General Conclusion' (ch. XXII). This long final chapter of the report opens with a version of a claim probably more familiar to readers from the late essay on 'Literature and Science' (1882) (see Chapter 1), where Arnold responded to Huxley's provokingly untrue portrait of him as an opponent of science by explicitly bringing science within the definition of culture as 'the best that has been thought and said'.[37] The fundamental distinction drawn by the report on *Schools and Universities* is not quite between literature and science, or between culture and science as Huxley put it, but between two related though not identical educational interest groups on the Continent. Education in Europe, Arnold observes, evidences time and again 'the conflict between . . . the partisans of the old classical studies and the partisans of what are called real, or modern, or useful studies' (289). Each side has a tendency to be unjust to the other—the humanist being 'loth to believe' that man has any access to vital knowledge except through poetry, philosophy, history; the realist that anything matters except knowing the physical sciences and the operations of nature (292–3). England, Arnold argues, is in a position to benefit from the comparatively undeveloped (non-centralized) condition of its own public education system, by observing that conflict and recognizing the desirability that each side 'abate [its] extreme pretensions' (289).

[37] 'Literature and Science' [14 June 1882], in *Philistinism in England and America*, ed. R. H. Super, *CPW* x (Ann Arbor: University of Michigan Press, 1974), 53–73. See also Huxley's implicit reference to Arnold's prioritization of the literary over the scientific in 'Science and Culture' (1880), in *Science and Education: Essays by Thomas H. Huxley* (London: Macmillan and Co., 1893), 134–59 (182).

Disputing the common view that the aim of education should be to form good citizens, or good Christians, enabled to do their duty and fill their place in life well, Arnold goes on to argue that we should view these as 'at best secondary and indirect aims' (290). The 'prime direct aim' of education 'is to enable a man to *know himself and the world*'. Humanists have long recognized the first part of this description, the Greek ideal of self-knowledge,[38] as 'the stronghold of their position'. But, Arnold continues, 'it is also a vital and formative knowledge to know the world, the laws which govern nature, and man as a part of nature'. This may look like an argument about to resolve into a predictable opposition between humanism and scientific realism, even as it provides the germ of *Culture and Anarchy*'s meditations on Socrates (88). But Arnold is at pains to insist that the two 'roads of knowledge' are better conceived of as access routes across 'the entire circle of knowledge'.

Every man is born with aptitudes which give him access to vital and formative knowledge by one of these roads; either by the road of studying man and his works, or by the road of studying nature and her works. The business of instruction is to seize and develope [*sic*] these aptitudes. The great and complete spirits which have all the aptitudes for both roads of knowledge are rare. But much more might be done on both roads by the same mind, if instruction clearly grasped the idea of the entire system of aptitudes for which it has to provide; of their correlation, and of their *equipollency*, so to speak ... (291)

What started as an observation of better-organized but also internally conflicted foreign educational systems, in which the classical confronts the 'real, or modern, or useful', is revised here as the description of an ideal system in which the philosophical and moral requirement for knowledge of the self will be matched with an equal requirement for knowledge of the external conditions of life, with the 'external' understood to embrace scientific, historical and anthropological study. It is a redefinition that at once dissolves the force of the humanities/ sciences polarization, and displaces as scarcely relevant (at most secondary) the useful/non-useful opposition.

As Arnold then describes his contemporary society, humanists have, indeed, nothing to fear from any pressure that might be brought to bear upon them from political economy. As long as the 'realists' go on

---

[38] 'Know thyself' (gnōthi seautón) was, famously, one of the injunctions carved into the Temple of Apollo at Delphi.

denying the importance of the humanities, he argues, the humanists will have the upper hand.

> The contemplation of human force and activity tends naturally to heighten our own force and activity; the contemplation of human limits and passivity tends rather to check it. Therefore the men who have had the humanistic training have played, and yet play, so prominent a part in human affairs, in spite of their prodigious ignorance of the universe; because their training has powerfully fomented the human force in them. And in this way letters are indeed like *runes*, like those magic runes taught by the Valkyrie Brynhild to Sigure, the Scandinavian Achilles, which put the crown to his endowment and made him invincible. (292)

This is a rare moment of silliness in the report—Arnold showing his true colours, no doubt, as a prejudiced advocate for the humanities over the sciences. But then he is, as so often, disarmingly overt. 'I, like so many others who have been brought up in the old routine', he confesses, 'know nothing else, and my judgment may therefore be fairly impeached.' The remaining pages of the 'General Conclusions' restrain themselves to a more sober and detailed elaboration of a 'liberal training' as a training in 'knowledge of ourselves and the world' (300).

If the report on *Schools and Universities* downgrades talk of utility, *Culture and Anarchy* comes close to effacing it altogether. But not quite. Through most of *Culture and Anarchy* considerations of utility cast scarcely a shadow on Arnold's prose; they are rather a telling absence, a consistent refusal to engage on that terrain. But one notices their absence from the main body of the argument the more because Arnold opens with, in effect, a parody of utility. *Culture and Anarchy* begins, famously, with an attack on that reductive idea of culture (identified with the liberal orator John Bright) which associates it with 'a smattering of Greek and Latin'[39]—useless in any obvious instrumental sense, but covertly instrumental as a sign of a gentlemanly education (in short, as a demarcator of class). Arnold proceeds then to take issue with Frederic Harrison's similarly dismissive treatment of culture as mere *belletristic* show—'a turn for small faultfinding, love of selfish ease, and indecision in action'. In short: a lack of competence in the 'active' exercise of 'common sense' which makes the man of culture a disaster in the sphere of politics. 'No end is too unpractical for him' (87).

---

[39] Matthew Arnold, *Culture and Anarchy, with Friendship's Garland and Some Literary Essays*, ed. R. H. Super, *CPW* v (Ann Arbor: University of Michigan Press, 1965), 87.

When Arnold came to revise 'Culture and its Enemies' in 1869 as the introduction and first chapter ('Sweetness and Light') of *Culture and Anarchy*, he added a preface which, in effect, takes this same way into his argument: setting up the definition of culture by means of a prior attack on those opponents of culture who would have us understand it as either thinly useful (socially) or not useful at all (politically). Pressing for a larger understanding of 'the essential inwardness of the operation' of culture, Arnold observes that 'it is not easy so to frame one's discourse' as to avoid giving the impression that one is, in fact, pursuing 'some rival plan of doing, which we want to serve and recommend', and in aid of which one might erect an institutional machinery for its measurement (a 'centre of taste and authority like the French Academy'). The worry (though Arnold doesn't have much time for the language of anxiety) is that those aspects of the English national character that ought to defend us against this error (apparently, anti-authoritarianism, egalitarianism, conscience, right reason) will be overtaken by philistinism of the kind Arnold sees operating in the education system. Hence what might otherwise seem a somewhat gratuitous attack on Mr Oscar Browning, an assistant master at Eton.

The usefulness of the true advocates of culture depends, Arnold argues, upon 'our being able to clear...away' the sort of misunderstanding which 'Mr Browning' (the 'Mr' is a sneer) had propagated in a recent article for the *Quarterly Review*: that is, the idea that education consists of keeping boarding houses for boys, training them for competitive examinations which their parents care about intensely but which the boys themselves in all likelihood care for not at all, and selling a great many school books to the parents. This is the kind of educational experience, even at the upper end of the class system, that perpetuates the idea of culture as mere acquisition of mental rules and habits. 'Our task' must be to break the stranglehold of habit, and 'to convince those who mechanically serve some stock notion or operation, and thereby go astray, that it is not culture's work or aim to give the victory to some rival fetish, but simply to turn a free and fresh stream of thought upon the whole matter in question' (530–1).

The passage is one of several references to individuals that disappeared between the 1869 edition (still widely reprinted) and the 1875 edition. In Browning's case there was particular reason for leaving well alone: he had been dismissed from Eton earlier that year, 'on the pretext of administrative inefficiency but actually because his influence [his encouragement of sexual confidences, and his cultivation of close friendships with some of the boys] was thought to be sexually contagious'.[40] Perhaps more relevantly, Browning's devastating review of Arnold's report on *Schools and Universities*, for the *Quarterly Review* (October 1868), made it clear just how badly Arnold had underestimated him.[41] It is, nevertheless, more generally the case that as the text of *Culture and Anarchy* developed over the years Arnold gradually steered its prose further away from direct opposition to the practical value of education, even in the form of parody.

The manuscript of 'Culture and its Enemies' (in Balliol College, Oxford) shows him repeatedly revising the word 'use' in favour of something else: 'Now, then, is the moment for culture to be of use', the first draft reads, but 'use' is scored out and replaced with the term 'service' (fo. 4ʳ) (secular as much as Christian in its implications here). A passage cancelled entirely from the final text bothers repeatedly over the same word:

Bishop Wilson is careful to warn the seeker of light against this waste of his light, just that it may all ~~be used be applied~~ be used 'for no end but that he may better see and not miss his way'; just that it may all ~~be used~~ serve simply 'to make reason and the will of God prevail'. (fos. 4ʳ–5ᵛ)

Arnold struggles particularly hard with the wording of a direct assertion, towards the end of the lecture, that the purpose of culture is not just 'to make all live in an atmosphere of sweetness and light,' but also (as the final 1883 text reads) to 'use ideas, as it [culture] uses them itself, freely—nourished and not bound by them'. The manuscript wrestles with the remit of that 'use': '~~to fit all for a use use and shape through ideas, judgements, and watchwords, even its own, as freely as it uses and shapes[?] through them itself~~' (fo. 21ʳ).[42] It is noticeable that 'function' is not one of the alternatives he seems to have considered, despite its standing (famously) in preference to 'use' in the title of the

---

[40] Richard Davenport-Hines, 'Oscar Browning', *New DNB*, online edition. Accessed 27 January 2010.

[41] *Quarterly Review* 125 (October 1868), 473–90.

[42] The final MS version reads 'to make all live in an atmosphere of sweetness and light, [... scored out passage as above] and use ideas, as it uses them itself, freely, to be nourished and not bound by them. This is the social idea.' The *Cornhill* text reads: 'to make all live in an atmosphere of sweetness and light, and use ideas as it uses them itself, freely—to be nourished and not bound by them.' The 1883 text (Super's copytext) belatedly clarifies (or corrects) the agency: 'to make all men live in an atmosphere of sweetness and light, where they may use ideas, as it uses them itself, freely—nourished and not bound by them.'

1864 essay 'The Function of Criticism at the Present Time'.[43] In this
context, 'function' suffers by association with the uncultured functionary.
'[H]ow,' he asks, shall we convince 'the Barbarian' that we do not 'want
for ourselves his pre-eminency and function?... we want [him], and
others uninterested in the cause of a public and national culture] to
believe, that the intelligible law of things has in itself something desirable and precious, and that all place, function, and bustle are hollow
goods without it' (227).

In one prominent place the term 'utility' is allowed to stand. The
definition of culture near the start of *Culture and Anarchy* has three
stages. True culture is neither mere curiosity ('a desire after the things
of the mind simply for their own sakes') nor only 'a study of perfection'
('the desire for removing human error, clearing human confusion, and
diminishing human misery'), but a joining of the two in a 'culture...
possessed by the scientific passion as well as by the passion of doing
good'. When Arnold upholds this third, conjoined, model of curiosity
with the study of perfection, he makes it clear that he is recommend-
ing it because curiosity would be 'selfish, petty, and unprofitable' without the addition of the 'great and plain utility' of 'the study of
perfection' (93). One way of reading this is to say, as Nick Shrimpton
does, that it is 'an argument with Utilitarianism but it's not an exclusion of it' (a tendency Shrimpton locates in several areas of Arnold's
writing[44]). Another is to say that it is, exceptionally in *Culture and
Anarchy*, a moment at which Arnold chooses to meet economic instrumentalism on its own linguistic ground, but to take one of its favoured
terms and harness it to an effort that is idealistically aspirational, and by
any common standard of economic usefulness, immeasurable.

The very shadowy place permitted, in most of *Culture and Anarchy*,
to the idea that culture may be useful is not, in short, an accident—it
is the outcome of a deliberate process of revision. Getting rid of it was,
apparently, not an easy process. The language of use comes readily to

[43] In *Lectures and Essays in Criticism*, ed. R. H. Super, with the assistance of Sister Thomas Marion Hoctor, *CPW* iii (Ann Arbor: University of Michigan Press, 1962), 258–85.

[44] In ch. III of *Culture and Anarchy*, 'Barbarians, Philistines, Populace', he engages with
the Utilitarian value of 'happiness' ('All of us... imagine happiness to consist in doing what
one's ordinary self likes') (*Culture and Anarchy*, 145). This too is an argument with Utilitarianism but it's not an exclusion of it. In 'Porro unum est necessarium' he praises (while
responding to a criticism from) the most distinguished Utilitarian philosopher of the new
generation, Henry Sidgwick.

hand, as Arnold clearly found: it is, indeed, a good example of the kind
of mechanical or merely habitual thinking that he held it culture's
role to expunge. In place of the occasional claims found in the manuscript for culture's utility, the final text consistently stresses that view of
culture which has become famous (and which I don't need to rearticu-
late here, except in summary): culture as a life-long process of seeking
perfection in the Socratic sense—the free exercise of intelligence and
reason; the cultivation, and not just the mechanical learning, of 'the best
that has been thought and said'; the pursuit of 'sweetness and light'.

This last, notoriously unsatisfactory descriptor of culture brings into
focus perhaps the greatest problem faced by advocates for the humanities—as much a problem now as it was for Arnold. How does one find
a language of validation that accurately captures the qualities of the
humanities without becoming vulnerable to overuse. Succinctly: one
cannot. Arnold, who succeeded as well as anyone for a time, also, and
inevitably, failed.

the Greek word, euphuia, a finely tempered nature, gives exactly the notion of
perfection as culture brings us to conceive it: a harmonious perfection, a perfection in which the characters of beauty and intelligence are both present,
which unites 'the two noblest of things,'—as Swift, who of one of the two, at
any rate, had himself all too little, most happily calls them in his *Battle of the
Books*,—'the two noblest of things, sweetness and light.' The euphyês is the
man who tends towards sweetness and light; the aphyês is precisely our Philistine. The immense spiritual significance of the Greeks is due to their having
been inspired with this central and happy idea of the essential character of
human perfection; and Mr. Bright's misconception of culture, as a smattering
of Greek and Latin, comes itself, after all, from this wonderful significance of
the Greeks having affected the very machinery of our education, and is in
itself a kind of homage to it. (99)

Lionel Trilling's footnote on 'sweetness and light', in his classic 1939
study of Arnold, states the problem succinctly: 'This phrase has fallen
into such disrepute that it has come to mean a smirking, simpering
flabbiness of attitude, a kind of Pollyanna hypocrisy.'[45] Or, scarcely less
negatively, from Stefan Collini's Past Masters volume on Arnold: 'it is
unfortunate that the words "sweetness and light" now have a somewhat
unctuous, almost genteel, even anaemic air about them; they suggest

[45] Lionel Trilling, *Matthew Arnold* (London: George Allen and Unwin Ltd, 1939), 268.

too much the mild uplift dispensed by that kind of wet do-gooder who never seems to have felt the pull of any real human appetites.'[46] Did Arnold recognize that there might be a problem? Not immediately, or one assumes he would not have employed them at all, but he certainly came to recognize within a fairly short space after the publication of *Culture and Anarchy* that the words might be a liability as well as (gratifyingly) that they had passed into common currency.

In early December 1869 he writes to his mother that 'Dizzy' [Disraeli], 'in high force' and 'agreeable' at a dinner party the previous night, had leaned across the table apropos of something and teasingly remarked ' "Sweetness and light I call that, Mr Arnold, eh?" ' It is one of several instances in Arnold's letters after *Culture and Anarchy*, in which the phrase 'sweetness and light' is made to perform a kind of rhetorical flourish, acknowledging its own success but also admitting a hint of irony at Arnold's expense. The irony and the flourish grow over the years. When the phrase 'sweetness and light' first appears in his correspondence, outside its original context in *Culture and Anarchy* (1869) it is entirely straight faced: a letter to the prison reformer William Tallack, later that year, warning that no amount of philanthropic energy, or gathering of information, 'or even vigour of mind' in the reforming cause, will be 'sufficient to give what I call "sweetness & light"; something more is needed, and this something is delicacy of perception'.[47] By 1870 Arnold is starting to pick up a whiff of irreverence towards the phrase. Attending the Oxford Commemoration in June of that year to receive an honorary doctorate he is mildly ragged by the new Chancellor, Lord Salisbury: 'He told me afterwards it had been suggested to him that he ought to have addressed me as *Vir dulcissime et lucidissime*. He is a dangerous man...'[48] Not long afterwards Arnold has taken over the role of the ironist, writing to James Martineau to recommend a housekeeper by the Dickensian name of Tuffin, and joking that 'if he would not think I was too much pressing him with sweetness and light I would add to my account of Mrs Tuffin that she had remarkably pleasing manners'.[49]

Arnold was well aware that there is a risk to being associated with a catchphrase. That 'sweetness and light' had passed into the common

---

[46] Collini, *Arnold*, 83.   [47] 10 October 1869, *Letters* iii. 368–9 (p. 369).

[48] Letter to Mary Penrose Arnold, 25 June 1870, *Letters* iii. 425–7 (426).

[49] Recounted letter to Mary Penrose Arnold, 1 November 1871, *Letters* iv (1871–1878), 58–60 (59).

conversational currency of educated England was already apparent within months of its publication, as Disraeli's wink across the table indicates.[50] The currency was something to be exploited: 'You have no idea how Culture & Anarchy is improved', he told his publisher, 'by throwing it into chapters, with headings supplied by the phrases in the book which have become famous: "Sweetness and Light," "Hebraism & Hellenism,["] &c.'[51] But Arnold also acknowledged privately that the phrase's transportability and saccharinness might be a liability. So, when he was accosted by Disraeli, now Lord Beaconsfield, again at a dinner party in 1881, and told that 'I was doing a very great good, and... that I was the only living Englishman who had become a classic in his own lifetime', he was inclined to be sceptical:

The fact is that what I have done in establishing a number of current phrases— such as Philistinism, sweetness & light, and all that—is just the sort of thing to strike him; he had told Lady Airlie [their hostess] before I came that he thought it a great thing to do, and when she answered that she thought it was rather a disadvantage for people got hold of my phrases and then thought they knew all about my work he answered: 'Never mind—it's a great achievement!'[52]

By 1881, when Arnold agreed to substitute for Lord Derby as the speaker at the opening of the Session of the University of Liverpool, he was prepared to mock himself rather more robustly than a modesty topos would normally accommodate. 'You were to have... an address from an eminent man of science':

You have in his stead, many people would tell you, a nearly worn out man of letters... with a frippery of phrases about sweetness and light, seeing things as they really are, knowing the best that has been thought and said in the world, which never had very much solid meaning, and have now quite lost the gloss and charm of novelty.
... I wish I could promise to change my old phrases for new ones,... I wish I saw a prospect, that, within the term of life which can yet remain to me, phrases such as 'sweetness and light', 'seeing things as they really are,' were

---

[50] Park Honan, *Matthew Arnold: A Life* (London: Weidenfeld and Nicolson, 1981), 350 notes how quickly the newspaper press took up the phrase. Rosemary Tate has discovered several further examples of the phrase circulating through the newspaper press in the early months of 1869 alone. 'The Aesthetics of Sugar: Concepts of Sweetness in the Nineteenth Century' (Oxford D.Phil. thesis, University of Oxford, 2010), 165–6.

[51] Letter to George Smith, 20 August 1875, *Letters* iv. 279.

[52] Letter to Frances Bunsen Trevenen Whately Arnold, 21 February 1881, *Letters* v. 135–6 (135).

likely to cease to sum up, to my mind, crying needs for our nation. . . . But I fear there is no chance of this happening. What has been the burden of my song hitherto, will probably have . . . to be the burden of it till the end.[53]

There are various ways, most of them by now well explored, by which one might try to rescue 'sweetness and light'. Irony is not commonly one of those ways, and it works only to the extent that it makes Arnold himself seem less 'wet'. A more conventional approach is to do as Trilling suggested and recall the phrase's origin in Swift: 'Aesop, in Swift's *Battle of the Books*, moralizes thus on the bee's quarrel with the spider: "Instead of dirt and poison, we [the Ancients] have rather chosen to fill our hives with honey and wax, thus furnishing mankind with the two noblest of things, which are sweetness and light"' (419–20n.). Sweetness and light are, then, the attractive and valuable qualities given to us by the true scholar of the classics (the one who respects the wisdom of the ancients, 'Hellenic' wisdom, in Arnold's phrase). In the context of the *Battle of the Books*, 'sweetness and light' is, in other words, not a token of vague sentimentalism about high culture but a weapon in the armoury of the satirist. The phrase knows its own excess, as it were. What Arnold valued in Swift was, he tells us, the light (sweetness being in short supply). As he put it in a cross letter to an American correspondent near the end of his life: 'No great writer is to be disposed of as your friend disposes of Addison and Swift; he says, nothing is to be learned from Swift; why, a sense for the blatant nonsense and clap trap which constitutes three-fourths of our public writing, and which is a greater curse to your country than even to ours, is to be got from him.'[54]

To trace the origins of 'sweetness and light' back beyond Swift into the classics is, in the same mode, to find a long history not of cultural complacency but of joined debate about the value of poetry. So, Pindar repeatedly exploits the analogy between the divine sweetness of his own writing and that of the bee ('honey-sounding hymns', 'honey-sounding songs'). Plato, in a famous passage in the *Ion* (534a ff.), then takes up the comparison and twists it into a witty putdown to the excessive claims of the poets, declaring that the bee is sufficiently unpredictable and irresponsible to be a fair symbol of that 'light, winged, and airy thing', the poet. When Horace subsequently took

---

[53] 'A Liverpool Address' [30 September 1882], *Philistinism in England and America*, 74–88 (74–5).

[54] To Frank Preston Sterns, 7 January 1886, *Letters* vi. 110.

over the image, as part of his defence of poetry as *dulce et utile*, he was deliberately inverting the Platonic associations again.[55]

Dulce et utile was, by Arnold's time, the most famous of these classical allusions to sweetness—so much so that when Arnold invokes Swift's 'sweetness and light' he is also, surely, invoking Swift's deliberate transformation of 'sweetness and usefulness' into something which both is and is not an apt translation. In Swift's parable, 'sweetness and light' are utilities. They are what the bee gives that is pleasing and useful to man: in the first case, honey (food, palatable nourishment); in the second, wax or paraffin (literal light). At the same time, of course, the terms reach much higher: they are claims about beauty—about something well in excess of a merely instrumental utility value.[56] When Arnold substitutes 'light' for 'utility', he thus both respects the Horatian dictum for poetry and refuses the second of its terms, substituting another which honours the original purpose but asks us to look to another more diffusive meaning of light—illumination, knowledge, insight, the perfection of God's revelation (though it is worth repeating that Arnold's model of education is secular in content). For the first audience of 'Culture and its Enemies' the word could serve to acknowledge gracefully Arnold's role as Professor of Poetry at Oxford, taking in the university's ubiquitous motto—'*dominus illuminatio mea*', God is my light. The words are from Psalm 27.[57] Like so much of the vocabulary of *Culture and Anarchy*, the phrase 'sweetness and light' thus

[55] For all these classical references see Steele Commager, *The Odes of Horace: A Critical Study*, foreword by David Armstrong (London: University of Oklahoma Press, 1995), 48–9.

[56] At several points in *Culture and Anarchy*, Arnold expands upon 'sweetness and light' to include also 'beauty' or to make beauty stand as a kind of summary equivalent of 'sweetness and light'. Almost the last words of 'Cultural and its Enemies', and thus of Arnold's final lecture as Oxford's Professor of Poetry, are a reassertion of culture as a reassertion of 'sweetness and light'—'only it must be real thought and real beauty; real sweetness and real light'.

[57] Arnold read and reread the Psalms continually. His *Note-Books* contain numerous quotations from them, including (in 1868) Psalm 36: 9: 'In thy light shall we see light'; and Psalm 13: 3: 'Lighten mine eyes, O Lord, that I sleep not in death'. *The Note-Books of Matthew Arnold*, ed. Howard Foster Lowry, Karl Young, and Waldo Hilary Dunn (Oxford: Oxford University Press, 1952), 72, 86. Psalm 27 is quoted several times over the years; the opening words are excerpted with other verses in the second of the larger general *Note-Books* (545) but probably date from 1877 or afterwards, given that they follow a quotation from Georges Sand's *Dernières pages* (1877). In 1881 Arnold, perhaps struck by the similarity to 'sweetness and light', also takes down a passage from Ecclesiastes 11: 7–10, beginning 'Truly the light is sweet…' (366).

draws on the values of religion, but rearticulates them in more secular terms, seeking to make culture the guarantor of a set of values which (Arnold held) the language of religion was no longer well equipped to defend before a society at once increasingly secular and increasingly sectarian.[58] In the process it both acknowledges utility as a good, and declines to pay it the attention that contemporary political debate and economic exigency, if nothing else, would expect it to be paid.

The question of the competence of 'sweetness and light' as a valuation of culture nevertheless stands. The phrase is, from one perspective, vulnerable to its own density as much as to its ethereality. Too much is packed into it by way of historical and intellectual argument over the centuries—and not all was likely to be apparent to Arnold's first audience, let alone to ours. There is, however, one final argument that can be made on its behalf, and which has bearing on its deflection of standards of utility, as well as its more general appeal or want of it. Just possibly, the lexical incompetence itself does work. 'Sweetness and light', that is, marks the place at which no terms will sustain their value for long as descriptors of certain things about culture which Arnold wants us to understand are valuable, but which depreciate as soon as they pass into a language of critical appreciation or evaluation. If that argument has any purchase, it matters that Arnold himself came to feel, acutely, the phrase's vulnerability to irony, and, latterly, to employ that irony on his own behalf as part of a defence of culture that was ongoing, not rigid.

Lest you are becoming alarmed: I am not arguing that Arnold offers us a way out of our present difficulties. As has been said so often, there is too much about *Culture and Anarchy* that is unpalatable and unfeasible for a defence of culture, or of the university as a location for that defence, in the twenty-first century. But I am making a case for an 'Arnoldian' modernism that could take up the task of defending the free play of mind in ways that are not simply hostile to instrumentalism—and yet that can still refuse to see higher education confined by it, or to give more than a small part of the humanities' valuation to it. It is worth asking why the 'Arnoldian' cultural contract proved such an effective

---

[58] See a Notebook entry for 1866: 'We can use any language of established religion, but at certain epochs the effort of translation thus necessary, the partialness of the language's hold on the facts, strikes us forcibly. The language is then drawing near to the time when it must undergo a change.' *Note-Books*, 66.

argument for government policy, lasting at least until the 1960s, when it was put under pressure by expansion and the Wilsonian emphasis on technology, and, arguably, until the 1980s, when it was definitively superseded by more aggressively commercial models. Nothing in the humanities' language of justification has dealt as effectively since with the problem of how, and in what measure, to recognize the value of practical ends without making them a defining, or a distorting, purpose. For all that is unworkable and undesirable now in Arnold's understanding of culture, *Culture and Anarchy* has much still to offer on the question of what should be our response to the pressures of economic instrumentalism in government, both as a diagnosis of a problem and as an extension to the range of ways by which we might react.

Robert Young's suggestion that we recognize a deconstructive logic of the supplement in the centuries old opposition of usefulness to uselessness that has structured our debates about the value of the university and of culture offers another way of reacting. It's not obviously a way that will give us much practical assistance in resisting a mistaken pressure to demonstrate economic or social benefit—though it may offer us the consolations of modern philosophy, and it may encourage hesitation before re-enacting argumentative patterns of mere repetition. The alternative, until recently, has usually seemed to be direct rebuttal of the claims of usefulness. This, too, has a place. But to those arguments we should, I think, add Arnold's perception that economic instrumentalism, like other forms of mechanistic or reductive thinking, takes its grip most powerfully at the level of our language and in the way we are educated, and go on to educate others, in thinking through language. If we speak too often in terms of applied uses, of instrumentalism, of standards of excellence bereft of content, of impact—even in the act of speaking against those things we cede too much of our own ground.

Arnold would willingly have conceded that all educational purposes can be expressed as usefulness if one pursues the notion of use finely enough. To know oneself and to know the world will alike serve the 'secondary aim' of enabling one to fulfil one's place in the world. Similarly, the characterological aspects of *Culture and Anarchy*—its belief that culture's aim should be the development of that 'best self' which exercises the 'free play of thought' and checks the mechanical following of any 'mean master-concern'—will in a refined sense of 'use' be 'useful' to the society and the state, providing more curious, less dully habituated employers and employees. But, for Arnold, this too would have been at most a secondary consequence of the development of the individual and, with the individual, the culture.

Nothing has been more striking in the discourse of the UK academy over the past few years than the astonishing rate at which 'impact' and (to a lesser degree) 'social benefit' have become part of our everyday talk. It's not necessary to think of the ground we are thereby ceding as the high ground of Arnoldian culture in order to recognize that the better position might be to keep instrumentalism, in the main, at a clear remove from our language—to prioritize individuality of style, as the mark of independent intelligence (or 'reason' as Arnold would have put it) and to concede as little as possible to the formulaic language of the bureaucratic statistician. Arnold did not succeed in finding such a language, or rather did not find one that could last for very long before it began to seem elitist, complacent, soft, in varying measures. But he himself knew that this fate will befall, perhaps should befall, any language that offers to define the value of the humanities for us in permanent measures of taste and value.

3

Socrates Dissatisfied

The Argument for a Contribution to Happiness

Arguments to the effect that the value of the humanities rests not on their usefulness to society but on their contribution to utility are less commonly advanced now than in the past. The utilitarian claim proper, that their value lies in something we can recognize, define, perhaps in certain limited ways also quantify as a contribution to individual or collective human happiness, is perhaps the least trusted and certainly among the least developed lines for their defence now— this despite all the work in and attention given to positive psychology and the economic measurement of happiness. Utilitarianism offers the humanities a constellation of possible arguments rather than one single defence. Any version of it is beset by definitional difficulties— even putting to one side the problem of metrics. 'Happiness', like 'pleasure', is, to echo Plato's Socrates, a 'many' not a 'one' (*Philebus*, 12c). Nevertheless, apology for the humanities by way of hedonism, or something closely related to it, has a distinguished history and one especially famous formulation from John Stuart Mill. It is specific, in the first instance, to literature, and its status as a 'defence' is at one remove, rather than direct and polemical; but it is implicitly and strongly a defence, nonetheless, in the course of a larger reaction against a reductive economic and political conception of the human good. In principle, the viability of Mill's arguments extends beyond the predominantly Romantic works he himself valued to embrace all forms of literature, including historical and philosophical writing that engages the imagination.[1] His views were shaped by a now outdated associationist psychology,[2] but the core claims need not be hostage to it.

If Mill's claims for the contribution of literature (by modern extension, the humanities) to our individual happiness are strong, and deeply engrained in the history of resistance to narrow economic conceptions of the human good, it is important to recognize at the outset that he did not seek to make them in terms of the collective experience of society; nor did he think that they were arguments relevant to the description of what we should look for from a well-designed university education. On the contrary, they arose in response to a peculiar deformation of his own character by a highly unusual—perhaps unique—experiment in early education. The question for anyone interested, today, in a revised hedonism that would comprehend additions to happiness as one measure of the public good, is whether what was an account of a highly idiosyncratic individual experience has any wider application to public life: in other words, whether we are warranted in treating the individual characterological description as either a microcosm of, or an analogy for, the character of society, or educated elements in society.

There is a very large literature on happiness within contemporary economics and behavioural psychology. The most influential contributions to that literature, however, are puzzlingly free of reference back to the most intense period of earlier philosophical and political debate about the idea that a good society should do what it can not just to promote the prosperity of its inhabitants but to enable them to be happy. When I first envisaged writing a chapter on this subject I had expected that it would need to engage closely with that modern literature,[3] but nothing I have encountered there pursues the claim that

---

[1] When treating questions of educational content, Mill himself used the word 'literary' in a 'wider' sense to embrace study of the classics and languages, philosophy of history, and historical criticism or historiography. 'Inaugural Address Delivered to the University of St. Andrews 1867', in *Collected Works of John Stuart Mill* (hereafter *CW*), editor of the text John M. Robson, 33 vols. (Toronto: University of Toronto Press; London: Routledge and Kegan Paul, 1963–91) (hereafter *CW*), xxii: *Essays on Equality, Law, and Education*, 215–57 (220).

[2] Having said that, associationist ideas still pervade a great deal of psychology and related disciplines (for example, in the understanding of connectionism).

[3] The most influential distillations of the academic literature for wider public consumption have been the work of Richard Layard, *Happiness: Lessons from a New Science* (London: Penguin Books, 2005), John F. Helliwell, and Wang Shung, *Weekends and Subjective*

education has a contribution to make to happiness with anything like the depth, or the clarity, to be found in Mill. The current literature standardly observes that there is a correlation between individuals being 'at the top of the income and education distribution',[4] and their reporting higher levels of happiness (with no distinction made between the effects of education and those of prosperity); also, that the relation between happiness and education is reciprocal (education affects a person's happiness, but happiness also affects the ability to learn (60)). Economic theorists commonly describe education as an important support for building incomes, improving health, creating trust, and increasing the efficiency and accountability of government. Some have detailed more specific ways in which higher education (across the disciplines) can be seen to alter behaviour—for example increasing the propensity of people to assume civic responsibilities.[5] Indeed, it is primarily through these important channels that education supports happier lives (*WHR* 93). There is some acknowledgement of the specific contributions education can make to knowledge of the kind that may,

---

Well-Being (Cambridge, Mass.: National Bureau of Economic Research, 2011), and (the leading exponent of positive psychology) Martin E. P. Seligman—see esp. *Authentic Happiness: Using the New Positive Psychology to Realize your Potential for Deep Fulfillment* (London: Nicholas Brealey Publishing, 2003) and *Flourish: A New Understanding of Happiness and Well-Being—and How to Achieve Them* (London: Nicholas Brealey Publishing, 2011). Also relevant is the publication of the first World Happiness Report, Commissioned for a United Nations Conference on Happiness, under the auspices of the UN General Assembly: ed. John Helliwell, Richard Layard, and Jeffrey Sachs (New York: The Earth Institute, Columbia University, 2012) <http://www.earth.columbia.edu/sitefiles/file/Sachs%20 Writing/2012/World%20Happiness%20Report.pdf>. Accessed 29 September 2012. For the most recent international overview of this strain of thinking about education, at the time of writing, see *Education at a Glance: OECD Indicators* (Paris: OECD Publishing, 2011). A helpfully sceptical review of the economic literature on the subject can be found in Wilfred Beckerman, *Economics as Applied Ethics: Value Judgements in Welfare Economics* (London: Palgrave Macmillan, 2010), ch. 10. The exception to the forgetting of Mill in the modern happiness literature is (in passing) John Kay, *Obliquity: Why our Goals Are Best Achieved Indirectly* (London: Profile Books, 2010).

[4] *World Happiness Report*, 4. In as much detail as is given: 'On average, the level of education has no clear direct impact on happiness, but education is of course indirectly related to happiness through its effect on income: education increases income and income increases happiness' (78).

[5] A classic work on this subject is Ernest T. Pascarella, *How College Affects Students: Findings and Insights from Twenty Years of Research* (San Francisco: Jossey-Bass, 1991). See also OECD, *Education at a Glance 2012* (Paris: OECD, 2012) (editorial summary p. 13); OECD, *Improving Health and Social Cohesion through Education* (Paris: OECD, 2010); OECD, *Understanding the Social Outcomes of Learning* (Paris: OECD, 2007); and OECD, *Social Capital, Human Capital and Health: What is the Evidence?* (Paris: OECD, 2010), 15.

for example, help one to be more healthy and prosperous than one would otherwise be, and to form 'values' conducive to positive participation in society.[6]

The negative correlations are more impressive than the positive: 74 per cent of 'deeply happy' people have some exposure to formal education, but 90 per cent of 'unhappy people' have none (*WHR* 140, 144). Almost nothing is said about the nature and means of the contribution education may make, and whether there are any more specific claims to be made according to the field of study pursued. The efficiency with which the *World Happiness Report* (2012) dispatches any complications here is astonishing:

> One obvious problem is that happy people may be more likely to persist in education and this effect cannot be controlled for in panel studies.... education may have some non-income benefits to the individuals who get an education, especially in poor countries. But this is smaller than is often claimed by educationalists. On top of that there may be important social effects through an informed electorate and in poor countries through reduced birth-rates and mortality. (78)

End of analysis. And the data for higher education are simply not strong enough, as yet, to tell us anything reliable (148 n. 9). I realize that, coming from a member of an English literature department, the claim that there is a startling degree of historical forgetting going on here courts defensive protestations from the fields I am finding wanting, but I can see no way round the embarrassment.

The happiness argument is, after all, though strong in the collective memories of humanities departments, and frequently alluded to in the specific forms of justification sought for literature, not especially current or especially well detailed in the wider political debate today. That this is so is in part a consequence of the resurgence of economic instrumentalism as one of the primary political pressures on the humanities; in part also because for much of the time period post Leavis, the authority of the Romantic appeal to literature as a rendering of 'life itself' has, within the academy if not without, been an object of considerable scepticism.

---

[6] See, for example, OECD, *Education at a Glance 2012*, 203—though the claim here relates to secondary not tertiary levels of education.

Mill describes in his *Autobiography* (published posthumously in 1873[7]) how reading certain works of literature rescued him from the narrow ends-driven conception of happiness instilled in him by his utilitarian education. In 1826, at 20 years of age, he was the product of an experiment in home schooling that has since become notorious: 'an appalling success', in Isaiah Berlin's pithy phrase.[8] Under the tutelage of his father James Mill, political philosopher and dedicated Benthamite, Mill was raised in a radical school of reformist political thought and activism. He tells us that he studied ancient Greek from the age of 3. By his early teenage years he was a fluent reader of Latin, Greek, and French, and proficient in many branches of the classics, philosophy, law, history, economics, mathematics. Directed away from Cambridge at 15, on the assumption that he 'already knew more than he could learn' there,[9] he instead began a long and distinguished career in his father's department of the India Office. By 1826 he had considerable responsibilities at work while, outside office hours, he was overseeing the education of his eight siblings, studying, editing, taking a leading role in debates within his radical circle, and propagandizing zealously as a periodical writer for the Benthamite cause. Then, in the autumn of that year he experienced 'A Crisis in my Mental History':

it occurred to me to put the question directly to myself, 'Suppose that all your objects in life were realized; that all the changes in institutions and opinions which you are looking forward to, could be completely effected at this very instant: would this be a great joy and happiness to you?' And an irrepressible self-consciousness distinctly answered, 'No!' At this my heart sank within me: the whole foundation on which my life was constructed fell down.

...I frequently asked myself, if I could, or if I was bound to go on living, when life must be passed in this manner. I generally answered to myself, that I did not think I could possibly bear it beyond a year. When, however, not more than half that duration of time elapsed, a small ray of light broke in upon my gloom. I was reading, accidentally, Marmontel's *Memoirs*, and came to the passage which relates his father's death, the distressed position of the family, and the sudden inspiration by which he, then a mere boy, felt and made them

---

[7] It was written in stages: started 1853–4, revised 1861, completed 1869–70.

[8] 'John Stuart Mill and the Ends of Life', in *Four Essays on Liberty* (Oxford: Oxford University Press, 1969), 175.

[9] Michael St John Packe, *The Life of John Stuart Mill*, with a preface by F. A. Hayek (London: Secker and Warburg, 1954), 49.

feel that he would be everything to them—would supply the place of all that they had lost. A vivid conception of the scene and its feelings came over me, and I was moved to tears. From this moment my burthen grew lighter. The oppression of the thought that all feeling was dead within me, was gone. I was no longer hopeless: I was not a stock or a stone. I had still, it seemed, some material out of which all worth of character, and all capacity for happiness, are made.[10]

The critical literature on Mill standardly recognizes several aspects to the intellectual repositioning that followed from his crisis and gradual recovery. The most immediately developed, in the 1830s and 1840s, involved his thinking about psychological determinism and free will. More obviously and enduringly influential was the series of important philosophical revisions to Mill's account of utilitarianism so as to incorporate a more complex theory of human motivations, redescribing what the individual's proper relation should and can be to the goal of happiness. These revisions are primarily, but not exclusively, the business of his classic essay on *Utilitarianism* (1863).

That essay also introduces a famous distinction between quantitative and qualitative pleasure, by way of challenge to Bentham's strictly quantitative approach. 'Prejudice apart,' Bentham wrote, 'the game of push-pin is of equal value with the arts and sciences of music and poetry. If the game of push-pin furnish more pleasure, it is more valuable than either.'[11] Or, in Mill's terse redaction: 'Push-pin is as good as poetry.'[12] 'Higher pleasures', in Mill's revisionary account, tend to be those pleasures available to 'a being of higher faculties': they involve 'intellectual tastes'.[13] *Utilitarianism* says little about the content of these higher tastes (the only pursuits directly implicated are poetry and philosophy), but the belief that some pleasures are non-instrumentally better than others colours much of his post-crisis thinking about what a more persuasive account of happiness than Bentham's, and any

[10] *Autobiography* (Holograph MS Columbia University Library Text), Parallel Reading Texts of the Early Draft and the Columbia MS, in *Autobiography and Literary Essays*, ed. John M. Robson and Jack Stillinger, *CW* i (Toronto: University of Toronto Press, 1981), 139, 145.
[11] *The Rationale of Reward* (London: Robert Heward, 1830), 206.
[12] 'Bentham' (1838), in *Essays on Ethics, Religion and Society*, ed. John M. Robson and D. P. Dryer, *CW* x (Toronto: University of Toronto Press, 1985), 75–115 (113).
[13] *Utilitarianism*, with an introductory essay by D. P. Dryer, in *Essays on Ethics, Religion and Society*, ed. John M. Robson, introduction by F. E. L. Priestley, *CW* x (Toronto: University of Toronto Press, 1985), 203–59 (213).

adequate model of education, will need to comprehend.[14] Some exploration is needed of how Mill's emotional response to literature in the midst of psychological crisis prompted the revisions to his thinking on each of these fronts, before looking more closely at the ways in which the *Autobiography* might lead us to extend and deepen his own philosophical theory of what it means to aim at happiness.

The question that triggered 'one of the best-known identity crises in history'[15] can be reworded more explicitly: 'if society were granted everything that I, John Stuart Mill, a Benthamite utilitarian, think practically necessary to yield the greatest happiness for the greatest number, would I be happy?' To which Mill responded with an emphatic 'No!' Logically one would expect the response 'I might be happy, but I cannot be sure that I would be so.' The reply he gives is firmer than logic alone justifies: too emphatic, but it recognizes a deeper problem than offended egoism, and a level of distress that goes beyond the ordinary coordinates of a loss of political faith.

Mill's retrospective description of himself at this juncture in his life is overtly emotional, but it is also intellectual and political. The difficulty on all fronts was not simply that utilitarianism offered no guarantee of happiness in his individual case. It is a familiar objection to classic utilitarianism (and one Mill greatly helped to *make* familiar) that it computes happiness in the aggregate; it has no special concern with the condition of the individual. But Mill's problem was not just the lack of regard for his own agency: in giving him no reasons to care for his own happiness as an element in the larger social and political picture, Benthamism left him confronting the lack of any secure connection between the individual's immediate motive (his or her own happiness) and the espoused goal (the general happiness). And the general happiness mattered to Mill, even as he felt the loss of his own desire to pursue it. He wanted to want it. One striking feature of his mental crisis and the route he finds out of it is that there is no fundamental parting of the ways with Benthamism over what the goal should be, though some philosophers have thought that coherence should have required a parting. Indeed, the whole subsequent history of Mill's dealings with utilitarian philosophy

---

[14] The most relevant writings are the *Autobiography*, 'The Inaugural Address' given on his appointment as Rector of St Andrew's University in 1867, and his several literary essays, collected in *CW* i.

[15] Stefan Collini, introduction to *CW* xxi: *Essays on Equality, Law, and Education*, x.

can be read as an effort to reform and qualify Benthamite utilitarian claims from within, rather than to allow the greatest happiness to become the price paid for reclaiming the happiness of the individual.

The way in which Mill reacted to his own loss of motivational drive reveals the nature of the crisis to be deeper and stranger than his own description in the *Autobiography* quite registers. To all outward appearances he did not react at all. On the external biographical evidence, an acute distress of some six months' duration was not evident to anyone else. Mill continued to function publicly, doing his work at the India Office, tutoring, debating. 'None of his friends... was aware there was anything wrong with him'—a state of affairs that suggests the poverty of his experience of friendship to that date, his biographer Richard Reeves observes: a 'lack of intimacy in even his closest friendships'.[16] The philosopher Elijah Millgram draws out just how peculiar Mill's predicament was:

> the problem was not simply that he was depressed. If Mill's affliction had only been clinical depression, it would not have been nearly as bad as it was, and it would not have shaped Mill's life and philosophizing as it did.
>
> The deeper problem was that, although he was depressed and unmotivated, he could not act depressed.... People who are depressed mope around, can't get out of bed in the morning, and give up on the enterprises for which they have no heart; if Mill had been able to do any of this, he would not have been as desperate as he was. Instead, having realized that he simply did not care about his party's platform, he could not cease working to advance it. The pace of his labors did not slow perceptibly, and hardly any of his acquaintances seem even to have realized that anything was wrong.[17]

As Millgram describes Mill's case, in line with Mill's own understanding of psychology, the problem was the sudden perception of a gap between his commitment to the goal defined for him by his utilitarian education—not a 'higher pleasure' but an out-ranking 'highest pleasure'—and his ability to associate desire with the object.[18] A convinced empiricist (like his father) and an adherent of associationist psychology, Mill understood the psyche to be, at the time of a person's birth, a

---

[16] *John Stuart Mill: Victorian Firebrand* (London: Atlantic Books, 2007), 63.

[17] Elijah Millgram, 'Mill's Incubus', in Ben Eggleston, Dale Miller, and David Weinstein (eds.), *John Stuart Mill and the Art of Life* (Oxford: Oxford University Press, 2010), 169–91 (177).

[18] For the term 'highest pleasure' (not used by Mill), see Millgram, 'Mill's Incubus', 173.

blank slate, in Locke's famous metaphor, onto which are etched, by repeated experience, pathways or habitual 'associations' of sensation and perception. In his case, the main effort of all his early education had been 'to form the strongest possible associations... of pleasure with all things beneficial to the great whole, and of pain with all things hurtful to it' (*Autobiography*, 141). His personality had been 'structured around [that] single, overriding objective'.[19] But because the associations had been 'forcibly' instilled, using the 'old familiar instruments, praise and blame, reward and punishment', the feelings they produced were too weak to withstand the early inaugurated 'habit of analysis', which then became 'a dissolving force' as Mill puts it (141), a 'perpetual worm at the[ir] root' (143).

Millgram draws on Mill's later contributions to the second edition of his father's psychology textbook (*Analysis of the Phenomena of the Human Mind*, 1869) to separate out two routes by which a person's 'hedonic profile' (how far and in what ways they are happy or unhappy) may change under the Laws of Association. Commonly, an association that becomes merely habitual, or taken for granted, will weaken over time and 'fade away'.[20] Millgram calls this the 'hedonic drift' problem. But in Mill's case his desires and pleasures were also vulnerable to that early entrenched habit of submitting his own ideas to sceptical scrutiny. And one can add to Millgram's account here that the analytic habit is itself doubly (and, it may appear, contradictorily) a source of vulnerability: on the one hand it risks corroding all of its objects by its scepticism; on the other, it may itself lapse into a merely routinized response if it does not meet with resistance from other mental powers or faculties. A mind unsupported by the analytic habit would be without intellectual mettle; but one trained to employ it too exclusively will be in danger of believing in and caring for no sustained purposes. It will exhibit a merely mechanical competence, however impressive. As instilled in Mill at so young an age, without equivalent care to those other powers and faculties, the products of the analytic habit were (in his own later judgement) 'precocious and premature' (143).

Such an interpretation of associationism led Mill to a way of thinking about the capacity for individual flourishing and moral character

---

[19] Millgram, 'Mill's Incubus', 175.

[20] Millgram, 'Mill's Incubus', 176, summarizing James Mill, *Analysis of the Phenomena of the Human Mind* (1829), ed. John Stuart Mill (London: Longmans, 1869), i. 106–10, 231–2 with editorial footnotes by J. S. Mill.

development as entailing a fine balance between naturally acquired associations and the invigorating and educative power of self-scrutiny. The core of the 'crisis' in 1826–7 and, if Millgram is correct, the origin of Mill's abiding concern thereafter with liberty of mind (intellectual affiliation, moral choice, desire), was that, at this early point in his adult life, having experienced the loss of connection between his motives and the goal he subscribed to, he was initially unable to locate alternative motivations that could 'trump' those given to him by his education in utilitarianism. Habituated 'dispositions', he would argue some seventeen years later, in the *System of Logic* (1843), often overtake and suppress the operation of choice or conscious motive, so that feeling and, ultimately, character may be said to be largely determined by experience. But 'determinism' here describes only the invariable sequence of psychological causes and effects that operate in a character: 'given the motives which are present to an individual's mind, and given likewise the character and disposition of the individual, the manner in which he will act might be unerringly inferred.'[21] These are constraints on free will and self-motivation but they are not cause for concern: they are matters of ordinary psychological functioning and characterological coherence. The problem arises when a person is unable to exert his or her own free will—or, as Millgram prefers to express it, when they become 'morally unfree':[22]

Putting the characterization a bit more formally than Mill himself did, the will is free—that is, morally free—when, for any motivation you have, there are psychologically available to you further motivations that you could marshal to trump it. Because the phrase is slightly misleading to twenty-first-century ears, it is worth adding that the notion is not restricted to what we would think of as moral matters. Moral freedom is a state of character: a near-equilibrium, in which one's motivations are in relative balance with each other. (171)

The *System of Logic* provides a much quoted defence of our moral freedom against the exponents of necessitarianism: a person's 'character

---

[21] *A System of Logic Ratiocinative and Inductive: Being a Connected View of the Principles of Evidence and the Methods of Investigation*, 2 vols., ed. J. M. Robson, introduction by R. F. McRae, *CW* vii–viii (Toronto: University of Toronto Press, 1973–4) (viii. 836–7). Motives themselves the mature Mill understood to be the effect of an encounter between 'external inducement[s]' and certain established 'mental conditions' in a person, with which the mental conditions 'must co-operate, in the production of the act'. *System of Logic*, viii. 814.

[22] 'Mill's Incubus', 170.

is formed by his circumstances . . . ; but his own desire to mould it in a particular way, is one of those circumstances, and by no means one of the least influential'.[23] The Mill who found himself utterly demotivated in the winter of 1826–7 could not yet formulate that thought. Having 'locked his ends and activities into place' he scrutinized them and found them wanting. Of a sudden unable to care about those ends and activities he was also unable to break off from them: 'he found himself the helpless passenger of his own life'.[24]

Though the associationist psychology in which Mill's view of these subjects was cast makes much of the assumed mental functioning behind it sound historically remote, the core predicament is plainly summarized. The manner in which he found relief from his predicament is similarly attractive in its surface (though not superficial) emotional simplicity. The first glimpse of hope that there might be escape, and that he had within him still a capacity for feeling that could counter the corrosive effects of his own analytic cast of mind, came with the 'accidental' reading of Jean-François Marmontel's *Mémoires d'un père* (1804). A mix of didactic instruction for children, sentimental recollection, and social and literary history, the *Mémoires* (translated in 1805[25]) were well known in their time. Their many Victorian admirers included Ruskin—another high-achieving son educated (in part) by his father, and carrying complicated emotional baggage from childhood into adulthood.

The fortuity of Mill's happening upon the work ('I was reading, accidentally, Marmontel's *Memoirs*') is a curiously intruded observation, implying that whatever force pulled Mill out of his 'gloom' it was not (or not yet) characterological. Can we give no credit to Mill's agency in selecting, or putting himself in the way of, his reading? Should we not be curious about how it came to be recommended to him? Apparently not. Mill prefers the Wordsworthian thought (and Wordsworth will quickly supplant Marmontel in the crisis narrative) that this was a quasi-Providential rescue—the agnostic Mill having little truck with Providence. What followed was a gradual rebuilding of

---

[23] *System of Logic*, viii. 840. For commentary, see Dale E. Miller, *J. S. Mill: Moral, Social and Political Thought* (Cambridge: Polity Press, 2010), 25.

[24] Millgram, 'Mill's Incubus', 178.

[25] *Memoirs of Marmontel*, 4 vols. (London: Longman, Hurst, Rees, and Orme, 1805). Translator anonymous.

his own ethos, but the first awakening of inner powers could only come from without. Such was the extremity of Mill's debility, or his retrospective perception of his own debility, or both.

The scene that so moved Mill in the *Mémoires* is one of Marmontel's great sentimental set pieces, describing his own coming of age at the news of his father's death. The psychological rationale of the scene's appeal for James Mill's son has not gone unremarked by critics, many of whom read the episode as displaced wish fulfilment: imaginative gratification of an unconscious wish to murder the father.[26] Mill's point of identification in the story is with the 'mere boy' who convinces his family that he can 'be everything to them'—his 'making them feel' prompts the 'feelings' in Mill that then reassure him 'all feeling ' is not 'dead'. The significance (for Mill) of the tears shed over Marmontel is that they are a much needed reassurance that he has still a natural concern for his own condition—an 'irrepressible self-consciousness' not wholly absorbable into rational pursuit of the economic and political means to 'the greatest happiness'. In providing such reassurance, his response to literature initiates the discovery of new motivations for agency: the motivation to achieve some 'worth of character' and the conscious desire to realize some 'capacity for [personal] happiness'.

Mill is not saying anything so crude or implausible here as 'literature makes us happy'. Nor is he saying, with vague Romantic flourish, that feeling trumps reason. Indeed, he says pretty much the opposite. In his own case, the effect of happening upon a sympathetically engaging piece of literature at this critical moment in his life was to open him up to the experience of unhappiness. The first result of reading Marmontel is a 'vivid' apprehension of a complex of feelings: grief, 'distress' (perhaps economic as well as emotional), and then whatever it is that Mill means to convey as the content of the boy's 'inspiration'— determination certainly, love presumably, but also, surely, ambition to be equal to the task of replacing his father. That Mill can intensely feel, and express, such a complex of emotions and desires relieves him of the fear that he may have been made 'a mere reasoning machine' (III).

---

[26] See esp. Bruce Mazlish, *James and John Stuart Mill: Father and Son in the Nineteenth Century* (New York: Basic Books, Inc., 1975), 209–11; Élie Halévy, *The Growth of Philosophic Radicalism*, trans. Mary Morris (1928), new edn. with preface by John Plamenatz (London: Faber, 1972), 269–70.

It also proves to him (though at this point secondarily) that he possesses natural powers of sympathy: a capacity to feel for and like
others.

The 'secondary' recognition of sympathetic kinship with others is, in
the larger picture, at least as important as the 'primary' recognition of
his capacity to feel deeply. If the only point of Mill's encounter with
literature were that it rescued him, an exceptional case (even a bizarre
one), from a life nearly wrecked by excessive educational emphasis on
reason at the expense of feeling, it would be difficult to see what the
wider implications could be. In any more normal education, the cultivation of feelings would have happened through numerous channels,
starting with the daily affective life of familial and friendly relation-
ships. It would not have required the special cultivation of feeling as
assisted by a work of literary sensibility to act as a strong corrective.
That said, Mill several times insists that his own case is, however
extreme, indicative of a general intellectual limitation within classic
utilitarianism. He was not just the son of one man who 'undervalue[d]
feeling', and carried that undervaluation into an unusually exacting
educational programme; he was associated with an intellectual group,
and an intellectual enterprise, that was 'theoretically indifferent to'
poetry, and to 'Imagination generally as an element of human nature'
(115).
    Of Bentham himself, Mill notes that 'he used to say "all poetry is
misrepresentation": but, in the sense in which he said it, the same
might have been said of all impressive speech; of all representation or
inculcation more oratorical in its character than a sum in arithmetic'
(115). The failing of poetry (and of 'all impressive speech') was, specifically, a failure with respect to Reason. Insofar as the Benthamites were
hostile to poetry, they were hostile to it just as they were hostile to all
'sentimentality', 'declamation', and 'vague generalities' that indicated
the absence or failure of rational arguments, and they took the frequent attacks on utilitarianism's 'cold calculation' as something of a
badge of honour (113). Mill freely concedes that many in his utilitarian
circle were, as a matter of fact, 'great readers of poetry':

[Peregrine] Bingham himself [editor of Bentham, and a leading utilitarian
theorist of jurisprudence] had been a writer of it, while as regards me (and
the same thing might be said of my father) the correct statement would be

not that I disliked poetry, but that I was theoretically indifferent to it. I disliked any sentiments in poetry which I should have disliked in prose; and that included a great deal.... I was wholly blind to its place in human culture, as a means of educating the feelings. But I was personally very susceptible to some kinds of it. (115)

The larger implications of Mill's recognition that this undervaluation of poetry was a limitation, in fact an error, on the part of Benthamite rationalism, and his awakening to the power of poetry as an educator of feeling, emerge when he goes on after the paragraphs on Marmontel to attempt to connect the individual pursuit of happiness to the utilitarian goal, the general happiness. The meshed quality of egoism and compassion in his response to Marmontel, it then becomes apparent, is vital to the conclusions he draws from the crisis and the manner of his release from it, both at the level of autobiographical report and at the level of a 'theory of life'.

If the 'capacity for happiness' was to be realized, Mill insists, it could not be by sacrificing the 'public good' to egoistic pursuit of personal happiness. But how were they to be linked? The difficulties are multiple. For a start, it is a distortive effect of Mill's unbudging commitment to the utilitarian goal that whatever relationship he describes between feeling and reasoning cannot move causally from individual feelings to shared reasons: he cannot claim that we need the existence of certain sentiments (altruism, say, or an egalitarian sympathy for each other's interests) in order to identify utilitarian goals. In his own case he has, after all, worked 'backwards'. The goal was already identified; having been denied the natural cultivation of the affections that would support it, he had to nurture them belatedly so as to provide himself with properly rooted motives. This was unnatural, but it cannot be discounted or ignored on that ground: for all Mill's theory of happiness makes reference to 'forced' and 'artificial' associations, his account of mental development is not simply naturalistic. As an empiricist, he believes that we are formed through repeated associations instilled by experience, and his own experience is (again) not just weirdly specific to him (though it is that) but the cultural effect of the familial and intellectual environment in which he was raised.

A further difficulty for Mill in joining the individual to the general happiness (and for the reader of Mill in interpreting his changing relation to utilitarianism) is that it is disputable whether the axiological hedonism of Benthamite theory entailed psychological hedonism. The most important self-discovery to come out of Mill's crisis, and his discovery in Marmontel's *Memoirs* of the seeds of emotional recovery, is that he needs to make a place in his theory of the good and what he would later call his 'art of life' for *feelings* of pleasure and pain: that is, for individual psychology. But was this a recalibration of early utilitarianism, to draw out an already extant element of psychological hedonism? or was it an importation of psychological hedonism into a very different kind of theory (an axiological theory that identified happiness as the fundamental source of value)? In other words, is Mill creating a problem for utilitarianism by asking it to accommodate a psychological dimension not commensurate with the goods it already recognizes? If the latter, there is an obvious danger of incoherence: the two forms of happiness that Mill wishes to connect will require something more than verbal overlap to bind them.

Part of this difficulty has to be laid at Bentham's door. As Fred Feldman comments, 'Bentham's style is notoriously obscure: there are a few places, in the *Introduction to the Principles of Morals and Legislation* (1789), where he seems to endorse a hedonistic theory of happiness' ('happiness consists of... enjoyment of pleasures, security from pains'[27]), but much more prominently he tends to treat happiness as 'interchangeable' with a number of semantically non-equivalent terms.[28] 'By utility', he writes in the opening paragraphs of *Morals and Legislation*,

is meant that property in any object, whereby it tends to produce benefit, advantage, pleasure, good, or happiness, (all this in the present case comes to the same thing) or (what comes again to the same thing) to prevent the happening of mischief, pain, evil, or unhappiness to the party whose interest is considered: if that party be the community in general, then the happiness of the community: if a particular individual, then the happiness of that individual. (12)

[27] An authoritative edition by J. H. Burns and H. L. A. Hart, with a new introduction by F. Rosen and an interpretative essay by H. L. A. Hart (Oxford: Clarendon Press, 1996), 74.
[28] Fred Feldman, *What Is This Thing Called Happiness?* (Oxford: Oxford University Press, 2007), 23. The definition of 'pleasure' in Bentham's writings is equivalently and notoriously elusive. Many philosophers interpret 'Good is pleasure', and similar statements as tautological: that is, they take Bentham to be defining pleasure as good (or goods). For a more careful consideration of the non-equivalence of the terms according to Bentham's theory of language (pleasure is a 'real indefinable' but good a 'fictitious definable'), and the conclusion that pleasure is a 'paraphrase' of good, see Amnon Goldsworth, 'Bentham's Concept of Pleasure: Its Relation to Fictitious Terms', *Ethics* 82/4 (1972), 334–43.

Taken as a group these are not reliably commensurable goods—though Bentham wants us to think of them as such (they 'come to the same thing' under his economic calculus[29]). At the level of the individual, one may be advantaged without taking any pleasure from it (hence, 'a hollow victory'), and one may be benefited without being made at all happy (a legacy, say, from someone whose survival mattered incomparably more to one than the bequest). Particularly difficult problems arise when one tries to measure individual experiences of happiness and unhappiness on the same scale with benefits to the public good. For utilitarians, the general happiness cannot be psychological in the same way that individual happiness may be. The good of all just is the good of individuals.

Mill effectively recognizes this problem when he provides one of the most authoritatively experiential testimonies to the insufficiency of the utilitarian privileging of the greatest happiness. As he puts it most simply in the *Autobiography*: 'to know that a feeling would make me happy if I had it, did not give me the feeling' (143). The stress of disconnection reverberates in that pained ambiguity, 'make me happy': the approved (and achieved) Benthamite meaning is 'give me reasons to be happy'; the felt (and failed) meaning is 'make me feel so'. The disconnection is not solved by Mill's simply coming to recognize that 'having the feeling' in one's own right and on one's own behalf matters. If things were going well for Mill in later 1827 (if, by then, he were restored to equanimity) that would not mean to say that things were going well for everyone 'on average'—whoever 'everyone' is, and however 'on average' might be calculated. One cannot meaningfully ask whether a society 'feels' happy or unhappy. In modern terms, one is usually talking about economic prosperity as aggregated in GDP or about mean levels of 'self-reported happiness'—which come with their own set of interpretative challenges.[30]

---

[29] I am perhaps being uncharitable here to Bentham, who is stipulating a deliberately narrow reading of 'advantage' and the other terms in play here: an advantage, 'in the present case', is something that will promote the balance of your pleasure over your pain. Still, the unresolved relation to psychological hedonism seems somewhat exposed here.

[30] For a start, it often fails to correlate with what those same self-reporters will say about their definition of happiness. See Beckerman, *Economics as Applied Ethics*, 114–18. On the difficulties with interpreting and making use of self-reported happiness see esp. p. 118: 'Even if it can be shown that certain measurable physiological changes inside the brain are correlated with certain self-reported states of mind, one can question how far these self-reported states of mind correspond to one's own definition of "happiness", whatever the respondents may say. And a given physiological change inside the brain may correspond to

Depending upon how one deals with Bentham's lack of clarity, Mill either inherits an already apparent uncertainty about the importance of individual psychological happiness within utilitarianism's account of goods, or his interpretation of utility in more plainly psychological terms brings to light a latent uncertainty. It is of the essence of Mill's crisis that it makes him in some ways acutely alert to the problem of why the individual should care about the greater good, but in others arguably not quite alert enough. A very large number of his critics have held that, even in *Utilitarianism* (written some seven years after these passages of the *Autobiography*), he never provided a sufficiently persuasive explanation of how the happiness of individual persons connects to the general happiness. Certainly, the logical proof he offered there that the general happiness is desirable *because* the happiness of each individual is so has widely been thought unsatisfactory:

happiness is a good:...each person's happiness is a good to that person, and the general happiness, therefore, a good to the aggregate of all persons. (234)

It is a sentence that seems oddly to have been written by a man who might as well never have experienced a crisis over utilitarianism's failure to recognize each individual's happiness as a different kind of priority for him or her from the general happiness. Treating happiness as a simply additive quantity, it pays no regard to motive.

Mill did answer his critics, but only (so far as is known) on one occasion, in a private letter to Henry Jones (a teacher in a private school in Bristol):

As to the sentence you quote from my *Utilitarianism*, when I said that the general happiness is a good to the aggregate of all persons I did not mean that every human being's happiness is a good to every other human being; though I think, in a good state of society & education it would be so. I merely meant in this particular sentence to argue that since A's happiness is a good, B's a good, C's a good, &c., the sum of all these goods must be a good.[31]

different reported levels of happiness. In any case, most—and possibly all—concepts of happiness would distinguish it from the satisfaction or pleasure obtained by temporary experiences. A statistical analysis of how particular experiences make people happy at the time provides little guide to what makes a happy life over any significant period of time.' It is worth noting that the objection does not cover analyses of subjective well-being based on retrospective report ('life-satisfaction').

[31] 13 June 1868, in *Later Letters of John Stuart Mill, 1849–1873*, ed. Francis E. Mineka and Dwight N. Lindley, 4 vols., *CW* xiv–xvii (Toronto: University of Toronto Press, 1972), xvi. 1413–15 (1414).

'If that letter had been more widely known', Alan Ryan comments, 'the critical literature would have been somewhat thinner; on the other hand, the casual way Mill responded to his critics is itself somewhat dispiriting.'[32] Well, possibly, but there is a substantial literature written in full knowledge of this explanation that still finds Mill's account incomplete, and perhaps incapable of completion. Roger Crisp, arguing that it *is* capable of completion, observes that one would have to fill in a number of assumptions: the 'moral assumption' that his readers 'are already taking morality seriously'; the 'aggregative assumption' that (as Mill put it in a footnote to chapter 5 of *Utilitarianism*) 'the truths of arithmetic are applicable to the valuation of happiness, as of all other measurable qualities'; and the 'impartiality assumption' that, 'when summing happiness, the distinction between persons is irrelevant', and the 'teleological assumption' that 'moral rules are justified only to the extent that they promote some end or good'.[33] Each of these assumptions may be disputed, and neither separately nor together do they quite preserve him from the charge of failing to demonstrate that the individual who naturally cares for his or her own happiness ought also to care for the happiness of all.

The *Autobiography* offers a different kind of answer to the problem of how to connect them. Mill moves on from the account of his mental crisis, and the start of his rehabilitation through reading Marmontel, to offer a summary statement of his revised theory of happiness. 'The experiences of this period', he reflects,

led me to adopt a theory of life, very unlike that on which I had before acted, and having much in common with what at that time I certainly had never heard of, the anti-self-consciousness theory of Carlyle. I never, indeed, wavered in the conviction that happiness is the test of all rules of conduct, and the end of life. But I now thought that this end was only to be attained by not making it the direct end. Those only are happy (I thought) who have their minds fixed on some object other than their own happiness; on the happiness of others, or the improvement of mankind, even on some art or pursuit, followed not as a means, but as itself an ideal end. Aiming thus at something else, they find happiness by the way.
(145–7)

[32] Introduction to J. S. Mill and Jeremy Bentham, *Utilitarianism and Other Essays* (London: Penguin, 1987), 50–1.
[33] Roger Crisp, *Routledge Philosophy Guidebook to Mill on Utilitarianism* (London: Routledge, 1997), 79–81.

The 'I thought' could be mistaken as an ironic signal that his ideas subsequently changed; it is, rather, an affirmation of the enduringness of the revised view of happiness ('I never, indeed, wavered'). A good individual life may embrace the general happiness as its political and ethical goal, but other choices remain open, including dedication to 'some art or pursuit'. In Mill's own view, to aim at the greatest happiness would be the best political choice (all his philosophical writing rests on that belief, and the *Autobiography* attests to his own fidelity to it) but he does not seek here to persuade everyone else to agreement, and he explicitly admits the validity of the life of art on equal (or almost equal) terms to the life of politics. '*Even on* some art or pursuit'… It is, the phrasing suggests, an unexpected admission for a man schooled in Benthamite utilitarianism.

As importantly, Mill asserts here that the relation between the individual's happiness and the happiness of society can only be indirect: 'Those only are happy…who have their minds fixed on some object other than their own happiness.' It is noteworthy that Mill does not frame this indirect connection with reference to the Benthamite standard: at no point in the autobiographical account of his own re-energized commitment to the goals of utilitarianism does he employ the phrase 'the greatest happiness'. In its stead he invokes 'the happiness of others', 'the public good', and a variety of similar expressions indicative of a greater but not necessarily 'the greatest' good.

There are two reasons why the *Autobiography* should verbally loosen the Benthamite goal from its status as the *telos* of utilitarianism at this juncture. The first arises from the recognition of the different force of motive—somewhat eased but not solved by the explanation that the relationship is indirect, and may in any given case be no stronger than an enabled fortuity. To invoke 'the happiness of others' rather than 'the greatest happiness' implicitly goes some way towards acknowledging the problem; it also allows for liberty of choice in the individual's selection of his or her goal in life. To insist upon the 'greatest happiness', especially in the context of this autobiography, would be to constrain the theory of life as James Mill had sought to constrain his son's mental development.

The second reason involves the kind of document Mill is writing. Were this a work of philosophy, he would be in some trouble at this point—and to the extent that the *Autobiography*'s difficulty in securing a logically binding relation between the personal and the collective happiness is replicated in *Utilitarianism* and other writings, it can be taken as support for criticisms of those works (in other words, it can be seen as pointing the way to difficulties that would—as some will see it—never be formally resolved). But Mill has made a deliberate choice to write something other than a philosophical treatise or a political tract: in his own words, 'a sketch' of an education (5) and of the 'moral influences' on a life that are, for everyone, the most 'complicated, and the most difficult to specify with any approach to completeness' (41). The *Autobiography* is not a formal justification of Mill's ideas. It is, instead, an attempt to demonstrate their consequences in his own life—not least through the series of adjustments made, after the narration of the crisis and first stage of recovery, to his account of the contribution reading literature may make to the experience and the theoretical understanding of happiness.

The role of the literary in assisting Mill's pursuit of happiness quietly shifts after the initial release from the depths of despair. Literature ceases, in the wake of the Marmontel episode, to be simply the lever that opens up his private capacity for feeling, and becomes important in at least two distinct ways. As we have seen, art (generally) is admitted as one of the 'ideal end[s]' that a life may aim at, and that, if the person is lucky, may yield happiness 'along the way'. More importantly, poetry is valued as a mode of apprehension available to everyone in the culture, a way of seeing and describing the world that goes beyond analysis, and if properly incorporated *into* a culture will serve to correct any distortive bias towards the analytic. The danger, evident in that formulation, is that the role of literature in Mill's revised theory of life will seem as narrowly functionalist as the habit of analysis he wants to correct and redeem. This is, indeed, a common view of the Mill who wrote that famous pairing of essay portraits, 'Coleridge' v. 'Bentham': the poet philosopher with the amply humane understanding of emotion and imagination set up in opposition to the narrow systematizing rationalist. Terry Eagleton mocks Mill, in 'Ideology and Literary Form' (1975), on just that score: his is a 'mechanistic' harnessing of 'the symbolically fertile, metaphysically coercive resources of Romantic humanism' to 'an impoverished empiricist liberalism'.[34]

---

[34] *New Left Review* 1/90 (1975). <http://www.newleftreview.org/?page=artivle&view=403>. Accessed 24 June 2011.

This is a misreading, on several counts. For a start, Mill himself acknowledged the element of polemical exaggeration in the Coleridge/Bentham pairing. The essays were written for the radical liberal journal the *Westminster Review*, where Bentham could have expected a much easier ride, and Coleridge a much harder one. Neither essay is as straightforward as the oppositional casting of the two men suggests (Coleridge gets short shrift as a political economist, for example, and his 'inner sense' psychology is anathema to the empiricist Mill; the criticisms of Bentham's limitations do not diminish Mill's very high regard for the political and legal theory). Similarly, to look closely at the passages of direct literary discussion in the *Autobiography*'s account of a post-crisis change in Mill's outlook on life is to find something subtler than a functional yoking of poetic humanism to calculative analysis, more complex than the basic awakening of sympathies described in the Marmontel episode.

Wordsworth enters Mill's narrative at that critical point where he has begun, post Marmontel, 'to find meaning in the things which I had read or heard about the importance of poetry and art as instruments of human culture', but has not yet come to know their importance 'by personal experience'. Though no longer at that nadir of distress in which continuing with his life had seemed intolerable beyond another year, he was still in a bad way. Among the more agitating of his symptoms was being 'seriously tormented by the thought of the exhaustibility of musical combinations'. To his later self, this Swiftian anxiety (resembling 'the philosophers of Laputa, who feared lest the sun should be burnt out') looks at once abjectly 'egoistical' and yet 'connected with the best feature in my character':

I felt that the flaw in my life, must be a flaw in life itself; that the question was, whether, if the reformers of society and government could succeed in their objects, and every person in the community were free and in a state of physical comfort, the pleasures of life, being no longer kept up by struggle and privation, would cease to be pleasures. And I felt that unless I could see my way to some better hope than this for human happiness in general, my dejections must continue; but that if I could see such an outlet, I should then look on the world with pleasure... (149)

The importance of Wordsworth's *Poems* (1815) at this juncture in early 1828 is that they assist Mill to the 'better hope'. They do not merely, as Marmontel did, show him that he has powers of self-assertive and

compassionate feeling; they produce in him fresh and positive feelings
of connection to the world. Byron (whose works were completely
reread by Mill in 'the worst period' of his depression) was no help at
all: his 'state of mind was too like my own. His was the lament of a man
who had worn out all pleasures' (149–51). Wordsworth, by contrast,
offered a timely appeal to 'one of the strongest of my pleasurable sus-
ceptibilities, the love of rural objects and natural scenery'—'not mere
outward beauty, but states of feeling, and of thought coloured by feeling, under the excitement of beauty. They seemed to be the very culture of the feelings, which I was in quest of' (151). Above all, they
provided the looked for answer to Benthamism's failure to connect the
individual to the general condition:'I seemed to draw from a source of
inward joy, of sympathetic and imaginative pleasure, which could be
shared in by all human beings; which had no connexion with struggle
or imperfection, but would be made richer by every improvement in
the physical or social condition of mankind' (151).

This, then, is the more developed answer the *Autobiography* offers to
the problem of how the happiness of the individual can be drawn into
credible alliance with the general happiness.[35] Once again, it is not a
formal philosophical answer. Arguably, all it does is to replace one
unhelpfully pliable term, 'happiness', with at least two others, 'joy' and
'pleasure'. Bentham's 'happiness' gives place to the poet's phrase 'inward
joy'[36] where 'inward' seems close to 'immanent'—an apprehension,
internal to each individual, of 'sympathetic and imaginative pleasure'
capable of being 'shared in by all human beings'.

Among the many difficulties the new formulation presents is that it
is not entirely clear whether sympathy is an action imported by the
reader to the contemplation of such states of feeling, or whether it is
understood as a quality of the pleasure itself—poetic pleasure being,
then, inherently or intrinsically sympathetic in character or tendency.
Another is that, in shifting attention from happiness as a goal to happiness as an 'inward' state, it may seem to weaken the teleological clarity
of the utilitarian model. Teleology isn't entirely abandoned (an inward
state can of course be a goal; and the joy to be shared in will, as Mill

[35] But see also ch. 3 of *Utilitarianism* on utilitarianism's capacity to remove the unsatisfactory conflicts we feel between our own good and that of others.
[36] The 'source of inward joy' recalls both 'Surprised by Joy' and 'the inward eye' prompting the heart to pleasure in the daffodils, in 'I wandered lonely as a cloud'.

sees it, grow 'richer' with 'every improvement in the...condition of mankind'); but even as Mill repositions the starting point for utilitarianism from the end it aims at to the state of mind of its adherent, the drivers that will direct him or her towards that end seem to have been somewhat weakened. There is no impulsion felt in perceiving a general state of 'struggle or imperfection'; there is only a positive inspiration drawn from the 'excitement of beauty'. The danger is that Mill has rediscovered individual motive, understood as a reason for action, but lost sight of motivation as an energizing force.

This may seem an unsympathetic way of responding to Mill as he records what it was like to be newly and vulnerably happy. What is so objectionable about 'inspiration'? But a guarded reading of this passage that does not entirely surrender to its appeal to sympathy over analysis is not out of step with Mill's own double perspective on this stage in his restoration. 'I felt myself at once better and happier as I came under [the poems'] influence', he recalls; '[f]rom them I seemed to learn what would be the perennial sources of happiness' (151). Unlike the earlier 'Those only are happy (I thought)', there is genuine qualification here. The harking on 'seems' and 'thought' is part of the close verbal homage paid to Wordsworth's diction in the passage, but it also leaves room for later demurral. The particular literary texts Mill found of assistance psychologically at any given moment in the process of his recovery were, as he makes amply clear, closely related to the point at which he found himself in that process (which entailed several relapses, though never again to the low point of the winter of 1826–7). The reasons for his responding to Wordsworth's *Poems* with such intense pleasure in early 1828—his love of scenery, the fact that Wordsworth's landscapes were also his own (the Lake District, the Pyrenees)—are, accordingly, of less importance for gauging his changing view of happiness here than the tonal and perspectival distance he preserves on his Wordsworthian phase. He is strikingly ambivalent: wanting to register the force of the poems' appeal to him at that time, wanting to pay homage to Wordsworth through the allusiveness of his own style, but markedly unwilling to conceal later, more mature tastes and judgements.

No judgements were passed on Marmontel's *Memoirs*, whose value for Mill derives solely from their role in reawakening his capacity for feeling. But appreciation of Wordsworth is repeatedly subject to qualifications. *The Excursion*, Mill tells us, had failed to interest him two or three years prior to the crisis, though he had 'looked into' it then; had

he tried again in 1826, he speculates, he would not have changed his
opinion (151). The parts of 'Ode to Intimations of Immortality' singled
out as especially delightful because, along with the usual 'sweetness of
memory and rhythm', they offered a record of a disenchantment with
youthful hopes and ambitions similar to Mill's own (and sound teaching about where to seek compensation) are nevertheless accompanied
by quite a lot of quibbling. The 'Ode' is 'falsely called Platonic';[37] the
two passages of 'grand imagery' most often quoted are 'bad philosophy'
(153). Wordsworth is 'the poet of unpoetical natures', Mill concludes.
'I long continued to value [him] less according to his intrinsic merits,
than by the measure of what he had done for me' (153). It is faint
praise. It is also ambiguous praise. Does 'long continued' mean that he
no longer values Wordsworth much? Or that he has reappraised him
again since and finds more of intrinsic merit than he once did? Or
that, however keenly Mill has responded to literature in his time, his is
self-confessedly an 'unpoetical nature'? Or is it a merely elegant use of
the past tense, the meaning being that he still holds Wordsworth in
high regard because the poems had a beneficial effect at a time of
need? The last reading is probably the right one, but there is room for
uncertainty.

The surface message of this part of the *Autobiography* is that Wordsworth was important to Mill in early 1828 because he opened him up
to positive pleasures capable of being shared by everyone. But Mill is
also, as importantly, demonstrating in these paragraphs that the analytic
habit was not banished, even if it now had something to contest its
influence. Wordsworth is consistently the object of a form of dual
vision that corrects the younger Mill's vague sentimentalism with the
conclusions of a more mature analysis. It matters that the later correc-
tion is not simply hostile to or disqualifying of the earlier response.
Mill can remark Wordsworth's faults as a philosopher without losing
sight of the pleasures and consolations of the poetry. So, he rather
quaintly tells us that the first thing he does, publicly, with his new
found openness to the literary cultivation of the feelings is to throw
himself and Wordsworth into the ring of the London Debating Society. Specifically: he gave the *Poems* to his friend and fellow Benthamite
John Roebuck, and then debated with him the relative merits of
Wordsworth and Byron (Roebuck's candidate). Roebuck seems to

[37] The term is used by Wordsworth in his headnote to the poem.

have been recruited as a kind of avatar for Mill of his un-reformed self: open to the pleasures of poetry, but unwilling to admit that 'these things have any value as aides in the formation of character' (155). The debate was, Mill tells us, the first time the two men 'had been on opposite sides'—and the 'schism between us widened from this time more and more' (153–5).[38]

Later, and by his own lights better, intellectual judgement led Mill to rank Coleridge above Wordsworth. This discovery does not, however, play a role in the narrative of his mental development comparable to that of the earlier opening up to Marmontel and Wordsworth. The evidence of the mature preference is there in his twice turning to Coleridge for assistance in describing the despair endured in 1826–7:

> A grief without a pang, void, dark and drear,
> A drowsy, stifled, unimpassioned grief,
> Which finds no natural outlet or relief,
> In word, or sigh, or tear.
>
> Work without hope draws nectar in a sieve,
> And hope without an object cannot live.[39]

These were lines fastened on by Mill months or years afterwards, during 'a later period of the same mental malady', but they are read backwards into the initial crisis as the truest available articulation of his emotional and intellectual condition: in him 'of all writers I have found a true description of what I felt'. For the rest, Coleridge appears in the *Autobiography* as a philosopher, and only secondarily (and by implication) one of 'the greatest poets'. Warmly admired though he is, in those terms, and with the more sustained praise of the 1840 essay in the background, his intellectual and poetic stature does not go unchallenged: Mill compares his abilities, rather to his disadvantage, with the unfulfilled but 'decidedly superior' mental gifts of Mill's friend, and one-time Coleridgean disciple, F. D. Maurice.

---

[38] It is worth remarking that the long account of Roebuck's character and career, in the early draft of the *Autobiography*, is subject to some of the most substantial cuts made when Mill revises in 1861—reducing the embarrassingly exposed egoism of the comparisons between Roebuck's cast of intellect and his own. See 154–9.

[39] 'Dejection, an ode', in *Sibylline Leaves* (London: Rest Fenner, 1817), 238; 'Work without Hope', *Poetical Works*, 3 vols. (London: Pickering, 1828), ii. 81. (Both sourced in Mill, *Autobiography*, 139, 145.)

This manner of Mill's incorporating his later, and deeper, poetic tastes and judgements into a narrative of gradually changing psychological needs, requires some rethinking of the initial picture given, via Marmontel, in which the literary cultivation of feeling presented a straightforward corrective to the analytic cast of mind. However strong the emotional impact of that initial picture, and however appealing (or not) the dualistic clarity it offers, Mill's mature account of the role of the literary in assisting us to happiness is not reducible to the idea that feeling (poetry) may be a 'medicine' for the analytic mind that has lost sight of all pleasures. On the contrary, the content and the style of the post-Marmontel reflections on literature strive towards a demonstration that feeling and analysis are simultaneously active modes of response to experience: correcting each other's excesses, yes, but also stimulating each other to more lucid, more flexible, and more comprehensive perceptions. The same development can be seen in Mill's literary essays and reviews spanning 1832 to 1844. He holds closely, at first, to the 'Marmontel' view of poetry as 'the delineation of the deeper and more secret workings of human emotion'[40]; later he is more willing to consider 'sentiment and purpose' together.[41] In the early 1830s one finds him drawing sharp distinctions between 'the poetry of a poet', which is 'feeling itself' (Shelley is the example), and the poetry of a 'cultivated but not naturally poetic mind' in which, however brightened by feeling, the 'thought ... is always the conspicuous object' (e.g. Wordsworth).[42] In 1843, by contrast, one finds him admiring Macaulay's ability to join poetic feeling with historical thought.

At the level of content, it would be easy to make the mature working together of feeling and analysis sound like only a subtler form of dualism. But at the level of style, Mill achieves something better: a complex voice at once confessional and self-critical, inward and outward looking, and all the while suffused with quiet allusiveness to the voices of past literary and philosophical writers in ways that reach well beyond the predominantly Romantic engagements recorded in the narrative. Swift (as we have seen) is explicitly invoked, as is Shakespeare on at least one occasion. Johnson is surely there, too, in the pitch and cadence of 'Those only are happy ... who have their minds fixed on

[40] 'Thoughts on Poetry and its Varieties' (1833), in CW i. 340–65 (345).
[41] 'Milne's Poetry for the People' (1840), in CW i. 517–21 (519). See also 'Macaulay's Lays of Ancient Rome' (1843), in CW i. 523–32.
[42] 'Thoughts on Poetry' (357).

some object other than their own happiness; . . . Aiming thus at something else, they find happiness by the way.' It is not a direct allusion, but
it is audibly the voice and the outlook of *Rasselas*: somewhat chastened
in its optimism, verging on the elegiac, but alleviated by irony at its
own expense.

Unsurprisingly, the philosopher, besides Bentham, who can be heard
most clearly in Mill's literary style is Plato. Specifically, the Plato of the
Gorgias. 'Is it incorrect to say, as people do,' Socrates asks, 'that those
who want nothing are happy?' 'No,' the oligarch Callicles responds, 'for
at that rate stones and corpses would be extremely happy' (492e).[43]
'I was not a stock or a stone', Mill affirms in relief as he recalls the tears
he shed on reading Marmontel. The phrase is a commonplace, but
given the nature of the questions Mill is asking, many of his first readers would have heard the echo of Plato. And Plato's presence brings
into sharper view the one aspect of Mill's account of happiness that has
given more trouble than any other over the years: the distinction
between quantitative and qualitative pleasure. It is an ineliminable
aspect of his hedonistic argument for the value of the literary.

Literary critics and intellectual historians rightly look to Romanticism
as the proximate source for the high valuation placed on feeling in
Mill's crisis narrative, and the challenge posed to Benthamite rationalism. But the basic situation—a confrontation with, and gradual revision to, a hitherto accepted account of happiness and the good—has
much deeper roots in classical hedonism.

The *Gorgias* was not among the very first works of Plato that Mill
was exposed to as a small boy (its length alone would make it an
unlikely place to start), but it is among the texts that James Mill went
to some trouble to locate for him early on, in (if Myles Burnyeat is
correct) the relatively unforbidding Bipont edition of 1781–7.[44] Mill is
known to have translated it by the age of 12 or 13. It receives one of
the longest and most admiring treatments in his 1834–5 *Notes on Some
of the More Popular Dialogues of Plato*. A middle-period Platonic dialogue, it marks one stage in the ongoing development of Plato's think-

---

[43] *The Dialogues of Plato*, trans. with analyses and introduction by Benjamin Jowett
(Oxford: Clarendon Press, 1875).
[44] M. F. Burnyeat, 'What was the "Common Arrangement"? An Inquiry into John
Stuart Mill's Boyhood Reading of Plato', *Utilitas* 13/1 (2001), 1–32 (25).

ing about hedonism.[45] Some way in, a discussion that has focused until
now on the relative worth of rhetoric and philosophy widens its ethical remit to take up questions about the good and the bad life, the
distinction between pleasure and the good, and the proper relation of
intellectual to bodily desires. Responsibility for continuing the argument with Socrates shifts at this point from the rhetorician Gorgias
and his pupil Polus to Callicles—also a student of Gorgias but, more
pertinently, a spokesman for the power of the oligarchy, unrestrained
by consideration for the greater good. Callicles puts an unapologetic
case for the good life as a life dedicated to gratification of unrestrained
pleasures. There follows a lengthy dialogue with Socrates in which a
plainly irritated Callicles ('You always contrive somehow or other,
Socrates, to invert everything'...(511a)) is obliged to agree that pleasure is not identical with the good; that there are right and wrong
pleasures; and that the highest and best are those afforded by the life of
philosophical enquiry. As a first step in the refutation, Socrates
extracts that simple concession, from which all else will follow: a life
of satisfied desires would fall short of happiness. 'It is incorrect to
say...that those who want nothing are happy?', he probes. 'No,...at
that rate stones and corpses would be extremely happy.'[46]

It is this first, reluctant, chink in the self-image of the man devoted
to maximizing pleasure that is replayed at the turning point in the
Autobiography. The rebuff to Benthamism in Mill's 'I was not a stock or
a stone' gains in force from recalling a celebrated moment in a Socratic
dialogue. Insofar as we may be prompted to speculate about structural
similarities, it would seem that the older Mill is ironically casting his
younger (pre-crisis) self as the possessor of a philosophical confidence
that could not withstand sceptical scrutiny and that bordered on arro-
gance. Not being 'a stone', then, would mean 'not being Callicles'—
changing one's ideas, choosing the better life of philosophy. But it is a
glaringly imperfect analogy: the young Mill was no unrestrained
hedonist (a few more bodily pleasures might have made him rather
happier at 20); and the pressure to rethink his views works away from

---

[45] See J. C. B. Gosling and C. C. W. Taylor, *The Greeks on Pleasure* (Oxford: Clarendon
Press, 1982), ch. 4 and *passim*.

[46] Mill's own translation is blunter: 'Stones, and the dead, would by this account be the
happiest.' 'The Gorgias', in *Notes on Some of the More Popular Dialogues of Plato* (1834–5),
Essays on Philosophy and the Classics, ed. John M. Robson, *CW* xi (Toronto: University of
Toronto Press, 1978), 97–150 (127).

an earlier too exclusive emphasis on the general happiness to admit the needs of the individual. In Callicles' case all the pressure is the other way—to rein in self-interest and acknowledge the claims of the greater good (though it may be beyond even Socrates' powers of persuasion to induce Callicles to change his life: 'I do not heed a word of what you are saying, and have only answered hitherto out of civility to Gorgias' (505c)).

There is no warrant for claiming that the *Autobiography* is in sustained philosophical dialogue with Plato.[47] The presence of the *Gorgias* behind Mill's narration of his mental crisis does not obviously go beyond shared intellectual terrain and one direct echo at the turning point. That said, the spirit of Socrates is never very far from Mill's thinking about happiness, and nowhere more clearly than in the defence of higher- against lower-order pleasures that formed a major component of *Utilitarianism*'s revisions to Benthamism. 'Qualitative hedonism' is a tacit but powerful assumption in the *Autobiography*'s reflections on happiness. For Mill, as for the Socrates of the *Gorgias*, pleasure is not an indiscriminate good, nor is it susceptible to simple accumulation and quantification. Some pleasures are intrinsically higher than others, and no competent judge would sacrifice the higher for the lower however much of the lower were on offer.[48]

These are the key claims from a famous passage of *Utilitarianism*:

... some *kinds* of pleasure are more desirable and more valuable than others. Of two pleasures, if there be one to which all or almost all who have experience of both give a decided preference ... that is the more desirable pleasure. If one of the two is, by those who are competently acquainted with both, placed so far above the other that they prefer it, even though knowing it to be attended with a greater amount of discontent, and would not resign it for any quantity of the other pleasure which their nature is capable of, we are justified in ascribing to the preferred enjoyment a superiority in quality, so far outweighing quantity as to render it, in comparison, of small account.

[47] See Guy Fletcher, reviewing Nadia Urbinati, 'An Alternative Modernity: Mill on Capitalism and the Quality of Life', which attempts to make such a case in Eggleston, Miller, and Weinstein (eds.), *John Stuart Mill and the Art of Life*, Notre Dame Philosophical Reviews (16 April 2011),< http://ndpr.nd.edu/review.cfm?id=23469>. Accessed 3 June 2011.
[48] This is the 'standard view' of Mill's qualitative hedonism. It is defended by Jonathan Riley in (amongst other essays) 'Interpreting Mill's Qualitative Hedonism', *Philosophical Quarterly* 53/212 (2003), 410–18. A non-standard view is described by Christoph Schmidt-Petri, 'Mill on Quality and Quantity', *Philosophical Quarterly* 53 (2003), 102–4. I take Riley's rebuttal to be correct.

. . . A being of higher faculties requires more to make him happy, is capable probably of more acute suffering, and is certainly accessible to it at more points, than one of an inferior type; but in spite of these liabilities, he can never really wish to sink into what he feels to be a lower grade of existence.

. . . Whoever supposes that this preference takes place at a sacrifice of happiness—that the superior being, in anything like equal circumstances, is not happier than the inferior—confounds the two very different ideas, of happiness, and content. It is indisputable that the being whose capacities of enjoyment are low, has the greatest chance of having them fully satisfied; and a highly-endowed being will always feel that any happiness which he can look for, as the world is constituted, is imperfect. But he can learn to bear its imperfections, if they are at all bearable; and they will not make him envy the being who is indeed unconscious of the imperfections, but only because he feels not at all the good which those imperfections qualify. It is better to be a human being dissatisfied than a pig satisfied; better to be Socrates dissatisfied than a fool satisfied. And if the fool, or the pig, is of a different opinion, it is because they only know their own side of the question. The other party to the comparison knows both sides. (211–12)

A great deal of ink has been spilled on these paragraphs. For those who react against Mill's account of qualitative pleasures, the problems can seem multiple. Which pleasures, specifically, are we to understand as 'higher' (or, a synonym for Mill, 'nobler'), which baser? Is it really possible to make distinctions in qualities of pleasure without 'importing criteria foreign to hedonism'—moral criteria, for example. How can we verify that higher pleasures are indeed higher? How can we know competent from incompetent judges (what is required for a person to become competent)?[49] Even setting aside the verification questions as unavoidably to be decided by experience, the very tone and manner of Mill's account of qualitative pleasure has seemed to many off-putting in its elitist disdain for the pig (and the swinish fool), its tendency to make one wonder whether this was, sufficiently, a man who had experienced 'both sides of the question', and above all its capacity to make happiness sound a pretty flat condition.

It is not necessary to try to solve all the difficulties Mill's qualitative hedonism raises in order to isolate the implications it has for his mature thinking about the contribution the humanities may make to a happy life. Mill gave some fairly clear indications, both in *Utilitarianism* and elsewhere, about how we can tell a higher from a lower pleasure. The

---

[49] Riley, 'Interpreting Mill's Qualitative Hedonism', 410.

primary distinction is between bodily and intellectual pleasures (hence the inferiority of the pig in muck); but intellectual pleasures (including aesthetic and moral sentiments[50]) are also internally ranked. Higher pleasures are connected with beauty, with sublimity, justice, and 'certain highly impressive and affecting ideas': (following Ruskin here) 'anything which suggests vividly the idea of infinity', for example, 'of magnitude or power without limit', or which 'stimulates the active power of the imagination to rise above known reality, into a more attractive or a more majestic world'.[51] Mill (as one might expect) says next to nothing about lower pleasures, but they are, by implication, any pleasures that fail to meet the higher standards: literature that merely aims at entertainment, for example, or that is content with clichés of style and sentiment; or, to follow a suggestion from one of his early reviews, any artistic representation that is merely 'imitative' rather than 'creative', belonging to 'the mechanical rather than ... the fine arts'.[52]

Mill would have granted—does grant, in *Utilitarianism*—that the value placed on good poetry and other expressions of intellectual culture and refined feeling will go unrecognized by uneducated or undereducated people. For that reason it cannot be a generally available aid to happiness—at least not in an imperfectly egalitarian world. That education better equips one to lead a qualitatively happy life was part of his case for a national reformed education system and for the extension of education to women on equal terms with men—in much less patrician tones than those just cited.[53] In Mill's ideally reformed world, everyone would be 'highly-endowed' by the culture they were born into and the education they received.

---

[50] *Analysis of the Phenomena*, 223–36, 239–42. On the ways in which Mill had to modify his father's associationism so that the distinction of higher order (moral and aesthetic) pleasures would not come to rest on a nativist or intuitionist account of mind, see Fred Wilson, 'Mill on Psychology and the Moral Senses', in John Skorupski (ed.), *The Cambridge Companion to Mill* (Cambridge: Cambridge University Press, 1998), 203–54 (215).

[51] See Mill's note at the end of *Analysis of the Phenomena*, ch. XXI, sect. 3 (*CW* xxxi. 226) citing Ruskin's list of the 'lofty or lovely ideas' which give us 'the emotion of the Beautiful'—namely, appreciation of 'Unity, Repose, Symmetry, Purity, and Adaptation to Ends'. The 'moral pleasures' can also be ranked, according to Mill. For his distinction between the feeling of 'ordinary expediency and inexpediency' and 'the feeling of right and wrong' see *Utilitarianism*, 251. See also *Analysis of the Phenomena*, 239–41 for Mill's supporting analysis of the grading of feelings under Associationist theory.

[52] 'Thoughts on Poetry', 351.

[53] 'Reform in Education' (1834) and *The Subjection of Women* (1869), in *Essays on Equality*, *CW* xxi. 259–340.

One of the reasons why Mill liked Plato was that he saw in him a philosopher for whom 'morals are but a branch of intelligence': 'no evil is ever done . . . voluntarily; but always involuntarily, from want of knowledge, from ignorance of good and evil; . . . whoever had knowledge to *see* what was good, would certainly *do* it.'[54] Something of the same perception colours Mill's claim that a person educated into the use of their higher faculties 'can never really wish to sink into what he feels to be a lower grade of existence'. On the basis of *Utilitarianism* alone, one would have to assume that the same verdict applies to Mill's qualitative hedonism and its implications for literature: for him 'aesthetic sentiments are but a branch of intelligence'.

This is a limitation, but no small part of the interest of the *Autobiography* is that, in the course of explaining to us the development of Mill's mind, it repeatedly places itself at an angle to his philosophical views. An account of how one got to one's mature views is not the same thing as a formal justification of those views. The *Autobiography*'s description of the kinds of pleasure Mill himself obtained from literature requires one to modify not only the formal account of how individual happiness relates to the general happiness, but also the standard view of qualitative pleasures. Specifically, it becomes necessary to modify the standard view to allow for the temporal and often uneven development of an intellectual and ethical life.

Reading Mill's formal claims about qualitative hedonism and higher- and lower-ranked aesthetic pleasures in *Utilitarianism* yields a pretty strenuous account of how the higher pleasures offered by literature and the arts more generally may contribute to happiness. They elevate our imaginations, individually and collectively: awaken our sense of sublimity, make us (valuably) conscious of the imperfections of the world as it is currently constituted. Put simply, they raise the bar for happiness. They assist us in aiming above mere contentment to a hope of genuine happiness, even if what comes within our reach may be only 'bearability'.[55] To read the *Autobiography*, by contrast, is to find a more attractive account of how literature can help

---

[54] John Stuart Mill, 'The Protagoras', *Notes on Some of the More Popular Dialogues of Plato* 1834–5, in *Essays on Philosophy and the Classics*, CW xi. 39–61 (61).

[55] For John Grote's objection that Mill, having pointed out the distinction between happiness and contentment, does not sufficiently 'bear it in mind' and asks us to pitch too high, see *An Examination of Utilitarian Philosophy*, ed. Joseph Bickersteth Mayor (London: Bell and Daldy, 1870), 32, 35–6.

us to improve not only our appreciation of our ideal ends but also our lived experience.

What part it plays exactly depends upon where one is in one's life, and what one's psychological needs are at that moment. Qualitative pleasures are an important element in the story, but primarily as the endowments of a mature mind: one that has learned to practice, or at least to look for, a right balance of feeling and analysis. The qualitative response to literature is not as important to Mill in his early twenties as the more basic emotional response. His reading of Marmontel is not indiscriminate—some discrimination has gone on in the fact of his responding to Marmontel rather than another, less eloquent or knowledgeable memoirist—but that isn't the point of this part of the narrative. Subsequent stages in the life story, by contrast, describe and, increasingly, demonstrate the gradual development of Mill's tastes and aesthetic judgements as a component of the pleasure he takes from literature. Once we get to Wordsworth, and even more strongly to Coleridge, he is constantly demonstrating to us that the mature mind simultaneously exercises feeling and analysis: its feelings have become qualitatively refined, its analyses humanized by being tested against those feelings.

Mill is not, however, describing a straightforward process of graduation from the dualistic, remedial model of engagement with literature to the conjoined feeling-analytic model. If nothing else, a strong sense of the claims of memory—the ability to recall what it felt like to be profoundly unhappy and then to recover the possibility of happiness—would prevent him from equating the ethical value of literature only with the achieved higher tastes and judgements. He goes on valuing Wordsworth 'not so much for his intrinsic value', which more mature judgement qualifies, as 'by the measure of what he has done' for him. It is not irrelevant that Mill refers us to the man rather than, more accurately, the poems. Wordsworth is a metonym or synecdoche for his own writing, but he is also a figure for the ethical power of poetry as it may meet the needs of a particular person, at a particular point in the narrative of their life.

A defence of the humanities by way of axiological hedonism cannot be a complete defence. In the form—or forms—Mill gave to that broad terrain of argument, it has evident attractions but inevitable limitations. His *Autobiography* offers one of the most powerful personal testimonies and one of the most authoritative intellectual arguments we have for the incompleteness of any analytic culture that is not tested and extended by constant contact with the culture of expressive feeling. An obvious limitation is the tendency of that argument to resolve, in spite of Mill's efforts to prevent it doing so, into a 'two cultures' dualism that risks misrepresenting our intellectual life—now and then. Mill's concern with a relatively narrow and 'elite' range of cultural tastes is another limitation, though not fatal. He might have conceded that his own understanding of a liberal education ought to admit a broader set of agreements on the objects of culture, and the different spheres in which they find value.

The lack of any developed account of reasons for valuing literature *other than as an educator of the feelings* is more of a problem. The *Autobiography* says almost nothing about the pleasures of expressive form in its own right, or the practice and recognition of technique, or the value attaching to the thought content as well as the incitement to feeling in literature, or indeed about the pleasures of reasoning about literature and its effects. For Mill, technique was mere 'mechanics'. On the other hand, it is abundantly clear from his intellectual practice and his comments on education throughout his life that the education of the feelings is not the only end of education, any more than is the education of analytic reason. The mixed quality of analysis and feeling in his practice as a reader and critic may supply the gap, demonstrating not only the interrelation of sentiment and cognition but the mixed nature of pleasures derived from objects of culture that elicit sympathy and analysis together. He provides also, in the *Autobiography*, a reminder, if needed, that the relation of the two will, for the individual, vary according to personal context, including time of life. (The mature relationship to the objects of culture that one has learned to care for and to value as a younger person carries a component of remembered pleasures that may qualify or even contradict one's response to them now.)

There is a strong and growing body of recent writing that would encourage an addition to Mill on the relation between emotion and cognition by asking us to see the emotions and passions as themselves goods. Among the most prominent contributors to this way of thinking at present are those who subscribe to a cognitive theory of the emotions: who see the emotions as, themselves, forms of intelligence. The account of the humanities' contribution to happiness developed here does not prohibit that addition, or the conclusion that might follow that the humanities make a contribution to happiness that is simultaneously a contribution to knowledge. I myself retain a degree of scepticism about the cognitive theory of emotions, however,[56] and that scepticism finds support from reading Mill. A core component in his account of his personal crisis, and the recurrence of unhappy periods subsequently, is his realization that a feeling about a situation or an object is something more and quite other than an intellectual appraisal of that situation or object.

One need not subscribe to the 'intelligence of emotions' in order to advance the claim that culturally developed sentiments are among the basic human goods, and (more importantly in this context) that an educated familiarity with the range and depth and variety of human emotions and ways of understanding them constitutes one of the goods of education. Adjusted to a wider range of tastes, and a more modern sense of the kinds of cultural materials worth our intellectual attention, Mill's account of qualitative hedonism supplies moreover something that the current critical literature on education and happiness is strikingly lacking: namely, a sense of what a higher education might provide 'above' a basic or secondary education. Put simply, he tells us that some kinds of pleasure are only available to those who possess sufficient education. A higher level of education brings higher intellectual and aesthetic pleasures within our grasp. (To say that 'higher education brings higher pleasures' would be glib, on the other hand, since the two meanings of 'higher' are not identical. A higher [more advanced] education today is not definitively an education in higher [more sublime] intellectual tastes.) One can jettison or leave as optional most of Mill's assumptions about what raises a pleasure to a higher order (sublimity, the sense of infinity, nobility) but retain the central perception that a higher level of education brings more complexly valuable kinds of cultural experience within our reach.

All defences are circumstantial. Mill's defence of poetry in the course of a larger reaction against Benthamism's reductive definition of the

---

[56] See esp. Martha Nussbaum, *Upheavals of Thought: The Intelligence of Emotions* (Chicago: University of Chicago Press, 2001). For reasons to be sceptical, see Simon Blackburn, 'To Feel and Feel Not', *New Republic* 24 December 2001, <http://www.tnr.com/article/feel-and-feel-not#> (accessed 24 December 2012). And for an exploration of the cognitive theory of emotion in relation to the mediating power of language: Isobel Armstrong, 'Thinking Affect', in *The Radical Aesthetic* (Oxford: Blackwell Publishers, 2000), 108–48.

human good was an argument forged *in extremis*. Inevitably it privileges certain questions and certain claims over others, but then the observation made by his friend Grote remains true: 'There are wants of our animal nature the satisfaction of which is happiness in the view of the economist: but human life develops wants and feelings much beyond all this, and here it is as hard to find universally accepted pleasures as it is to find universally accepted notions of duty.'[57] Among the strongest reasons for keeping Mill in the frame of contemporary discussion about the value of the humanities is that the problems with utilitarianism that provoked his attention are, once again, topical. In the two fields that have had most marked influence on recent political thinking—behavioural economics and positive psychology—Mill is a near-total absence. The revisions he made to utilitarianism remain, however, canonical, with different emphases, in literary criticism, philosophy, and political history. Any theory of human happiness that holds out to us now the possibility of accounting for happiness, or that offers individual and collective happiness as the goal at which we should all be aiming, needs reminding that we have been here before.

[57] Grote, *Examination of Utilitarian Philosophy*, 28.

4

'Democracy Needs Us'

The Gadfly Argument for the Humanities

Insofar as the humanities possess a strong piety about their own value, at present, it is the piety that they, of all the faculties of the university, are a force for the democracy. So strong has been the commitment to this terrain of advocacy in recent years in the UK (and for much longer within the American liberal arts system) that it seems necessary to approach this of all claims—as its philosophical origins require—with some presumption of suspicion.

Rex Warner's 1938 novel *The Professor* indicates some of the reasons why suspicion might be warranted. Warner's hero is a distinguished classicist at an unnamed university in an unnamed minor European state, loosely modelled on Austria between 1932 and 1938. 'The greatest living authority on Sophocles, rich in the culture of many languages and times', the professor finds himself called upon to lead the nation at a moment of crisis when the imminent possibility of fascist takeover by a neighbouring country threatens the future of his nation's democracy.[1] Though an eloquent exponent of the history and philosophical ethos of a democratic polity, he proves 'for his own time . . . most inapt' (7). His conception of the ancient Greek polis as the first 'safety zone' for a 'liberal organization' of citizens against 'the barbarism of others' fails to connect with the seriousness of his democracy's predicament. There is, his son remonstrates with him publicly, 'no enclosed space in Europe. The enemies of democracy are in control of our democracies. . . . [Y]ou, my father, with all your wisdom, sympathy and culture are,

---

[1] (London: Penguin Books, 1945), 7.

however little you may like the idea, helping to destroy us.... The
word "Polis" suddenly seem[s] ... like a joke over a dying man' (12).

The plot that follows justifies the son. The professor lasts two
days in power before being forced to flee from office when his Chief
of Police conducts a coup on behalf of the fascists. In a symbolic
assault on the liberal educational aspirations to which the professor
has dedicated his life, he must watch from the shadows of the university quadrangle while some of his students enact a satiric repetition of his lecture on the polis and burn his library. The *Iliad*, the
Odyssey, Herodotus, Thucydides, and—picked out for special attention—Keats all go up in petrol-fuelled flames. 'Something about "an
unravished bride"', says the student leader: 'I call that rather dirty.
What do you say then, boys? Shall we bung it in with the rest? Of
course, I shall abide by your democratic decision.' 'Bung it in, and
damn democracy!' The novel is, such scenes notwithstanding, something other than didactic allegory. In its refusal fully to undermine
the professor's idealism, its evident intellectual commitment to his
culture of philosophic debate, scholarly preservation of knowledge,
and aesthetic judgement, even as it depicts his unfitness to lead the
democracy in wartime, it speaks at once for and against the importance of the humanities as the cultural bedrock of a democratic
polity.

The Professor has never, as far as I can see, made it onto any of the
great books lists associated with American liberal arts teaching,
though Warner's 1944 translation of *Medea* has. Depicting a moment
of crisis at which the democratic culture is put in suspension by the
exigencies of fighting fascism, it is not a comfortable fit with the
work of sustaining and enhancing a democratic culture that has been
the purpose of liberal arts curricula, past and present. In key respects
it hardly represents a fair test of the educational values it both defends
and mourns. The movement of the humanities professor from his role
as critic of government to governor is by the novel's (and his own)
lights a mistake. It is unsurprising that a man who has spent his life in
scholarship proves a poor political leader; nor is there any real difficulty with the thought that democratic values need to be backed up
by strong armies (the Athenians would have agreed). Nevertheless, in
asking so explicitly 'what are the limits of the humanities' democratic
influence?' *The Professor* can serve as the contrarian's way in to assessing the most ambitious argument for the public value of the

humanities now regularly heard in America and Britain at what is, for quite different reasons, widely seen as a moment of crisis for liberal education.

Martha Nussbaum's *Not for Profit* (2010) is the most high profile of several efforts in recent years to persuade governments and publics historically committed to liberal educational ideals that a good reason, even the primary one, for preserving that commitment is that a healthy democracy depends upon it. Her manifesto is an eloquent restatement of the founding principles of the American liberal arts system. But if her main claims would not have been alien to the deans and professors who promoted liberal arts curricula, in the aftermath of Rex Warner's 'coming war', as a cultural bulwark against external and internal threats to 'Western civilization', the air of beleagueredness might have surprised them:[2]

Thirsty for national profit, nations, and their systems of education, are heedlessly discarding skills that are needed to keep democracies alive. If this trend continues, nations all over the world will soon be producing generations of useful machines, rather than complete citizens who can think for themselves, criticize tradition, and understand the significance of another person's sufferings and achievements.[3]

It is no accident that this, the most polemical form of the 'democracy needs us' argument, is also the most defensive form. *Not for Profit* is an urgent appeal to university leaders and the wider public for renewed commitment to the liberal arts, across the American secondary and tertiary education systems, at a time when that commitment is under pressure from falling enrolments, cuts in budgets, prioritization of 'useful skills' over humanistic studies, and increasingly corporatist university administrations presiding over and reinforcing those priorities. In other words, the perceived enemy of democracy today is not an alternative political system such as fascism, but the effect of a global capitalist system that ignores or discounts reasoned debate about the aims and ideals of the polis in favour of market forces (forces that are at once theoretically 'unrestrained' and in practice deeply distorted by political policies).

---

[2] See Louis Menand, *The Marketplace of Ideas: Reform and Resistance in the American University* (New York: W.W. Norton, 2010), 29–43.

[3] *Not for Profit: Why Democracy Needs the Humanities* (Princeton: Princeton University Press, 2010), 2.

What does it mean to write a manifesto for a kind of education that already exists? Or does Nussbaum believe that the liberal arts model has, like some political theories one could think of, never been fully tested? Certainly her idea of a fully liberalized education, from primary to tertiary level, that would ensure the health of the democracy involves a more strenuous mission statement than any institution has yet to put its name to. She has a seven point plan (two up on Dewey) for educating the emotions, and thereby yielding better, more tolerant, more responsible citizens who will be skilled in critical thinking, courageous in dissent, willing and able to argue free of the constraints of deference or the assumptions of authority (see 45–6). She bases that plan in part on a theory of healthy moral development in childhood as involving 'positional thinking' about the perspectives of others: learning empathy, controlling one's own aggression, rejecting those pernicious adult norms that might impede open-mindedness, compassion, and reciprocity (a subject she has made her own in earlier work on the intelligence of emotions[4]). From this model of early education she extrapolates many of her claims for what a higher education should do, though it is not entirely clear why a higher education should be considered a necessity in the same terms that a primary and secondary education may be.

Some lines of scepticism do get a hearing, but the answers move fairly quickly past potential difficulties:

Does global citizenship really require the humanities? It requires a lot of factual knowledge, and students might get this without a humanistic education—for example, from absorbing the facts in standardized textbooks... and by learning the basic techniques of economics. Responsible citizenship requires however, a lot more: the ability to assess historical evidence, to use and think critically about economic principles, to assess accounts of social justice, to speak a foreign language, to appreciate the complexities of the major world religions. The factual part alone could be done without the skills and techniques we have come to associate with the humanities. But a catalogue of facts, without the ability to assess them, or to understand how a narrative is assembled from evidence, is almost as bad as ignorance, since the pupil will not be able to distinguish ignorant stereotypes purveyed by politicians and cultural leaders from the truth, or bogus claims from valid ones. World history and economic understanding, then, must be humanistic and critical if they are to

---

[4] See especially *Upheavals of Thought: The Intelligence of Emotions* (Chicago: University of Chicago Press, 2001).

be at all useful in forming intelligent global citizens, and they must be taught alongside the study of religion and of philosophical theories of justice. (93–4)

This is a prose powered by imperatives ('requires' × 2, 'must' × 2) and by moral plain speaking (good/bad, true/bogus). It is, in other words, a strikingly unSocratic defence of a Socratic education—though that is a sacrifice mandated by the genre of the manifesto. More problematically, it is an argument that moves fairly deftly to elide 'humanistic' and 'critical', so that economics and law, for example, become honorary branches of the humanities as soon as they start scrutinizing their own knowledge claims. The reference to 'skills and techniques *we have come to associate with* the humanities', however, indicates, at least gesturally, that we may be in the terrain described in Chapter 1, whereby the field is pressed to show its more 'aggressive edge' in response to relative neglect of its skills and techniques in other areas of the university or in public life. What currently looks 'humanistic' about certain kinds of education, then, is so not by virtue of the humanities' definitive ownership of historical argument or comparative cultural understanding or philosophical scepticism, but because such intellectual and (for Nussbaum) ethical practices seem now underrepresented and under-regarded in disciplines, and even whole faculties, where they once had a prominent place: most pertinently the social and political sciences.

In the main Nussbaum's case rests on her view of the humanities as having a much longer historical and political importance than would be explained by such relatively recent changes in the character of our disciplines. The roots of her defence lie not just generally with the Socratic mode of argument, but specifically in Plato's account of the true philosopher's role within the political state. In Benjamin Jowett's translation of the famous passage from the *Apology*:

And now, Athenians, I am not going to argue for my own sake, as you may think, but for yours, . . . For if you kill me you will not easily find another like me, who, if I may use such a ludicrous figure of speech, am a sort of gadfly [μύωπος τινος/muopos tinos], given to the state [πόλις/polis] by the God; and the state is like a great and noble steed who is tardy in his motions owing to his very size, and requires to be stirred into life. I am that gadfly which God has given the state and all day long and in all places am always fastening upon you, arousing and persuading and reproaching you. And as you will not easily find another like me, I would advise you to spare me. (30d–31a)

A literal translation of the central metaphor would be 'a sort of gadfly [or spur: μύωπα/moupos puns on "spur" and "gadfly"] given to the city [πόλις/polis]'. Jowett renders 'polis' imperfectly but conventionally enough as 'state'. Nussbaum substitutes another Greek word— δημοκρατία/demokratia. As she has it: 'I am a sort of gadfly, given to the democracy by the gods...' (47).

Attention to the figure of the gadfly is, in justice to Nussbaum, not much more than a passing note in her discussion: something beyond a grace note, but rather less than a major theme. The main emphasis is on the wider Socratic inheritance conditioning the humanities' sense of their own vocational and social function. On the other hand, it is worth considering the effect of this small sleight of the translating hand. Making the substitution of 'the democracy' for 'the polis' (not found in any standard translation) clearly assists Nussbaum's case for the importance of Socratic pedagogy to a democratic 'political culture' (53): she goes on to chart a genealogy of educational reformers in his long wake—from Rousseau, through Johann Pestalozzi, to Friedrich Fröbel, in Europe, Bronson Alcott, Horace Mann, and above all John Dewey in America, and Rabindranath Tagore in India. But reaccenting Plato's terms also enables her to cast into relative shadow aspects of the Socratic model that do not as readily recommend themselves to modern democratic theory and practice.

It is necessary to step back at this point in order to gauge what is non-conventional about Nussbaum's argument, for all its continuities with standard liberal arts claims about education helping to cultivate informed civic consciousness. The classical claim for the political value of education (long pre-dating the more specific aspirations of a liberal education) was that it functions as a 'cultural qualification for the exercise of political and administrative power'. More important than any practical considerations of training here is the idea that education may instil what Ian Hunter calls 'a common set of discursive and moral reflexes'.[5] That claim makes no particular assumptions about knowledge content, or (pre-dating such disciplinary divisions) about the value of the humanities compared with law, or politics, or economics, as core elements of the curriculum—though most of the models derived from antiquity reserved a prominent place for rhetoric as the

[5] 'Literary Theory in Civil Life', *South Atlantic Quarterly* 95/4 (1996), 1099–134 (1099–110).

art of political persuasion.[6] This view is, in its essentials, fairly bland: it makes few assumptions about the kind of polity involved. Unless one invokes the extreme case of tyranny, no kind of government will prosper better with ignorant leaders or administrators than it will from having at its disposal intelligent and informed individuals. Oligarchy, aristocracy, even one-party dictatorship, require, in that broad outlook, educated members. They will differ crucially from democracy, of course, in how far they wish to extend the goods of education to the populations governed, and how far they attempt to use education as a means of ideological control (that is, how far they encourage independent critical thought), but all of them will hold in some measure that education is a desirable qualification for the exercise of political and administrative power.

The distinctive claim made by advocates of an education in and for democracy is that because, in a democracy, it is the people who govern, the people must be equipped by education to govern well. It is not a coincidence that extension of the franchise in Britain and America over the nineteenth and early twentieth centuries ran in tandem with extension of the right to a free state education.[7] That democracy might benefit from the general educational provision associated with liberal arts curricula has been an important claim, especially in America from the 1940s.[8] That democracy has any specific need of the humanities is a much less common assertion, despite its superficial similarity to other statements sometimes yoked to the humanities' defence, including Derrida's 'No democracy without literature; no literature without democracy'.[9]

---

[6] See Hunter, 'Literary Theory in Civil Life', 1110.

[7] See J. Ree, 'Socialism and the Educated Working Class', in C. Levy (ed.), *Socialism and the Intelligentsia 1880–1914* (London: Routledge & Kegan Paul, 1985), 211–18; and, with particular focus on the extension of adult education '[i]nitially intended . . . to make responsible democratic citizens of the working classes' but increasingly harnessed by the Labour movement to enabling the working classes to exercise power, see Lawrence Goldman, 'Education as Politics: University Adult Education in England since 1870', *Oxford Review of Education* 25/1–2 (1999), 89–101. For a contemporary source (discussed in Goldman), see A. H. D. Acland, 'The Education of Co-Operators and Citizens', in *The Co-Operative Wholesale Society Ltd Annual Diary 1885* (Manchester: Co-operative Wholesale Society, 1885).

[8] The classic statement of that view is the report of the Harvard Committee on the Objectives of a General Education in a Free Society: *General Education in a Free Society*, with an introduction by James Bryant Conant (Cambridge, Mass.: Harvard University Press, 1945).

[9] *On the Name*, ed. Thomas Dutoit, trans. David Wood, John P. Leavey Jr, and Ian McLeod (Stanford, Calif.: Stanford University Press, 1995), 28.

The claim that, beyond all this, democracy has any specific need of a higher education in the humanities is still less conventional. It presents an immediate problem of access—one highly politicized in its own right. The most ambitious target for participation in tertiary education in the UK has been 50 per cent of 18- to 30-year-olds; the highest achieved figure is 43 per cent.[10] Latest US Census Bureau statistics do not give consolidated projections for the same age band, but show 50.1 per cent of 20–21-year-olds attending undergraduate or graduate college.[11] Of the total enrolment in both countries, a diminishing percentage majors in the humanities (currently just over 15 per cent in the UK,[12] just under 16 per cent in the USA—with the important difference that US liberal arts curricula give all students at least some exposure to humanistic studies).[13] In both systems, imperfect realization of the democratic goal of access (the right of any individual to seek to realize the potential of his or her intelligence as a resource and reward not reducible to the potential economic rewards of education) therefore puts certain ongoing difficulties in the way of any claims one might want to make for the contribution of a higher education in the humanities to the democracy. Structurally, at least, such claims currently

[10] David Turner, 'Call for Review of 50 per cent Target', *Financial Times* 30 March 2010. <http://www.ft.com/cms/s/0/d5e1bfc8-3b3a-11df-a1e7-00144feabdc0.html#axzz1E2rdtrG9>. Accessed 15 February 2011.

[11] US Department of Commerce, *United States Census* (October 2009), table 1, 'Enrollment Status of the Population 3 Years Old and Over, by Sex, Age, Race . . .', <http://www.census.gov/population/www/socdemo/school/cps2009.html>. Accessed 15 February 2011. The figures most commonly cited to describe access to higher education in the USA cover the age range 25 and older, which give no indication of the increase in college attendance over the past two or three generations.

[12] Percentage calculated from Higher Education Statistics Agency, Statistical First Release 130, 26 January 2009, <http://www.hesa.ac.uk/dox/pressOffice/sfr130/sfr130r_table7.pdf>.

[13] William M. Chace, 'The Decline of the English Department: How It Happened and What Could Be Done to Reverse It', <http://www.theamericanscholar.org/the-decline-of-the-english-department/>. Accessed 15 February 2011. See also <http://news.bbc.co.uk/1/hi/education/1789500.stm> on the definition of the target. Accessed 15 February 2011. All the economic and ideological pressure from the UK government is now to reduce the numbers going to university on grounds of 'cost-efficiency', but with the STEM subjects (Science, Technology, Engineering, Maths) protected because they are perceived as producing evidently needed benefits to the economy. The mixed economy of public and private universities in the States theoretically allows for more independence from government, but numerous commentators have remarked on the growing encroachment of instrumentalist conceptions of education on liberal arts ideals.

require us to see the democracy as dependent on the contributions of what John Stuart Mill defensively called 'the instructed few'.

With Mill in view, it is worth noting again (see Introduction) that one of the distinctive features of the 'democracy needs us' argument, historically considered, is that it has little direct precedent in that high period of Victorian argument that provided the liberal arts tradition with so many of its frames of reference for debating the idea of the university and the use value or otherwise of literature. Arnold, Mill, Newman, Ruskin, Pattison all would have agreed that a school and university education should involve training in skills that have a potentially valuable political application: a critical understanding of history, knowledge of other cultures, some competence in other languages. All these writers held that the possession of an idea of culture, in which the arts had a guaranteed place, was crucial to the flourishing of the individual and the progress of society. All would have agreed in seeing the Socratic model as the origin of modern forms of liberal argument and, in its accent on the character and ethos of the teacher's influence on the pupil, still the ideal educational model.[14]

Some, but by no means all of them, held that the objectives of education should include the formation of good citizens.[15] Mill, for example, thought that a university education should have 'a direct bearing on the duties of citizenship'.[16] Ruskin argued that European school education, as then constituted, paid inadequate attention to politics, and that enough of the principles of philosophy, social relations, jurisprudence, labour, and commerce should be taught to every individual to enable them to 'ac[t] wisely in any station of life'.[17] He had a frankly

[14] H. S. Jones, *Intellect and Character in Victorian England: Mark Pattison and the Invention of the Don* (Cambridge: Cambridge University Press, 2007), 182.

[15] Arnold was more sceptical, writing in the report on *Schools and Universities on the Continent* (1869) that 'The aim and office of instruction, say many people, is to make a man a good citizen, or a good Christian, or a gentleman, or it is to enable him to get on in the world, or . . . to do his duty in that state of life to which he is called.' But these are 'at best secondary and indirect aims'. The 'prime direct aim' of education 'is to enable a man to *know himself and the world*'. *The Complete Prose Works of Matthew Arnold*, iv, ed. R. H. Super (Ann Arbor: University of Michigan Press, 1964), 290.

[16] 'Inaugural Address Delivered to the University of St. Andrews', in *Collected Works of John Stuart Mill*, ed. John M. Robson, 33 vols. (Toronto: University of Toronto, 1963–91), xxii: *Essays on Equality, Law, and Education*, 215–57 (245).

[17] 'Modern Education', 'Appendix, 7', *The Stones of Venice*, vol. ii (1853), *The Works of John Ruskin*, ed. E. T. Cook and Alexander Wedderburn, 39 vols. (London: George Allen, 1903–12), xi. 258–63 (260).

conservative concept of social station (and thought ordinary people should possess only one book—beautiful, and deeply read by them), but many of his admirers found in his writings support for more radical democratic views of education as a 'training for citizenship'.[18] Even Newman allowed for the 'formation of the citizen' as part of the 'proper function of the University' (though his conception of citizenship was primarily philosophical and theological rather than practical).[19] But none of these writers thought that the arts and humanities had a privileged, let alone primary, role to play in training people for civic responsibility, though they reserved a vital place for them in the pursuit of happiness. The one well-remembered exception is William Morris who did argue, much more radically than Arnold or Mill, for the education of the common people as a necessary condition for 'the realization of a new society with equality of condition for its basis'.[20] Morris, however, accented the artisanal aspects of a humanistic education much more strongly than the intellectual.

The absence of specific claims here for the humanities in part reflects the relative weakness of the disciplinary divisions that shape today's debates.[21] Ruskin's inclusion of science, politics, economy in an 'Arts' education indicates such a comparatively flexible outlook on knowledge. But it is worth noting that Mill's 'Inaugural Address' on becoming Rector of St Andrews (cited by Nussbaum as one of the inaugurating expressions of the 'democracy needs us' argument and a model for the defence of a liberal education[22]) does not in fact give priority to those subjects we now classify with the humanities when it considers the civic role of education. Mill afforded first place to Political Economy

[18] See Francis O'Gorman, 'Ruskin's Science of the 1870s: Science, Education, and the Nation', in Dinah Birch (ed.), *Ruskin and the Dawn of the Modern* (Oxford: Oxford University Press, 1999), 35–55 (50).

[19] John Henry Newman, *The Idea of a University*, ed. I. T. Ker (Oxford: Clarendon Press, 1976), 146. To which could be added the more darkly pessimistic voice of Mark Pattison who, in 1877, deplored the loss of the idea of liberal education in which a boy was not taught narrowly what would be 'useful to him' but 'moulded into a man and a citizen'. Quoted in Jones, *Intellect and Character*, 213.

[20] *Commonweal* 9 June 1888, quoted in Stephen Coleman, 'William Morris and "Education towards Revolution": "Making Socialists" versus "Putting them in their Place" ', <http://www.morrissociety.org/JWMS/AU94.11.1.Coleman.pdf>. Accessed 13 February 2011.

[21] O'Gorman, 'Ruskin's Science'.

[22] See esp. Martha Nussbaum, 'Being Human', *New Statesman* 1 June 2010. <http://www.newstatesman.com/ideas/2010/05/liberal-education-arts-mill>. Accessed 10 December 2010.

in the training for citizenship—after which he added International Law and only then 'the principal systems of moral philosophy'.[23]

Insofar as any of the major British advocates for a liberal education in the nineteenth century tied it to the good functioning of democracy they saw education as a means of easing and controlling the transition towards democracy.[24] A majority of them had doubts either about the democratic ideal or about how far society's educators could be expected to bring current practice closer to the ideal.[25] 'Civic' cannot be taken in any of their writings as a synonym for 'belonging to the democratic polity'. The incompleteness of franchise reform even at the end of the Victorian period is less germane here than the distinction each of them made, quite independent of their support or otherwise for reforms of the ballot, between equality of representation and (as they saw it) the necessary superiority of intellect, character, and education desirable in the people's representatives and those involved in the administration of the state's affairs. As Mill put it, in *Considerations on Representative Government* (1861) (I select Mill because he is, in other respects, famously, the most egalitarian of the major Victorian thinkers in his views on democratic representation):

The natural tendency of representative government, as of modern civilization, is towards collective mediocrity: and this tendency is increased by all reductions and extensions of the franchise, their effect being to place the principal power in the hands of classes more and more below the highest level of instruction in the community. But, though the superior intellects and characters will necessarily be outnumbered, it makes a great difference whether or not they are heard. In the false democracy which, instead of giving representation to all, gives it only to the local majorities, the voice of the instructed minority may have no organs at all in the representative body.[26]

Most Victorian reservations about the democratic purposes of education are no longer relevant considerations in the debate today about the contribution of the humanities to democracy. As observed in the Introduction, they are of interest primarily because they reveal the

---

[23] 'Inaugural Address', 245–8.

[24] The most extended argument in this vein is Arnold's *The Popular Education of France* (1861), in *Democratic Education*.

[25] John Sparrow, *Mark Pattison and the Idea of a University* (London: Cambridge University Press, 1967), 119; Jones, *Intellect and Character*, 57, 89, 198, 208–9.

[26] In *Essays on Politics and Society*, ed. John M. Robson, 2 vols. *CW* xix (London: Routledge and Kegan Paul, 1977), ii. 371–577 (457).

historically recent arrival of the democratic claim in the debate—the extent to which we are even now arguing on new terrain. In one respect, however, the questions they raise about the relation of educa- tion to the good running of government identify a problem still to be reckoned with. There is a familiar objection to views of the kind Mill expresses that afford a privileged political place to 'the instructed few'. To prefer, as he would have preferred, 'the principal power' to be in the hands of those 'classes' who have received 'the highest level of instruc- tion in the community' is to support a guardianship model of democ- racy about which, presumably, most of us have proper doubts. The exacting educational requirements set out for rulers in Plato's *Republic*, most obviously, are key to defining a version of democracy that would exclude much the larger part of the demos from power.

Opponents of guardianship democracy standardly argue that in requiring a level of education for its representatives above the ordinary provision for citizens, the guardianship model sets the bar for entry too high. If democracy is to retain its founding connection with a belief in political equality that argument has to be clinching. Yet Robert Dahl, famously sceptical of guardianship democracy, thinks many educated people will instinctively try to wriggle out of it. He asks us to imagine a debate between the representative of the demos and the representa- tive of the aristoi. 'Aristos' defends guardianship via an appeal to the collective wisdom of modern philosophers of democracy, Mill promi- nent among them:

you ['Demos'] really *do* agree with me that the process of governing the state ought to be restricted to those who are qualified to govern. I know most democrats recoil from such an idea. You fear that by openly admitting this assumption you'll give the game away at the start to those of us who support guardianship. Certainly in your democratic theory, philosophy, and argument this dangerous premise is rarely made explicit, precisely because it is so dan- gerous to your case. Yet, I don't believe that any important political philoso- pher in the democratic tradition—Locke, Rousseau, Jeremy Bentham, James Mill, for example—has ever rejected it, though perhaps only John Stuart Mill made it fully explicit.[27]

But such a political arrangement would, in truth, be not democracy but hierarchy—so the imagined riposte from 'Demos' then goes. Nor will the critic of guardianship easily be appeased by the response Mill

---

[27] *Democracy and its Critics* (New Haven:Yale University Press, 1998), 55–6.

would have made: that if privileged access to education by class is removed from the picture, we are dealing acceptably with meritocracy, not guardianship.[28] Does not education (as Bourdieu and others have told us) too commonly conceal the reproduction of social class with an illusion of democratic openness?

Outside the parameters of Rex Warner's novel, no one is suggesting that 'the principal power' in the democracy should lie with the humanities departments of universities and those they educate. Nevertheless, a suspicion that the guardianship model haunts the 'democracy needs us' argument would be consistent both with Plato and with a long line of adherents to the gadfly model after him. Neither Plato nor Socrates, as the *Apology* above all ought to remind us, was an admirer of democracy— however tempered their views by recognition that the restored Athenian democracy from 403 BC was stable, and without obviously feasible alternatives.[29] If the Socratic gadfly is, famously, the irritant conscience of the state, it is by no means clear that his role is particular to democracy, since his function would be as valid under oligarchy, or indeed under any political system with the possible exceptions of dictatorship and theocracy. (Which may be why Socrates does not specify to the king archon's court and its jurors the kind of polis on which the philosopher acts by divine licence.) Nor is it at all clear that his role is distinctively aligned with the humanities, given the pre-disciplinary articulation of a Socratic method that has bearing on all aspects of intellectual, social, and political life (in terms of content, the Socratic dialogues belong in modern politics, social science, law, and theology, at least as clearly as they belong to the humanities).

The Socratic gadfly is the ur form of Julien Benda's intellectual, 'speaking truth to power', of Karl Mannheim's ideal intelligentsia, charged with correcting the narrowly class-and party-bound interests of the rest of society, and of many other romanticizing accounts of the intellectual as a quasi-external authority on the structure and operations

---

[28] See *Considerations on Representative Government* (1861), in Mill, *Essays on Politics and Society* ii, *CW* xix (Toronto: University of Toronto Press, 1977), ch. 12 (esp. 509).

[29] The *Laws* is sometimes read as expressing a late accommodation to democracy, but is more persuasively understood as an attempt to safeguard democracy against many of its own weaknesses (including the limited power of rational persuasion) by rooting the state's laws in natural theology. See Malcolm Schofield, 'Plato', in E. Craig (gen. ed.), *Routledge Encyclopedia of Philosophy Online*, version 2.0 <http://www.rep.routledge.com/article/A088SECT17>. Accessed 15 December 2010. Also Schofield, *Plato: Political Philosophy* (Oxford: Oxford University Press, 2006), 74–89.

of political life. And with Benda in mind, one could outline a less flattering genealogical account of the humanities' relationship to democratic ideals than Nussbaum provides. Such an account might follow
the lines indicated in Francis Mulhern's *Culture/Metaculture* (2000):
from Thomas Mann's *Reflections of an Unpolitical Man* (1918), through
Benda's *La Trahison des clercs* (1927), Mannheim's *Ideology and Utopia*
(1929), Ortega's *The Revolt of the Masses* (1929), to Leavis's *Mass Civilization and Minority Culture* (1930). The story, then, would be much
more in line with Socrates' reluctant assent to democracy, though
revised as the story of a specialist cadre or (to use Coleridge's preferred
medievalism) a 'clerisy' rather than an exceptional individual 'not easily' replaced. The philosopher-critic is imagined (in Mulhern's words)
'supervening over [the political space], from a higher plane of social
judgement' rather than involved in its deliberations on terms of equality of status.[30] And lest anyone assume that the 'higher plane' assumption is self-evidently self-discrediting, or that the changes in the
understanding of culture from Raymond Williams onwards have rendered the idea of a clerisy obsolete, it is worth observing that it has
prominent advocates even now: most credibly, in Britain, Jonathan
Bate, who has defended the 'humanising work' of universities by
appealing to the Coleridgean view (connecting Coleridge's emphasis
on the distribution of knowledge to the more modern political demand
for knowledge 'dissemination').[31]

   None of this means that there is no way of adapting or modernizing
the Socratic role so that it does relate a higher education in the humanities to democracy without smuggling in an assumption of guardianship, but it leaves us quite a lot of work to do in the way of adaption
and modernization. Collectively we cannot all be gadflies, Annette

   [30] *Culture/Metaculture* (London: Routledge, 2000), 12.
   [31] See esp. 'The Costly New Idea of a University', *Standpoint Magazine* December 2010:
'Reading Coleridge's definition of the clerisy in the light of 21st-century debates about
university funding, what is most striking is the huge emphasis that he places on what is
now called "dissemination". The humanising work must be "distributed throughout the
country, so as not to leave even the smallest integral part or division without a resident
guide, guardian, and instructor". What that might mean today is a major university working in collaboration with a local further-education college or making its lectures available
to everyone through podcasts. The responsibility—the public duty—placed upon the
latter-day clerisy is heavy, but in the "knowledge economy" and faced with the global
insecurity of the 21st century, the return upon a modest continuing national investment
in their work of teaching is potentially vast.' <www.standpointmag.co.uk/node/3577/
full>. Accessed 11 December 2010.

Baier has warned, or we run the risk of being no better than a 'plague' (why, in Richard Rorty's approving gloss, should 'the rest of society [then] not merely tolerate but subsidize our activity'?).[32] There is an obvious opening here to counter that bent of the metaphor with Hardt and Negri's conception of the global democratic multitude or swarm. (UK media reports on student protests in 2010 against the government's abandonment of the principle that higher education should be paid for by the state had frequent recourse to such metaphors.) We do not have to endorse Hardt and Negri's 'inebriate' vision of 'power through [political] faith' (I quote Tom Nairn[33]), to claim, contra Baier, that the humanities might be, as it were, a large collective gadfly, for example by reminding present-day society of inconvenient but pertinent facts about its past and its cultural heritage. This sounds more promising but, again, it is not self-evident that the humanities have special rights or responsibilities here, over disciplines with more obvious claims to understanding the operations of modern government and modern economies.

The potential redundancy of criticism that Baier and Rorty fear can be discounted. Why place limits on the amount of critical self-scrutiny a democracy can bear? A more legitimate difficulty with a plague of modern Socratic gadflies operating out of our universities involves the stark conflict between the isolated agitant role of the Socratic philosopher and the institutionalized and professionalized function of the modern academic. If we want nearer models for the kind of professional scholarly and structuredly educational work we do, Bruce Robbins has suggested, we might have to start by rethinking the Socratic animus towards rhetoric and sophistry.[34] We also need a sharper account of how the anti-authoritarian attitudes of Socrates can yield a model of critical enquiry that is a 'social practice', rather than (as Macaulay jadedly saw it) the charismatic performance of one man with 'a thorough love for making [other] men look small'.[35] More immediately

---

[32] Annette Baier, 'Some Thoughts on the Way We Moral Philosophers Live Now', *Monist* 67/4 (1984), 490–7; discussed in Rorty, *Truth and Progress* (Cambridge: Cambridge University Press, 1998), 173n.

[33] 'Make for the Boondocks', *London Review of Books* 27/9 5 May 2005, <http://www.lrb.co.uk/v27/n09/tom-nairn/make-for-the-boondocks>. Accessed 26 January 2011.

[34] *Secular Vocations: Intellectuals, Professionalism, Culture* (London: Verso, 1993), 112.

[35] Diary for July 1853, excerpted in *The Life and Letters of Lord Macaulay*, ed. G. Otto Trevelyan, 2 vols. (London: Longmans, Green, and Co., 1876), ii. 361–3 (363).

(since we do not lack good accounts of the social and political respon-sibilities of our profession[36]), we need an account of our characteristic intellectual objects and activities that more accurately allows us to identify our role in relationship to the democracy. As classically imag-ined, the gadfly figure makes us both anti-authoritarian and anti-statist in a way that does not help us to that end. Nor does it enable us to articulate why the humanities might be particularly well equipped to meet certain of the democracy's current needs.

Justification by way of cultural distinctions between intellectual dis-ciplines quickly leads, as Chapter 1 argued, to mis-description. A draft version of this chapter, for which I retain some affection and convic-tion, pursued the claim that the humanities have a particular gadfly role to play as a corrective to the dominance of quantitative modes of reasoning in political life. For example, if we believe that the sheer quantity of information gathering and information provision that attends government is inimical to coherent debate about policy, we might claim that it is within the remit of the humanities to show where the democratic interest in open government may be misdi-rected into obfuscatory proceduralism; or where supposed devolution of power to the people in what Britain's Prime Minister at the time of writing likes to call a 'post-bureaucratic' age can misrepresent a dis-mantling of the state; or where the economistic assumptions at work in the audit culture that shapes not just our universities but all our professions and public services start damaging public values (including the value of education) by translating them into the language and val-ues of demonstrable public 'impact'—or, indeed, by making the work of assessment so time-consuming that the cost of accounting to gov-ernment outweighs the value of the public monies given. The draft pages also pursued the suggestion of one sympathetically inclined UK economist (Hamish McRae) that it is surely within the remit of the humanities to remind our colleagues in the social sciences that econometricians ignorant of history are liable to make serious political and economic errors.

[36] See esp. Robbins, *Secular Vocations*; Fish, *Doing What Comes Naturally*; John Guillory, *Cultural Capital: The Problem of Literary Canon Formation* (Chicago: University of Chicago Press, 1993), 'Preprofessionalism: What Graduate Students Want', *Profession* (1996), 91–9; and 'The System of Graduate Education', *PMLA* 11 (2000), 1154–63; Michael Bérubé, *Rhetorical Occasions: Essays on Humans and the Humanities* (Chapel Hill, NC: University of North Carolina Press, 2006).

Some or all of these suggestions are indeed opportunities for the humanities to serve the public good. But it is insufficiently clear that the democracy needs the humanities, specifically, to do the job. Most of the needs they identify are needs any critically educated member or group of the democracy could respond to intelligently—whatever their educational specialization. If secondary education has been broad and included enough of the skills being associated here with the humanities, but not solely theirs, then is there really a case for the special democratic force of a humanities higher education? In one of these instances, the need for a higher education in a humanities discipline is clear: a secondary education in history some years back probably will not have imparted the knowledge necessary to identify the relevant historical ignorance in economic theory today. But the more general protections of democracy look rather less obviously in need of higher humanities training. Moreover, if supplying a lack, or remedying a failure, in the governance of the democracy is presented as the humanities' primary justification of ourselves, it heavily skews what we do in one direction, aligning us with political work that is unquestionably important, but not obviously exclusively or even distinctively ours to do, and likely to be done better by others.

That 'us' is a problem. The first person plural is the regularly preferred point of view for much writing about the academic profession for the academic profession. It is a rhetorical sleight of hand by which the concerns of the profession can be made to seem entirely congruent with those of the democratic polity as a whole. But the profession is not a representative body of the democracy, and quite who is included as the agents of the humanities' claim to be a bulwark of democracy is very often unclear. If the 'us' in 'Democracy Needs Us' is taken to refer to those of 'us' who are scholars or students of the humanities in the universities, it does seem to commit 'us', willingly or not, to a guardianship model of democracy. Rational coherence requires 'us' then to accept, however reluctantly, that Plato and Mill were right, and that democracy left to itself is a noble but sluggish beast in need of our goading. But if the 'us' is a bid for all members of the democracy to protect the good operation of the democracy by exercising our critical capacities, humanities departments will be one place among many nurturing those abilities. The humanities academic, much as he or she can claim expertise in critical thinking, will have no special (no additional) authority in the political domain above that of ordinary citizens.

If the distinction between the higher-level practice of the professional few and the sufficiently educated practice of the many goes unmade, humanities scholars risk falling into the error Ian Hunter identifies when he warns against mistaking the 'prestigious ethical comportment' available within the university to literary theorists (more broadly, cultural critics) for our 'roles as citizens'.[37] They also risk confusing the kinds of critical capacity that it is desirable a democracy should have available within it with the critical capacities requisite for its survival or for individual participation in it. This does not mean that the work of humanities departments should not be political, or that it cannot seek to change 'actual social and cultural life', as Louis Menand puts it.[38] It certainly does not mean that their scholars have no responsibilities, as members of a profession, to the ideal of democratic equality or, more particularly, that their work should not recognize and respond to the serious imperfections in that ideal as witnessed in today's actual social and cultural arrangements. Nor does it mean that fidelity to democratic ideals should not be part of the university's professional discourses of legitimization. But the ideals that characterize humanities scholars' professional life and work are not the same thing as the discipline's justification for being—or (in the more specific UK context) its justification for being in receipt of public funds.

The most persuasive effort to date to make the case for the democratic force of the humanities in the UK, keeping in view that distinction between the academy as the home of expert practice and the academy as the place that nurtures skills widely practised beyond it, is Francis Mulhern's paper for a one-day conference at Birkbeck College, London, entitled 'Why Humanities?'[39] One of the strengths of Mulhern's position is that he recognizes the degree of under-definition in any appeal to the humanities' 'democratic commitments' as evidence of their contribution to the common good. People who seek to defend the work of humanities departments, he observes, regularly invoke their ability to foster skills and values that are essential to a democratic society. In doing so they have tended to align themselves

[37] Hunter, 'Literary Theory in Civil Life', 1110.

[38] *Marketplace of Ideas*, 158.

[39] But see also Thomas Docherty, *For the University: Democracy and the Future of the Institution* (London: Bloomsbury Academic, 2011), which makes a case for the democratic purposes of the university, with the accent on the work of literature and philosophy departments.

with an obviously desirable ethical comportment on the part of individuals and institutions in a way that confers easy benefit (one might add, easy esteem) on the speaker or institution but does little to identify the current needs of the democracy.

So: 'something akin to democracy turns up under the heading of equality of opportunity' in recent British accounts of humanities education, Mulhern notes—but this 'quickly becomes an economic good'. Something else 'akin to' democracy 'turns up under the heading of tolerance, and quickly becomes a cultural good—a putative British identity'.

What is far less in evidence is any conviction about the demands of a properly functioning democracy: the culture of democratic practices by which, in however limited a sense, the population is said to govern itself. A democracy is a form of polity in which alternatives are conceived and propagated, interpreted and evaluated in open debate, then decided on directly or according to various norms of representation; one in which this central deliberative process is embedded in a wider culture of free investigation, criticism and advocacy, with a media appropriately organized and supported; one in which the general culture supports an open play of suggesting, imagining and evaluating the possibilities of the common life.[40]

The argument for the humanities contribution to democracy is not (as Mulhern expresses it) a *definitional* defence, and does not seek to be one. It puts democracy first, and the contribution of the humanities second. It is the product of a particularly bleak moment in the recent history of higher education in the UK, at which some humanities departments had recently faced closure, many were and are seeing their work distorted by administrative efforts to maximize government funding, and the idea that universities might have a gadfly function in relation to the governing of the polity has played no part in the governors' sense of what public funds are to be used for. In response to these deformations of the political and institutional cultures in which the humanities do their work Mulhern selects some out of the many intellectual practices pursued by the humanities—trained deliberation, criticism, advocacy, evaluation, mediation of ideas with respect to norms of representation—and identifies them as having special

[40] Francis Mulhern, 'Humanities and University Corporatism', paper delivered at the 'Why Humanities?' conference, Birkbeck College, University of London, 5 November 2010; podcast at <http://backdoorbroadcasting.net/2010/11/francis-mulhern-humanities-and-university-corporatism/>. Accessed 9 November 2010.

importance for the good political functioning of a democracy. It locates the common ground of the humanities in their attention to critical reason. (This is necessarily a wider claim than the one sometimes made for literature and language departments on the basis of their shared attention to language.[41] Given that our lives are 'carried on to a large extent through language', as Deborah Cameron puts it, 'the power to name and define is an important arena for reproducing or challenging' our current political arrangements.[42] This is a substantial claim for critical attention to language in a highly mediated world, but not I think entirely generalizable across the humanities.)

The primary complaints Mulhern makes, then, about the current state of our universities are less uttered in alarm at a 'world crisis' in educational values than they are aimed at particular national policies that may have (do have) parallels elsewhere but that remain specific to particular democratic structures and particular elected governments:

One of the special frustrations of observing New Labour's adventures in university policy [in the UK] was the persistent confusion of the democratic demand for access with the instrumental requirement to retool the workforce, and the reduction of both to an arbitrary numerical target. Another feature of the period was the currency of ignorant and offensive comments about degree programmes such as media studies. What does it say about elected politicians that they cannot take seriously the idea of investigating the cultural forms that are their own most important plane of operation? The higher level intellectual practices that are the everyday core of humanities teaching and learning are also core practices of a democratic culture such as we supposedly have and value. And that, in general social terms, is one good reason 'why humanities'. If elected politicians still can't get the point, if university managements are too far advanced in their corporatist make-over to explain it to them, or even get it themselves, we will at least have been enlightened as to the effective reality of their commitment to democracy.[43]

This strikes a polemical note, especially in closing, but it is polemic qualified by an awareness of the limits of its power and its likely audience. It grants the humanities a special interest in the critical examination of the cultural forms vital to the democracy, but eschews the

[41] See esp. Isobel Armstrong, *The Radical Aesthetic* (Oxford: Blackwell Publishers, 2000) and Said, *Humanism and Democratic Criticism*, 28–9.

[42] 'Feminist Linguistic Theories', in Stevie Jackson and Jackie Jones (eds.), *Contemporary Feminist Theories* (Edinburgh: Edinburgh University Press, 1998), 147–61 (148).

[43] 'Feminist Linguistic Theories', 148. The valuation of communication studies would be the nearest US equivalent to that of 'media studies' in the UK.

language of moralism in favour of the operation of critical reason. For Mulhern the key practices involved are 'interpretation and evaluation', not least of the role of media in assisting any decisions about matters affecting 'the common life'. That he avoids the more ethically laden phrase 'the common good' is, I suspect, symptomatic of a care not to be seen to assert that the activities of the humanities are necessarily ethically driven, or endowed with special merit (though I do not imagine he would reject the phrase 'the common good').

The accent here is not on safeguarding knowledge of the historical formation of Western culture and providing a 'kind of cultural lingua franca'[44] (as in the liberal arts tradition), or (as for Nussbaum) on the moral qualities cultivated in individuals or institutions by an education in the humanities. All this is much less specific than the liberal arts listing of subject-specific skills ideally nurtured within a general education, but the British system of specialization does not in the main admit of a defence of the humanities by way of their role within a humane general-education. Rather, Mulhern confines his attention to the humanities' support for that aspect of the wider democratic culture that is encoded in the structure or 'form' of open debate, and better summarized by the word 'polity' than the word 'ethos'. Mulhern foregrounds, moreover, aspects of the common pursuits of the humanities that have to do not with new knowledge or ideas, but with ongoing and to a degree repetitive disputation in our evaluation of the forms of cultural representation. One function of scholarship in the humanities is, after all, to go over ground that generations have been over before, not only because interpretations and evaluations may change but because it is part of the scholar's responsibility to keep reinterpreting and re-evaluating that cultural memory in the context of the now.[45] And this will involve, as Mulhern puts it, 'deep and abiding conflicts of understanding and commitment that criss-cross our disciplines as they do all cultural life'.

Mulhern's is the best defended articulation of the democracy argument, pitched as a general claim for higher study in the humanities, that we have heard to date in the British debate. It takes us beyond what has been, until recently, a standard complaint, often but by no means exclusively heard from the left, that we are experiencing a

---

[44] Menand, *Marketplace of Ideas*, 41.
[45] Michael Bérubé makes a similar point in *Rhetorical Occasions*, 85–6.

widespread 'democratic deficit': a growing gap between 'formal and substantive democracy' that can only be filled by a revitalization of participatory democracy at the national level, and the creation and protection of political spaces that allow for genuine communication, argument, agreement, across a global civil society.[46] By itself that last analysis has not been of great help to the defence of the humanities: little advance if any on the kind of easy claim to political kudos involved in aligning ourselves with obviously desirable aspects of democracy (for equality and inclusiveness now read 'substantive communication'). Mulhern keeps the argument relatively specific, asking us to recognize the political value of a culture competent to criticize the acts of mediation through which political representation does its work: conveying the concerns of the democratic electorate to its politicians, and the actions and intentions of the politicians back to the electorate (more and less fully, more and less honestly). He also points us to one indicative area in which recent British governments have specifically misrepresented the nature of the democracy's interest in higher education: the egalitarian interest in access to the goods of education (not all of them instrumental goods) has repeatedly been redescribed as the narrowly instrumental goal of 'retool[ing] the workforce'. (One can speculate that this redescription may itself have been instrumental: a way of selling enlarged access under New Labour to the more grudging or anti-intellectual among taxpayers.) Both points are a helpful advance in clarity for the 'democracy needs us' argument. They remind us, if we are inclined to worry about overstating the importance of higher education, that the standards for participation in a democracy are, though within the reach of all sufficiently informed and rational citizens, preferably quite high. To be capable of propagating, interpreting, and evaluating ideas in open debate is not a small competency.

Some of the reservations raised earlier are still not entirely laid to rest here. For all Mulhern's wariness about cheaply earned political prestige, this is an argument that makes the humanities look very high minded. He presents, explicitly, the humanities in one version of their

---

[46] See, among many others, Mary Kaldor, 'Democracy and Globalisation', Working paper series, WP 03/2008. Centre for the Study of Global Governance, London School of Economics and Political Science, London, UK. <http://www.lse.ac.uk/Depts/global/ PDFs/0708ch2mkaldor.pdf>. Accessed 2 February 2011.

best, 'and it is not in the nature of the best to be the usual'. As with Arnold, the appeal to the best brings an inevitable reply: Whose best? There is no mention here of the more fanciful lines of enquiry and expression that can be worth trying out and, sometimes, letting go; or about all the work that is assiduous rather than ingenious, or playful rather than serious (though any teacher knows that one good joke can sometimes get a point across to students better than a crafted critique). And when humanities departments start to look as politically serious as this it is worth recalling that they are centres of low satire as well as high thought, of education remedial as well as elite. Indeed, the reme-dial work—teaching basic competence and coherence in expression—may be as real a contribution to a democratic culture as the higher work of criticism.

Mulhern's account of us at our most politically serious may also leave one wondering, still, how much the humanities may distinctively claim, here, by way of self-justification. One straightforward defence of their position is that they preserve and continue the higher order prac-tices that are passed on to those who will go on to teach the humani-ties at school level ('they teach the teachers'). Primary and secondary teaching are, of course, only two of the many career paths pursued by humanities graduates, who take the knowledge and practices nurtured at university into very many areas of public life, including government itself (see Chapter 2). These areas are also, however, fed from the other departments of the university, and the critical work associated here with the humanities ('alternatives. . . conceived and propagated, inter-preted and evaluated in open debate, then decided on directly or according to various norms of representation') is, or should be, charac-teristic also of how students are educated in the sciences and social sciences. It is definitive of intellectual work per se rather than the pos-session of any one domain of scholarship. Such intellectual work war-rants the description 'humane', but as indicative of a critical cast of mind towards all cultural arrangements and expressions that should be found right across our domains of enquiry.

Mulhern, indeed, accepts this. At base he is articulating a defence not just of the humanities but of the university as a place of Enlighten-ment. In his account, the humanities are being practised whenever a scientist breaks off from the routinized practice of a method and starts to ask why the method has become a default practice (this is 'a kind of philosophy'), and whenever a health professional working in a

multicultural environment starts to ponder the authority of the dominant medical discourse (to do so is to embark on rhetoric and ethics).
The humanities differ only in that they practise these kinds of 'dubita-
tive and speculative' thinking in concentrated form, so that their disciplines stand collectively as 'a specialist agency of a defining general
ethos of learning and inquiry'.[47] Once again, the strength of the current political assertion that the humanities have a larger or more
important claim for value here rests on the observation (correct, but
also historically and politically contingent) that it has become theirs as
a consequence of the downgrading of those kinds of thinking in other
areas of the university and of public life.

In one of his more temperately gadflyish late essays, 'The Priority of
Democracy to Philosophy', Richard Rorty asks the question, 'Does
liberal democracy "nee[d]" philosophical justification'. His answer is
that those, like himself, John Rawls, and John Dewey, who view the
question pragmatically,

will say that although it may need philosophical articulation, it does not need
philosophical background. On this view, the philosopher of liberal democracy
may wish to develop a theory of the human self that comports with the institutions he or she admires. But such a philosopher is not thereby justifying
these institutions by reference to more fundamental premises, but the reverse:
He or she is putting politics first and tailoring a philosophy to suit.[48]

'Flesh[ing] out our self-image as citizens of [a liberal] democracy with
a philosophical view of the self' may well be something we want to do
in addition but 'this sort of philosophical fleshing-out' does not have
much importance for Rorty (242).

Whether democracy 'needs' the humanities is not the same question, since the humanities are offering not to justify democracy but to
keep it true to principles that have long possessed strong justification
(in one interpretation of Plato's gadfly analogy, to keep it in good
health). But the distinction Rorty is making between philosophical
work that articulates a justification for democracy and philosophical

---

[47] I take this to be, also, Edward Said's position in *Humanism and Democratic Criticism*.
See esp. Chapter 1.
[48] 'The Priority of Democracy to Philosophy', in *The Rorty Reader*, ed. Christopher
J. Voparil and Richard Bernstein (Chichester: Wiley-Blackwell, 2010), 239–58 (242). And
see E. D. Hirsch Jr, 'Rorty and the Priority of Democracy to Philosophy', *New Literary
History* 39/1 (2008), 35–52, for a characterization of the place of this essay in Rorty's wider
work.

work that puts the political commitment to democracy first, and fits its theories to that commitment secondarily, is pertinent. Mulhern does just that: he puts the common political commitment of the citizens of democracy to their own good government first, and asks what the humanities do that serves it. The connection between the humanities and democracy, then, rests not primarily on the claim that the humanities foster a distinctive knowledge content in those who study them, or even that they assist the development of particularly desirable psychological qualities, but that they teach in concentrated form the critical 'processes' of the wider democratic polity and in some measure they represent and model those processes. They are, collectively, a forum for intellectual and political argument of a 'high' order, 'embedded in' a wider culture that has those practices at its political 'core', and that has historically supported their higher pursuit in the university (not least financially). Advocates for the liberal arts system would not, I assume, resist this formulation, which is not at odds with their own traditions of defence though it takes a different argumentative path.

If Mulhern's argument makes much less of the idea of individual development than of nurturing a collective intellectual praxis in support of the polity, it is, in itself, nonetheless a distinctive rhetorical performance. The somewhat agonistic manner of the parting shot is worth attending to. 'If elected politicians . . . are too far advanced in their corporatist make-over [for us] to explain [the needs of the democracy] to them, or even get [the point] themselves, we will at least have been enlightened as to the effective reality of their commitment to democracy.' This implies (as I read it) a mix of despondency and anger about the extent to which the interests of corporate capitalism have replaced, or subsumed, the debate and critique that are the core practices of a democracy; anger and despondency also about the probable limits of our influence on the individuals who govern us or the corporate cultures we inhabit. It clearly expresses also a view from the political left that the governing class regards ordinary people, exercising their democratic right to hold the government of the day to account, as an inconvenience. The phrase may involve, more than this, something of Edward Said's characterization of the political intellectual as an exilic figure: disabused, comparatively enlightened, but conscious of a strictly limited political influence. But given Mulhern's criticisms, in *Culture/Metaculture*, of precisely that strain in the Kulturkritik tradition, as he defines it, I suspect the despondency, if not the anger, is a matter of personal tone, not a recommended professional or institutional posture.

Not everyone who works in the humanities divisions of universities will share Mulhern's prioritization of the political. Some will think that the case for a higher education remains unproven: that we should trust in a basic primary and secondary education to provide for the critical and evaluative capacities of ordinary citizens; also (captiously) that we should put more trust in the various kinds of value attached to the humanities that do not require the image of the democracy (noble and sluggish, or ailing) to justify them. To the counter-argument that, in Jonathan Arac's phrase, removing the democratic claim from the humanities would leave us 'nothing important to do',[49] they will reply that it leaves us plenty: some of which is important (and some but not all of that primarily political), but some of which might have to be content to be unimportant: just careful, or scholarly, or fanciful, or pleasurable but not particularly consequential. It is worth reiterating, however, that the justification of the humanities on the grounds that they teach and practise, at the highest level, the intellectual skills neces-sary for the good working of democracy, is not a definitional claim. It is a defence of their public value that works inward from the needs of the polity to the contribution the humanities can make. It assumes, as did Socrates, that democracy is strengthened by having a higher level of reasoning available within it—as Mill put it, that 'it makes a great difference whether or not [that higher reasoning is] heard' but it claims no special political authority for those who make the humani-ties their profession. Its advocates will undoubtedly feel impelled to articulate their political defence when that contribution is in doubt, but it does not require a state of emergency for their claim to have validity.

[49] 'Peculiarities of (the) English in the Metanarrative(s) of Knowledge and Power', in Bruce Robbins (ed.), *Intellectuals: Aesthetics, Politics, Academics* (Minneapolis: University of Minnesota Press, 1990), 189–99 (194).

5

For its Own Sake

If the phrase 'intrinsic value' is, as the philosopher Shelly Kagan puts it, 'something of a philosophical term of art', not 'in much use in ordinary conversation',[1] it is nevertheless familiar to literary critics and frequently resorted to by advocates for the humanities.[2] Its attractions are clear, though its meaning is, on any close inspection, rather less so. When employed in the defence of poetry and the defence of the humanities it tends to denote one or both of two things: (negatively) resistance to requirements for demonstrated practical or instrumental value; (positively) a way of speaking about value that refers us back to the object itself and offers to free us from the charge of mere subjectivism. Both usages are problematic; neither is commonplace in philosophy. But before detailing difficulties it is worth pausing a little longer over the question of what hopes may be entailed in the persistence of 'intrinsic value' in the vocabulary despite well-known reservations about its validity.

The major hope invested in 'intrinsic value' is, I take it, that we might, by invoking it, be enabled to stop the hard and unsatisfactory work of trying to justify the value of the humanities and the value of studying them. Large claims of external use or purpose, economic, philosophical, and political, would disappear or retreat to secondary

[1] 'Rethinking Intrinsic Value', *Journal of Ethics* 2 (1998), 277–97 (277).

[2] See, for example, *Achieving Great Art for Everyone: A Strategic Framework for the Arts* (London: Arts Council England, 2011), 4; Rónán McDonald, 'The Value of Art and the Art of Evaluation', in Jonathan Bate (ed.), *The Public Value of the Humanities* (London: Bloomsbury, 2011), 283–94 (esp. 283–4 examining the weaknesses of intrinsic value, and 293 cautiously reinstating it). For the AHRC's ambition to 'capture intrinsic value' with 'measures and indicators', see the outline for the 'Measuring Cultural Value' project, <http://www.ahrc.ac.uk/Funding-Opportunities/Documents/DCMSplacementnotes. pdf>. Accessed 24 September 2012.

place, and the value would become wrapped up in objects and activities, which could be deemed, as the first sentence of this book intimated, self-justifying. There is, after all, a problem, as the last chapter observed, with a defence of higher education in the humanities that, however pluralistic in scope, relies upon their effects (effects on us individually, on the culture, on political life). If advocacy for 'the humanities' can say nothing about their content—the things they study or curate, the practices they cultivate, the knowledge they own, the interpretations they make and continually remake—then it is in danger of asserting consequential importance at the expense of any account of the human-ities as good in themselves.

Bentham's much-disparaged view that 'the game of push-pin is of equal value with the arts and sciences of music and poetry' (discussed in Chapter 3) is one logical result of taking one's eye off content: the value of the state of mind enabled ('pleasure', for Bentham) is upheld but one gives up on any discriminations of worth at the level of what is actually done, laboured over, enjoyed, chosen as an object of studious attention. This outcome will trouble some humanities scholars much more than others, depending on the importance they attach to 'judgement' as a further step beyond 'interpretation'. But one doesn't need to raise so early in the argument the spectres of renewed dispute about the canon and the conditions for judgement. One can, more simply, observe that the technical skills associated with disciplines and groups of disciplines have evolved in relation to particular kinds of material. Hence Richard Rorty's provocatively banal defence of philosophy as an autonomous discipline: 'somebody's got to read these difficult books, and it takes a lot of time.'[3] By the same token: somebody's got to study the literature, the art, the films, the music, the historical archive, and so on.

Understandable though the impulse to secure 'intrinsic value' is, the endeavour comes beset with philosophical complications. No substan-tial contribution to the literature on the subject fails to foreground them, to the extent where the difficulty of reconciling the desire for intrinsic value to be true with the recognition of its entanglement in fallacy may be said to be part of the point. As the poet and critic Geof-frey Hill remarks (with decided regret) of Ruskin's attempts to defend

[3] 'A Talent for Bricolage: An Interview with Richard Rorty', Interviewer Joshua Knobe, *The Dualist: Undergraduate Magazine*, 2, 1995, 56–71; online at <http://pantheon. yale.edu/~jk762/rorty.html>. Accessed 20 September 2012.

intrinsic value as the self-contained 'power' or 'worth' of a thing: intrinsic value so understood is 'at best a promissory note, at worst a semantic relic to ward off the evil eye of commodity'.[4] To put things thus is to direct attention to a particular area of difficulty—that of purifying judgements of value from considerations of 'ulterior' value, which would mean, 'at worst', considerations of exchange value in the unstable marketplace of language and ideas (383) (others will be more concerned with purifying judgement from political or theological concerns or from the eccentricities of individual subjectivity)—but it aptly gauges the general character of the aspiration towards a self-contained, self-evident good.

Shelly Kagan is not alone among contemporary philosophers in thinking that much of the theory traditionally implied by the term 'intrinsic value' has, by now, exhausted its claim to philosophical respect. The specific claim that intrinsic value is based on intrinsic properties 'may well be false', and there is some danger 'that we will make a fetish out of philosophical beliefs' in it. Kagan defends the view that 'value *as an end*' (which he takes to be one conventional interpretation of 'intrinsic value') 'need not depend solely upon an object's intrinsic properties' (279–80). In some cases 'we can explain something having intrinsic value by noting the various properties that provide the basis of its intrinsic value' (277, 287). Some of those properties may be relational—and some of these may have instrumental value. Abraham Lincoln's pen (Kagan's example) has instrumental value as an implement for writing—other pens would have served as well for the signing of the Emancipation Proclamation—but the fact that this was the pen Lincoln used gives it, on that basis, intrinsic value (285). And if this is so, the 'traditional [philosophical] contrast between intrinsic value and instrumental value' is an error: 'in *some* cases instrumental value may ground intrinsic value' (287).

In pursuing a distinction between intrinsic value and value 'as an end', or valuing a thing 'for its own sake', Kagan is working an increasingly well-worn furrow in value theory. The extent of the doubts expressed in relation to 'the intrinsic' differs, but the broad conclusion— that we can substantially modify or even dispense with intrinsic value

---

[4] 'Translating Value: Marginal Observations on a Central Question' (2000), in Geoffrey Hill, *Collected Critical Writings* (hereafter *CCW*), ed. Kenneth Haynes (Oxford: Oxford University Press, 2008), 383–93 (383); see also 389 for Ruskin on self-contained power.

without having to give up on objective value—commands fairly wide agreement.[5] The proper contrast with intrinsic value as Christine Korsgaard points out, in one of the most influential contributions to the current debate, is not instrumental value but 'extrinsic' value: 'the value a thing gets from another source'.[6] The right contrast for instrumental value, on the other hand, is 'a thing that is valued for its own sake or end' (170). She considers 'intrinsic value' a viable concept, but her means of rescuing it may not attract general agreement given that it depends upon a Kantian metaphysical protection against infinite regress in the conditions for goodness. One thing only, 'the good will', is intrinsically good. Human beings possess this intrinsic value by virtue of their capacity for valuing things rationally; they identify 'good ends' by means of making rational choices about what to value ('things are good because we desire or choose them' (187) or 'take an interest in them' (174), rather than our desiring them because they are good). The attraction of this theory is that it allows us to define 'objective' value as something conferred by human beings, under the conditions in which we live ('psychological, economic, historical, symbolic', and so forth (195)). The drawbacks (as one might expect from a Kantian view) include perhaps too great an emphasis on coherence of reasoning as the basis of our relations with the things we care about; (relatedly) too strong an assumption about the capacity of universal laws to confer human identity; and (relatedly again) too buoyant an expectation of 'grounding ethical life in something like psychic health or a state of flourishing'.[7]

I am, of course, selecting from a very large contemporary literature on intrinsic value. It would be misleading to suggest that intrinsic

[5] See, for example, Wlodek Rabinowicz and Toni Rønnow-Rasmussen, 'A Distinction in Value: Intrinsic and For its Own Sake', *Proceedings of the Aristotelian Society* NS 100 (2000), 33–51; and Dale Dorsey, 'Can Instrumental Value be Intrinsic?', *Pacific Philosophical Quarterly* 93 (2012), 137–57 (pursuing a related argument that instrumental value may sometimes qualify as intrinsic value. See also Thomas Hurka, 'Two Kinds of Organic Unity', *Journal of Ethics* 2 (1998), 299–320, for a sceptical assessment of the degree of agreement between the conditionality interpretation of intrinsic value proffered by Korsgaard and the holistic interpretation associated with Moore and his followers.

[6] Christine M. Korsgaard, 'Two Distinctions in Goodness', *Philosophical Review* 92/2 (1983), 169–95 (170).

[7] Objections raised by, respectively, Thomas Nagel, Raymond Guess, Bernard Williams. See Korsgaard, with G. A. Cohen, Raymond Guess, Thomas Nagel, Bernard Williams, *The Sources of Normativity*, ed. Onora O'Neill (Cambridge: Cambridge University Press, 1996), 201, 192, 213. For Korsgaard's reply to these and other comments, see 219–58.

value has suffered a final philosophical defeat or (on the other hand) that reservations about it are of recent appearance. If the term now seems to many who employ it a failed enterprise, necessarily girded round with caution, irony, self-consciousness, then this is nothing new, the primary difference being the degree of cumulative erosion in conviction. *OED*'s first three recorded usages for 'intrinsic value' are presented within the third definition for 'intrinsic' in the adjectival form:

intrinsic adj. 3a. Belonging to the thing in itself, or by its very nature; inherent, essential, proper; 'of its own'.

1642 J. Howell *Instr. Forreine Travell* ix. 116 If one would go to the intrinsique value of things.

1661–98 R. South *12 Serm.* III. 57 As if every such single Act could by its own Intrinsick Worth merit a glorious Eternity.

1691 J. Locke *Money* in *Wks.* (1727) II. 67 The intrinsick Value of Silver consider'd as Money, is that Estimate which common Consent has placed on it.[8]

All three citations approach the term 'intrinsic' as a conditional effect, a hypothetical, a provisional result of consensus, not fixed. Howell, perhaps the least obviously complicating at first glance, is in fact writing of the advantages to France of remaining 'insular' from Spain in its political and trading arrangements—of keeping 'most' of its trade 'intrinsique', though the whole cannot be.[9] 'Intrinsic value' speaks from the start (or as far back as the dictionary has yet recorded[10]) of an impossible and probably undesirable isolationism in valuation.

Ruskin, as it happens, is not among the subsequent citations of 'supporting evidence' offered by the dictionary,[11] but his name has been crucial to recent attempts to make good 'intrinsic value' for the English language. If he deserves special notice even now, in spite of the 'historical inaccuracy' of his employment of the term, and with his paternalistic benevolence towards the added value of labour,[12] it is (Geoffrey Hill suggests) because his social writings lent the term an 'aura' that was distinctively forward looking where others had preferred elegy, or a fantasy of restoration. The elegiac version Hill finds encapsulated in Hobbes's dedication of *Leviathan* to the memory of the dead Sidney

---

[8] Accessed 24 September 2012.
[9] James Howell, *Instructions for Forrein Travell* (London, 1642), sect. ix, p. 116.
[10] 'Intrinsic' is one of the as yet unrevised *OED* entries, dating from 1900.
[11] Hill, 'Poetry and Value' (2001), *CCW* 478–89 (481).
[12] Hill, 'Translating Value', 389.

Godolphin's 'inhaerent' virtue; the restorative view is exemplified for Hill in Hume's account of the 'durable admiration' attending those works that survive 'the caprices of mode and fashion, . . . the mistakes of ignorance and envy' (388). Where for Hobbes intrinsic or 'inherent' value is extinct and mourned, for Hume it is under constant threat but potentially retrievable—inherent value is value that 'has always been there' though concealed by human error, caprice, misjudgement. Ruskin holds out, by comparison, a positive definition of intrinsic value as contained possibility or 'promise': that form of value bound up in things that support life, a power or worth that (used or unused) escapes reduction to the effects of supply and demand:

Intrinsic value is the absolute power of anything to support life. A sheaf of wheat of given quality and weight has in it a measurable power of sustaining the substance of the body; a cubic foot of pure air, a fixed power of sustaining its warmth; and a cluster of flowers of given beauty, a fixed power of enlivening or animating the senses and heart.

It does not in the least affect the intrinsic value of the wheat, the air, or the flowers, that men refuse or despise them. Used or not, their own power is in them, and that particular power is in nothing else.[13]

The Beatitudes ('Consider the lilies of the field. . .'[14]) blend into anti-utilitarian pastoralism here. The supporting of life is understood generously—not as a mere 'sustenance of the body' (though sustaining physical life of course matters) but as a vital sustenance also of the heart and mind through 'given beauty' and the power of sensory 'animation'.

No one has pressed the allure and the vulnerability of that 'aura' harder than Hill, who must, indeed, stand as the prime exponent of a modern intention to keep faith with the commitment to 'just' dealing with ideas and words expressed by the term 'intrinsic value', despite full knowledge of philosophical objections to the term's lack of clarity. Hill, it may be objected at this point, if not sooner, is scarcely a 'representative figure' in

---

[13] *Munera Pulveris: Six Essays on the Elements of Political Economy* (1872), in *The Works of John Ruskin*, ed. E. T. Cooke and Alexander Wedderburn, 39 vols. (London: George Allen, 1903–12), xvii. 118–293 (153). Michael McKie has some hard things to say about Hill 'misunderstand[ing]' Ruskin here—overlooking or denying a precision in Ruskin's use of 'intrinsic value' in opposition to Mill (and others). I cannot myself see that Hill is wrong about the 'aura' Ruskin gives to the term, or about its definitional incompleteness. Michael McKie, 'In Defence of Poetry', Review of David-Antoine Williams, *Defending Poetry* (2010), *Essays in Criticism* 61/4 (2011), 421–31 (426–7).

[14] Matthew 6: 28–9.

contemporary debate about value (though who is?), but the very distance at which he works from most others in the strenuously theological cast of his writing gives the more significance to those aspects of his
thinking that chime with more general concerns about the tenability or
otherwise of claims for the 'intrinsic value' of the things the humanities
study. I select him here over the most obvious alternative, John Dewey
arguing against intrinsic value and in favour of contextual valuation,[15]
for forensic reasons: partly because the pessimistic cast of Hill's thinking,
by contrast with the optimism of Dewey, allows me to press a harder
scepticism before trying to rescue a 'for its own sake' argument; partly
because Hill's poetry allows me to take the theoretical discussion of
value directly into the practical work of critical valuation.

'I do not myself see', Hill writes in 'Translating Value',

> that a longing for something indispensable is *per se* misguided; though I con-
> cede the dangers and would accept that most attempts to embody the 'longing'
> create metaphysical wraiths. Ruskin's 'intrinsic value' is, in and of itself, such a
> wraith; but, according to my argument, it remains a term which points in the
> right direction, towards semantic realizations that have some substance. (390)

For Hill substantive 'realizations' of value are less objects of desire than
cause for continual ethical striving. His endeavours to refine the term
over the years would be critically incomprehensible without recognition of their foundation in his Christianity. Hill believes in original sin,
and understands our efforts to secure meaning and value through language as inseparable from 'that terrible aboriginal calamity'.[16] 'I would
seriously propose a theology of language', he writes in 'Language, Suffering, and Silence' (1999): 'This would comprise a critical examination of the grounds for claiming (a) that the shock of semantic
recognition must be also a shock of ethical recognition; and that this
is the action of grace in one of its minor, but far from trivial, types;
(b) that the art and literature of the late twentieth century require a
memorializing, a memorizing, of the dead…'.[17] The primary realization

---

[15] See the *Theory of Valuation*, in Dewey, *The Later Works, 1925–1953*, Collected Works of
John Dewey, vol. xiii: 1938–1939, *Experience and Education, Freedom and Culture, Theory of
Valuation, and Essays*, ed. Jo Ann Boydston, with an introduction by Steven M. Cahn (Carbondale, Ill.: Southern Illinois University Press, 1988), 189–251. Dewey rejects intrinsic
value, asking us to see values instead as contextual judgements that cannot be wrenched
out of the contexts giving them value and meaning.

[16] 'Common Weal, Common Woe' (1989), *CCW* 265–79 (279) quoting Newman.

[17] *CCW* 394–406 (405).

of value that emerges from this theology of language takes the form of ethical work: the poetic and critical endeavour to gauge value through the accurate weighing of words—not least the weighing of their inevitable imprecisions and ambiguities. We are, in a metaphor sounded in depth within the poetic sequence *Scenes from Comus* (2005), accountants who cannot make ourselves or our words 'add up', but who will ultimately be held to account for our speech.[18]

The changing ways in which Hill's poetry and criticism have assayed 'intrinsic value' in language, in the hope of pointing us in 'the right direction', are substantial matter for study in their own right.[19] Hill wants our endeavours in the language—especially poetic and critical language—to have intrinsic value insofar as they can withstand the corrosions, debasements, falsifications of the world of commerce and our own fallen condition. Language is the medium in which that condition expresses itself but in which, still, we may hope to find succour, even grace. A problem, even for admirers of Hill (and they include many who do not share his theology or agree with all his judgments), is that it has sometimes followed that he has wanted to supplement and secure our efforts at virtuous action with a claim to the intrinsic value of the achieved poem—its value then standing, in some elusive sense, independent of our engagement with it.

My purpose here being a reckoning not only with the defence of poetry but with justifications for the humanities, one iteration of that endeavour (and probably the best known) will have to suffice. Given this chapter's concern with how we value the *content* of the humanities, there is evident merit in putting a specific work on the page. From *The Triumph of Love* (1998):

> *Active virtue:* that which shall contain
> its own passion in the public weal—
> do you follow?—or can you at least
> take the drift of the thing? The struggle
> for a noble vernacular: this
> did not end with Petrarch. But where is it?
> Where has it got us? Does it stop, in our case,
> with Dryden, or, perhaps,

---

[18] Quoted and discussed in David-Antoine Williams, *Defending Poetry: Art and Ethics in Joseph Brodsky, Seamus Heaney, and Geoffrey Hill* (Oxford: Oxford University Press, 2010), 166–7.

[19] The most extensive account to date is Williams, *Defending Poetry*, ch. 4.

Milton's political sonnets?—the cherished stock
hacked into ransom and ruin; the voices
of distinction, far back, indistinct.
Still, I'm convinced that shaping,
voicing, are types of civic action. Or, slightly
to refashion this, that Wordsworth's two
Prefaces stand with his great tract
on the Convention of Cintra, witnessing
to the praesidium in the sacred name
of things betrayed. *Intrinsic value*
I am somewhat less sure of. It seems
implicate with active virtue but I cannot
say how, precisely. Partaking of both
fact and recognition, it must be, therefore,
in effect, at once agent and predicate:
imponderables brought home
to the brute mass and detail of the world;
there, by some, to be pondered.[20]

The 'active virtue' involved in the poet's struggle for a noble vernacu-
lar Hill takes in starting, to be definite: definable, having achieved form
in the 'cherished' historical 'stock' or root of our poetry, such poetry as
has contained 'passion in the public weal' (Petrarch, Dryden, Milton,
Wordsworth). Active virtue requires the drawing of one's own private
'eccentricities' of powerful emotion and interest[21] into the public weal
or wealth (the word 'public' deliberately preferred to the false promise
of 'common'[22]). But the desired definition comes under quick suspicion of indefinition in the following lines and in the analysis of our
contemporary civic realm that they hold out for our contemplation.
So, the quasi-lexicographic opening statement is not strictly a definition: rather, the declaration of a future-directed ideal; or, perhaps, a
pronouncement that mimics a performative utterance (that disputed
power of poetry[23]). The desired definition drifts mimetically, but also
confessedly, towards indistinction. 'Active virtue' (distinct grammatical
subject) becomes 'the thing', 'this', 'it'.

[20] *The Triumph of Love* (1998) (London: Penguin Books, 1999) Sect. LXX, 36–7.
[21] On 'passion' see *CCW* 72, 107, 129, 190 (on Dryden's openness to passion as both
'the effect of cheating eloquence and the source of "noble eagerness" '), and, especially,
483–4 on language as 'a form of seismograph: registering and retaining the myriad shocks
of humanity's interested and disinterested passions'.
[22] See 'Common Weal, Common Woe', 269.
[23] See 'Our Word Is our Bond' (1983), *CCW* 146–69.

Against this tendency to lose our hold on active virtue, Hill will assert 'still' (even now, even so, allaying doubts) that the activities of shaping and saying are types (models, emblems, prefigurings) of virtuous civic action. But can he claim for them 'intrinsic value'? The pondering of the intrinsic through these lines works in reverse to that of active virtue: it starts in indistinction—announcing an object he would fain be certain of—and gradually accrues definition, or rather 'weight' would be the better word, since the lines are beset by evidence of a grammatical and lexical struggle for this to be an act of definition and not merely a talking into being or instantiation. (The overall structural effect is not quite chiasmus, but close to it.) This is an idea of 'intrinsic value' that Hill wants us to know he knows is in trouble, though he is prepared to press on. When something is given away with respect to it ('I cannot say how') it is quickly reclaimed ('precisely')—not the saying but the precision in question. If the language protests too much ('it must be') it concedes its own weakness ('therefore, in effect'), though without conceding the point. 'In effect' dissolves certainty but also directs us towards 'effects', achieved works where intrinsic value may be found. Hill's reliance on grammar here as both underpinning *techne* and a source of analogy invites us to think about grammar itself as at once part of the mechanism of the weighing and an element in what is being weighed. It structures the pondered relation between intrinsic value and attributed value, the thing itself and the qualities attached to it, but it also threatens to unmoor it—to discover the agent as properly a predicate, or, to put it another way, as just an aura effected by our attribution of qualities. (One could observe something similar with Hill's use of the troche in ways that moor and unmoor, declare weight and take it away. But I must move on.)

'Brute mass' is, presumably, Hill going back to C. S. Peirce's statement that 'Actuality is something *brute*: there is no reason in it'.[24] I confess, I am not at ease with these final lines, and not only because the notion of 'bringing imponderables "home" to where there is no reason' sounds, for the context, too like throwing in the towel altogether. The deixis—the 'there'—offers a grammatical bringing home of the subject that nicely ambiguates: it is 'there', achieved (intrinsic value upheld) but also 'over there', out of reach. The 'by some', however, gives trouble since it cannot but sound as 'by me, Geoffrey Hill' (picking

---

[24] See 'Our Word Is our Bond', 163; and 'Dryden's Prize Song' (1991), *CCW* 226–42 (229).

up on 'I am somewhat'). Hill wants the F. H. Bradley-esque pitch of 'some': not a 'planned evasion' or 'cop-out' but an act of apprehension that cannot make it as far as articulation—what would be apprehended in this case being as much the problem of value as value itself.[25] He also, presumably, wants the sonorousness of 'some . . . pond[er]', but for this reader the awareness of Hill putting a figure on the scales, nudging intrinsic value just that fraction towards apprehension, disturbs the pitch.

The intrusion of the first person explicitly on my own part, as (I detect) implicitly on Hill's, is deliberate. It is no disparagement of Hill, who knows this too, to say that the sorting out of good readers from bad, attentive weighers of semantics from the inattentive, admits the kind of contingency in judgement, despite all efforts to rise above contingency, that so bothered Hume. There are, after all, elements in judgement that cannot be 'realized' as if they were facts—cannot be apprehended or touched with the finger 'on the place', as Hill (in 1999) would have it. In part this is because, as Peter Robinson puts it, after Bradley, 'no one [not even Hill] has read enough to command the data;'[26] in part because there are legitimate differences in the judgements we may reach on the basis of the same evidence.

Hume attempted to get around the problem of how, then, one establishes public agreements about what is and is not worthy of valuation, through the pliability of the term 'taste'. 'Taste' is an old-fashioned and largely discredited term for the subjective response to art (and the term 'humanities' won't do here, though the point about subjectivity in aesthetic valuation is germane to the question of subjectivity in valuation generally—including as it bears on the aesthetic and non-aesthetic aspects of the humanities). 'Taste' smacks unappealingly now of Saintsbury comparing criticism with wine-tasting, but it is not obvious what other term in the critical lexicons of today is doing the work this word or its near companion 'sensibility' once did—work that cultural criticism has largely abandoned, though philosophy of value, of course, has not. Hill is an exception, weighing the word 'taste' closely, in his reading of Hume and Hobbes, as he considers the pressure of 'collective opinion upon individual judgement' ('Translating Value', 384).

---

[25] See 'Word Value in F. H. Bradley and T. S. Eliot' (2001), *CCW* 532–47 (533).

[26] 'Contemporary Poetry and Value', in Peter Robinson (ed.), *The Oxford Handbook of Contemporary British and Irish Poetry* (Oxford: Oxford University Press, forthcoming 2013).

Contaminated though 'taste', and 'sensibility', were, from the start, by social caste, Hume used both terms to open up the response to the aesthetic as a field of experience and judgement with its basis in the sense impressions of the individual mind and body—a move which then required convincing arguments to close the gap between the phantasm of individual sensation and the common social ownership of standards of taste. It is a weakness of Hume's account of subjectivism, David Wiggins points out, that it rests so heavily on 'an analogy between...aesthetic taste and ordinary sensory (gustatory, *etc.*) taste', an analogy which doesn't help us much with the *epistemological* difficulty of relating one's individual response to any 'true and decisive standard' in aesthetics or in morals. It is a *strength* of the metaphor, Wiggins observes, that it prompts Hume to think about 'the *condition of the judge*' ('strong sense, united to delicate sentiment, improved by practice, perfected by comparison, cleared of all prejudice') and to posit these qualities as substantial and demonstrable and possessed by large numbers of people.[27]

But this produces a paradox, or something close to a paradox: in order to deal with what is internal to the individual, a 'phantas[m] of the feelings' (192), Hume must produce a *non*-subjective foundation in an independent standard of taste, supported by a 'nearly homogenous human nature' (Wiggins 193; the term 'paradox' is his). To that degree, Hume might seem to anticipate the tendency now to treat individual responses as immediately generalizable—via, for example, a theory of emotion, or cognition, or the social conditioning of subjectivity.[28] But there seems to me an important difference in that the language of taste at least retains an acknowledgement of a double epistemological difficulty: the difficulty of connecting the qualities of the object to the response of the subject; and the difficulty, in turn, of connecting that individual subjective response to a true standard. As Hill puts it: 'The significance of Hume on Taste is that he sees it partly as "wrought", a

---

[27] *Needs, Values, Truth: Essays in the Philosophy of Value*, 3rd edn. (Oxford: Clarendon Press, 1998), 191–3. The quotation in parentheses is from Hume, 'Of the Standard of Taste', in *Essays Moral, Political, and Literary*, ed. Eugene F. Miller, rev. edn. (Indianapolis: Liberty Classics, 1987), 231–58 (247).

[28] For a much more extended discussion of this point in relation to aesthetic theory, see my essay 'Caprice: On Aesthetic Subjectivism', in Ronan McDonald (ed.), *The Values of Literary Studies* (Cambridge: Cambridge University Press, forthcoming, 2014). Also John Guillory, *Cultural Capital* (Chicago: University of Chicago Press, 1993), 276–84; and Isobel Armstrong, *The Radical Aesthetic* (Oxford: Blackwell Publishers, 2000), 157–61.

matter of prejudicates, and in part arrived at through a mental discipline, a self-knowledgeable understanding of how deeply prejudiced we are, even—or especially—in our common agreements' (385). Where I have to part company from Hill is at the implication that submitting ourselves to 'mental discipline' and understanding our own prejudices is enough by way of response to the non-intrinsic qualities that impinge upon what we would want to call intrinsic value.

Hill's efforts to redeem—not 'intrinsic value' but the notion of just dealing with the standard of value which it precariously enshrines—are (as far as I am aware) the furthest any contemporary writer has pressed 'intrinsic value' as a 'philosophical term of art'. That they are arduous efforts probably goes without saying. Some of that arduousness is unavoidable. We might well think that it would be better for us to be able to make arguments for intrinsic value that are not dependent on 'metaphysical wraiths' like Korsgaard's and Kant's intrinsically good will or a belief in final or basic value derived from belief in God. But, as Mill put it, 'Questions of ultimate ends are not amenable to direct proof.'[29] As he immediately went on to say, this does not mean that they are unamenable to considerations that will 'determine the intellect either to give or withhold its assent' (208).

There is no possibility of a non-metaphysical defence for the intrinsic value of the humanities. There is, however, ample room for a considered account of why the humanities are worthy of our valuing them 'for their own sake'. Mill's own preference for the 'for its own sake' idiom (alternatively, for things being 'desirable as ends', 'in themselves good', 'good as ends') is never directly explained in his writing. There is a reasonable case to be made that Moore was wrong in attributing to him a strong belief in 'intrinsic value' as dependent solely on the intrinsic properties of the thing in question.[30] There is also some evidence that he held reservations not unlike those Kagan expresses: namely, that he understood that non-intrinsic properties can contribute to the intrinsic value of a thing. (In utilitarian terms: that 'the intrinsic desirability of an experience may be enhanced by other components of it than the pleasure

---

[29] *Utilitarianism*, with an introductory essay by D. P. Dryer, in *Essays on Ethics, Religion and Society*, ed. John M. Robson, introduction by F. E. L. Priestley, *CW* x (London: Routledge and Kegan Paul, 1985), 203–59 (207).

[30] See Guy Fletcher, 'Mill, Moore, and Intrinsic Value', *Social Theory and Practice* 34/4 (2008), 517–32.

enjoyed in it',[31] though pleasure alone is deemed, by the utilitarian, 'intrinsically good'.) If this is right, his choice of terms may well reflect similar concerns about the false purity implied by the term 'intrinsic'.

But how far does the move to the more relaxed, less philosophically 'fetishizable' (because less ostensibly technical) idiom of 'for its own sake' help us? At least one late twentieth-century philosopher reflecting on the term has found it 'paradoxical'. Like other 'reflexive-related constructions', T. S. Champlin claims—especially those generated by the prefix 'self' (self-evidence, self-generation, self-explanatoriness)— 'for its own sake' looks like a philosophical cheat. In this instance, the problem lies with appearing to present something as the means to its own end.'Doing A for the sake of doing A.'[32] Does the term 'sake' have any purchase here?

It is an attractive feature of 'for its own sake' that 'sake', though not a technical term, has a degree of opacity about it taken in isolation. It is not readily paraphrasable, so that, though we generally think we know what the phrase means, the main term on which it leans requires some elucidation by way of lexicography. As an 'independent substantive' 'sake' is, OED tells us, obsolete. Meaning, in Old English, 'contention, strife, dispute;... a contention at law; a suit, cause, action', also 'A charge or accusation (of guilt); a ground of accusation' (hence often indicative in Old English of 'guilt, sin; a fault, offence, crime'), it survives now only in phrases:'for the sake of ';'for (one's, a thing's) sake'.[33] In these phrasal forms 'sake' is given the following glosses:'Out of consideration for; on account of one's interest in, or regard for (a person); on (a person's) account'; or, without special relation to persons,'out of regard or consideration for (a thing); on account of, because of (something regarded in the light of an end, aim, purpose, etc.); often = out of desire for, in order to attain, etc.'[34]

If 'for the sake of' is to mean 'on account of one's interest in' or one's 'consideration' or 'desire for something', then 'for its own sake' does indeed present a puzzling self-reflexivity:'on account of its interest

[31] See D. P. Dryer,'Mill's *Utilitarianism*', in Mill, *Utilitarianism*, lxiii–cxiii (lxxxix), and sect. III 'What is Desirable For its Own Sake' *passim*.

[32] T. S. Champlin,'Doing Something for its Own Sake', *Philosophy* 63/239 (1987), 31–47 (32, 33).

[33] See *OED Online: sake n. 1* I. I, 2, and 3a. Accessed 26 September 2012.

[34] See *OED Online: sake n. 1* 6a and 7a. Accessed 26 September 2012.

in or consideration for or desire for itself'? The old association with guilt complicates further, since it offers to ghost the phrase with a more conflictual self-reflexivity: 'on account of its being in contention with itself'. In either reading, 'sake' threatens to double the act of accounting. 'On account of its being on its own account'. But reading 'sake' off as a compacted phrase within a phrase rather misses the point, since one of the distinguishing features of the historically entrenched phrase (generally speaking) is that it can conjure not so much a unified notion as a portable effect of style. 'A phrase is a group of words', I was taught (with an understandable concern to simplify) by my primary school teachers; later grammar lessons admitted a degree of complication, 'which either doesn't have a noun attached to a predicate or doesn't have a finite verb' (compare 'clause'). But a phrase is also 'a turn of phrase' (a degree less exacting than a philosophical 'term of art'), 'a common or idiomatic expression', 'a striking or pithy expression'.[35]

Champlin's path through the philosophical problems this semantic 'inexactness' presents takes a very similar route to Korsgaard's (his paper was written with other aims in view, the coincidence of method here being testimony to the extent to which Kant attached his name to the idea of doing good 'for its own sake'). But where Korsgaard holds on to the Kantian metaphysical condition (the protection of the good will as the one stronghold of intrinsic value), Champlin is even less happy to accept the exclusion of 'ulterior considerations' from the definition of 'genuine' worth.[36]

Consider the Desert Island Discs scenario. (I update it from its 1987 form in Champlin):

You are cast away with Kirsty Young on a desert island and asked to choose eight pieces of music to take with you. 'Did you choose this piece of music for reasons of nostalgia or for its own sake?' asks Kirsty. 'I chose this piece, not as a peg on which to hang a memory, but because I find it very beautiful. Listening to it gives me great pleasure' is your reply. Kirsty, turned Kantian inquisitor, pounces. 'You claim', she says, 'to have chosen the music for its own sake, yet you also admit that you chose the music for the sake of its beauty and for the pleasure it gives you.' (Adapted from Champlin, 36)

---

[35] OED Online: phrase, n.: 1, 2, and 3.
[36] Immanuel Kant, Groundwork of the Metaphysics of Morals, ed. Mary Gregor, introduction by Christine M. Korsgaard, Cambridge Texts in the History of Philosophy (Cambridge: Cambridge University Press, 1997), 12.

'But this is, surely, quite mad', Champlin objects—presumably on the grounds that beauty is here a good-making property of something good in itself. It isn't of course mad, if one is pursuing a metaphysical security for final value—but it does look a bit that way if it is taken to express naive dismay not just at the impurity of the notion of the good but at the impurity of human motives for affirming value. The 'rule of action', as Mill put it, is one thing; the actual motive felt or espoused quite another. Or to put it another way, one has to distinguish metaphysics from psychology in matters of valuation, and 'for its own sake' may have an advantage in clarity over 'intrinsic value' here insofar as it keeps the psychological component in valuation more clearly in view.

The consequences of frankly admitting the psychological impurity of our motives for valuing things are liberating. Champlin puts it nicely in concluding that the temptation towards value 'isolationism' held out by the phrase 'for its own sake' is something we can and should guard against: when Wilde and other late nineteenth-century aesthetes adopted the phrase 'Art for art's sake' they were not 'divorcing art from life'; they were insisting that 'the artist is not in the service of religion, conventional morality, party politics, diplomacy, patriotism, the state or any of the other forces which try to reduce art to a means to their ends and to rob art of the status of an end in itself' (47). For present purposes, the important part of this description is the opening clarification: that 'for its own sake' declares free-standing valuation while not isolating the thing valued 'from life'. Once one allows that the rule (valuation of the thing 'as an end') admits of many different means (desire, interest, pleasure, memory, anxiety) by which an individual comes to observe the rule, in the non-dogmatic sense of 'observe', then the problem of falsely isolating the thing valued from its contexts disappears. One has, then, the possibility of our concurring, or indeed not concurring, with the value of a thing 'for its own sake' without the valuation being discredited by the variety, or even the incoherence, of the routes by which we approach it.

To say this much does not of course answer the question of how agreements about value are reached in the first place, or what degree of consensus is requisite to support continuing acceptance of them as (inter alia) worthwhile objects of study. 'There will be much argument, ultimately about value', Frank Kermode predicted in 1997 amidst agitated debate about falling numbers of students taking humanities courses in the USA (the apparent exceptionality of English courses thought to be explained by the large number of women students still excluded from entry-level science). In the end, we have to fall back on one thing, Kermode thought: intuitions of value, 'without which the task is nearly hopeless'.[37] But we can also put considerable weight (and I add to Kermode here) on long-standing cultural agreements and evolving local settlements about what in our culture has more and less durable worth for us and (not always the same thing) what will reward study. These might themselves be seen as 'intuitions', if intuitions are taken to be non-inferential, foundational beliefs.

T. S. Eliot thought that there was a distinction to be made between our valuation of the objects of our study and our valuation of the effects of studying them: a distinction, indeed, between intrinsic and non-intrinsic value. 'I do not deny that art may be affirmed to serve ends beyond itself', he writes in 'The Function of Criticism' (1923), 'but art is not required to be aware of these ends, and indeed performs its function, whatever that may be, according to various theories of value, much better by indifference to them. Criticism on the other hand, must always profess an end in view…'[38] Up to this point Eliot's claims for art have been conventionally aestheticist, in the sense that he wants art to be answerable only to itself. His most immediately visible interlocutor is Arnold, whose prescription for the disinterestedness of criticism Eliot here arrogates to art, thereby distinguishing it from criticism (a tightening up, rather than a dismissal, of Arnold's view).[39] Like Arnold, Eliot wants to oppose the idea that writing literature is just a matter of 'doing as one likes' (27). He wants to be able to say 'what is right', and to recognize a standard of authority 'outside [one]self' (29). So, having seemed to set art against criticism, Eliot now deepens the distinction even as he brings it into question. To differentiate art from criticism, he says,

[37] 'Changing Epochs', in Alvin Kernan (ed.), *What's Happened to the Humanities?* (Princeton: Princeton University Press, 1997), 162–78 (177, 169).

[38] In T. S. Eliot, *Selected Essays*, 3rd enlarged edn. (London: Faber and Faber, 1951), 23–34 (24).

[39] Arnold, 'The Function of Criticism at the Present Time', in *Lectures and Essays in Criticism*, ed. R. H. Super, *CPW* iii (Ann Arbor: University of Michigan Press, 1962), 258–85 (283): 'I am bound by my own definition of criticism: *a disinterested endeavour to learn and propagate the best that is known and thought in the world.* How much of current English literature comes into this "best that is known and thought in the world"? Not very much, I fear… Well, then, am I to alter my definition of criticism, in order to meet the requirements of a number of practising English critics, who after all, are free in their choice of a business? That would be making criticism lend itself just to one of those alien practical considerations, which, I have said, are so fatal to it.'

'overlooks the capital importance of criticism in the work of creation itself ':

> Probably . . . the larger part of the labour of an author in composing his work is critical labour; the labour of sifting, combining, constructing, expunging, correcting, testing: this frightful toil is as much critical as creative. (30)

The staginess of 'frightful' is a nice touch: a self-mocking Woosterishness that registers the neurotic risking of oneself involved in the 'chore' of getting it right. But the questionable move to internalize critical labour to the work of art, and indeed the language, seems very much in keeping with Hill's own defence of the intrinsic value of poetry: a defence that rests not just on knowing one's facts, and on technical mastery, but on the ethical integrity demanded by accurate gauging of the semantic weight of words through alertness to their history (it is not the only way of gauging accuracy, but the one that matters most to Hill). But Eliot's defence is, necessarily, vulnerable to the same objections, and in the context of valuing not art, not literature, only, but 'the humanities' it once again sets the bar of judgement too high or (more accurately) too exclusively in terms of aesthetic judgement.

The criteria for what will reward study in the humanities are in the main more relaxed than the criteria for aesthetic or cultural value. Long-standing cultural agreements and evolving local settlements, backed (where aesthetic judgements *are* concerned) by intuition and long study, are probably as good as we can get by way of accounting for the curricula of today's literature departments (Kermode's immediate concern)—often thought to be risibly lacking in agreed criteria for worth. In any subject where beauty may be one of the criteria for valuation—literature, music, the arts—judgements of aesthetic value will necessarily have to find a place among judgements of what deserves attention because it is part of the history of the subject's ongoing formation, or part of the rich diversity of cultural practices, or has political salience now, or represents one among many kinds of technical development. What is worthy of study in one area of the English or Music or Art or Cultural Studies department may fail entirely to warrant selection on grounds of the historical significance or analytic intelligence or logical exactness or ethical depth that would be reasons for admission to study within the History or Philosophy faculties, or even in other areas of the one department. Beyond this the work of justifying the value of curricula has to be pursued at the level of the discipline and cannot be generalized.

In saying this I can confess to a certain amount of relief at being able to sidestep the quarrelsome terrain that has been 'the question of the canon' in literature departments for many decades now, and that still intermittently provokes headlines in the press.[40] There is an especially unlovely genre that is the love letter to literature and to the humanities more widely, presented by a professor of literature, in the form of hate mail to the profession.[41] It is a standard observation of that genre, shared by many who do not endorse the pessimism or the anti-professionalism, that literary studies is the representative discipline of the humanities: the discipline in relation to which the wider public formulates ideas about the value of the humanities as a whole: what its true value is; whether the university today does or does not properly recognize that value.

Insofar as that claim has any justice at all (and it seems to me to have very little; it is typically made by professors of English, and not by those who might want to challenge their priority—say, the professors of History or Philosophy), there are evident reasons why it might be thought so. As Stanley Fish has repeatedly remarked, the fact that many people read and care about literature, with other interests and pleasures in view than those that belong to its formal study, means that they can be inclined to view academic statements about literature (whether theoretical or historical or 'just' technical) as obscurantist or, worse, as a deformation of the 'real' value of the subject. The sense of a cultural propriety in the object of study tends to be especially strong when it is attached to a Romantic-Arnoldian belief in the study of literature as the study of 'life itself' (see Chapter 1). Such protectionism of literature outside the academy, Fish observes, is often coupled with a tendency to deplore 'those aspects of the academy which smack of the marketplace—matters of publishing, tenure, and professional power'.[42]

To the problem of how the wider public perceives the contributions of literary criticism to the general good must be added the

---

[40] The best treatment of those problems remains, in my view, Guillory, *Cultural Capital.*

[41] The examples are too many to list, but for an indication, see Andrew Delbanco, 'The Decline and Fall of English Studies', *New York Review of Books* 4 November 1999: <http://www.nybooks.com/articles/archives/1999/nov/04/the-decline-and-fall-of-literature/>.

[42] 'Profession Despise Thyself: Fear and Self-Loathing in Literary Studies', in Fish, *Doing What Comes Naturally*, 197–214 (198). Fish defines anti-professionalism as 'any attitude or argument that enforces a distinction between professional labors on the one hand and the identification of what is true or valuable on the other'. 'Anti-Professionalism', in *Doing What Comes Naturally*, 215–46 (215).

peculiar incoherence that has long infected public understanding of the function of criticism. As Bruce Robbins remarks, the near para-doxical standing of literary criticism among the other disciplines as the 'staging ground for social critique when literature itself was losing its social influence' rests on its inheritance of a notion of culture as 'critical' (traced by Raymond Williams from Romanticism, through Arnold, Pater and their successors), where criticism is 'set against social activity—*by its very definition*'.[43] Declinism has been one rhe-torically powerful expression of this incoherence within the valuation of 'criticism', as manifested at the interface between the academy and the wider public sphere. There has been a tendency, especially pro-nounced in the States, where the professionalization of the subject was earlier codified and where the virtues of professionalization are historically more closely related to democratization,[44] to bemoan the supposed sequestration of the university from the public realm, even as the humanities departments enact their given role of providing critical distance. Hence the professional's sometime revulsion against what could only then appear hyper-professionalization; hence also the sometime wish to pull up an imaginary drawbridge between academy (ivory tower) and world.[45]

If this description looks less perfectly fitted to the UK in the early twenty-first century than it was to the USA in the late twentieth cen-tury, that may be in part because of continuing differences in the extent and the cultural valuation of professionalism in the States and not just the UK but many other countries in which the value of the humani-ties is being publicly debated at the time of writing. (America is, in that sense, a special case, and patterns of discussion originating there are potentially misleading when applied elsewhere.) The sense of some historical distance on the anti-professionalist rhetoric that was com-mon in the 1990s may also be evidence that well-placed criticism at the time had effect, and that asserting the value of the humanities at the expense of the humanities profession is less often the unthought through reflex, or own goal, it has often been.

---

[43] *Secular Vocations: Intellectuals, Professionalism, Culture* (London: Verso, 1993), 60–1.

[44] See Andrew Abbott, *Chaos of Disciplines*, 125, and *The System of Professions: An Essay on the Division of Expert Labor* (Chicago: University of Chicago Press, 1988), 324, 386n. Also Burton Bledstein, *The Culture of Professionalism: The Middle Class and the Development of Higher Education in America* (New York: W. W. Norton & Co. Inc., 1976).

[45] See Robbins, *Secular Vocations*, esp. chs. 2 and 3.

Other disciplines, after all, have their versions of conflict between the priorities of the academy and those of 'the general public'—History, for example, can find itself in similar difficulties when it deals with topics within living memory, or when it addresses subjects on which there are strong inherited beliefs (say, the rightness or wrongness of the historical prosecution of particular national interests). But it is at least clearer what the sources of historical 'knowledge' are, and in that sense history has sometimes claimed an advantage over literature when in the position of representing the humanities. 'Knowledge', as many have pointed out before me, is more of a component in what literature departments teach than we have sometimes been willing to say[46]—a point true also for philosophy, languages, the arts. If, as Chapter 1 explored, interpretation, judgement, and the performance of the scholar's own style are often deemed to be of more importance, these activities nevertheless supervene on, and would be impossible without, underlying disciplinary knowledge.

Newman, famously, thought that it was, in the final analysis, the apprehension of the value of knowledge 'for its own sake', that linked all the faculties of the liberal university:

I am asked what is the end of University Education, and of the Liberal or Philosophical Knowledge which I conceive it to impart: I answer, that what I have already said has been sufficient to show that it has a very tangible, real and sufficient end, though the end cannot be divided from that knowledge itself. Knowledge is capable of being its own end. Such is the constitution of the human mind, that any kind of knowledge, if it be really such, is its own reward...

Now, when I say that Knowledge is, not merely a means to something beyond it, or a preliminary of certain arts into which it naturally resolves, but an end sufficient to rest in and to pursue for its own sake, surely I am uttering no paradox, for I am stating what is both intelligible in itself, and has ever been the common judgement of philosophers and the ordinary feeling of mankind.[47]

---

[46] See esp. Guillory, 'Critical Response II', 540–1: 'Literary and cultural studies are not in a good position to defend the integrity of knowledge as an end in itself against the encroachment of market measures, or norms of efficiency and optimization, if they refuse to claim the status of positive knowledge, on the grounds that such knowledge is inherently "susceptible" to optimization. The humanistic disciplines might contribute more directly to the defense of disciplinary knowledge by drawing a closer analogy between scholarship as knowledge and the many examples of scientific knowledge that must be similarly enjoyed as the gratification of a desire to know, without answering necessarily to any further demand.'

[47] *The Idea of the University*, ed. I. T. Ker (Oxford: Clarendon Press, 1976), 96–7.

Newman strategically underestimated the extent of agreement between philosophers, then as now. He may have been right about the 'ordinary feeling of mankind' but that is rather less open to demonstration. If one excerpts the core claim, 'Knowledge is...its own end', he would certainly seem in danger of the kind of isolation of knowledge from its contexts that has bedevilled some versions of the claim to intrinsic value.

Stated without qualification, the claim would go too far, but it is hedged about, by Newman, with a high degree of caution not often remarked upon: knowledge is 'capable of being' its own end, though the 'real and sufficient end' to which it contributes is not made up of knowledge alone which is, rather, a contributing factor. Insofar as it is 'an end in itself' it has that status because of 'the constitution of the human mind' which leads us to take not pleasure exactly (pleasure not being high in Newman's lexicon of approbation) but 'reward'. These are, then, matters of psychology rather than logical exactness or even metaphysical security of definition (the fundamentally theological motive behind Newman's valuation of education notwithstanding). What we are offered, in sum, is not a perfect security but a 'sufficient intelligibility' in judgement for human purposes.

One can, and should, dispute Newman's insistence on the valuation of Knowledge as what finally unites us, but the manner of his apprehension of that value has surprisingly durable validity. By way of a strong recasting of Newman for the present day, this is John Guillory in 2003 (see Chapter 1) urging the humanities to be less quickly dismissive of their claim to knowledge.

Knowledge should be defended for its own sake, not solely for its instrumental benefits, because it is the object of a human desire, the desire to know, a desire that ought not to be frustrated any more than any other human desire.[48]

The order needs reversing: those who desire knowledge as good in itself will do so because they think that is good, not that it is good because they desire it. But desire has here the same rightly 'depurifying' effect on the 'for its own sake' claim that surety of reward had for Newman, reminding us that value as an end is still value as apprehended

<hr>

[48] Guillory, 'Critical Response II', 537.

by individual subjectivities within particular societies and cultures and at particular historical junctures. If one admits (*pace* Newman), alongside knowledge for its own sake, pleasure, work, interest, affect—all 'for their own sakes'—one has a range of modes of engagement with the objects of study that have, like those objects themselves, a legitimate claim to value as an end.

Conclusion
On Public Value

These, then, are the core reasons why the humanities have public value:

- they do a distinctive kind of work, preserve and extend distinctive kinds of understanding (broadly, qualitative understanding of the meaning making processes of the culture), and possess a distinctive relation to the idea of knowledge as being inextricable from human subjectivity. At moments when the public conversation about matters of common interest neglects or denies those distinctive modes of understanding (politically we are in such a moment now), this basic description of distinctiveness of intellectual labour may become a description of a political virtue, and the normally slight grounds for claiming characterological force for the humanities will become stronger than at moments when their modes of understanding are widely practised.

- their work is useful to society: it assists in the preservation and curation of the culture, and of the skills for interpreting and reinterpreting that culture to meet the needs and interests of the present; it trains students who go on to a wide range of practical activities; and its objects of study and the ways in which it studies them bring a variety of benefits to a culture well beyond that of the university itself. Usefulness is not to be sneered at, but it should be rated neither high nor low in the range of measures employed to gauge the public value of higher education in the humanities. This is a judgement about the prior relevance of other kinds of valuation, but it entails also considerations of language in the work of advocacy: any defence that gives primary place to the instrumental value of a humanities education will quickly disfigure the broader kinds of good it nurtures.

- the humanities may make a vital contribution to individual happiness and to the happiness of large groups. Some readers may want to incorporate this claim under the category of instrumental value, but the form of 'use' involved is not primarily economic and not directly instrumental, and it cannot be made to rest on the humanities' power reliably to make their students and scholars happier people. The contribution to happiness will sometimes be in the form of direct pleasures given, but it more importantly takes the form of deepening our understanding of what happiness consists in, how we may best hope to attain it, what the relation may be between the psychological happiness of the individual and the well-being of society, and how education may alter the quality as well as the range of pleasures available to the individual. This way of valuing the humanities has deep roots in the history of Western philosophy; it offers a richer and more accurate account of happiness than is recognized in most of the current economic and psychological literature on the subject.

- the humanities can make a vital contribution to the maintenance and the health of the democracy. That contribution rests on their role as centres for the higher study and practice of the skills of critical reasoning, debate, and evaluation of ideas that are 'the core practices of a democracy'. This is not a definitional description of the humanities but a claim generated by the perceived political needs of the democracy in the present moment. How far the humanities can claim special importance here depends very largely on the extent to which the kinds of intelligence they cultivate are respected and cultivated across all disciplines of the university, and across the wider society. When they are neglected by other disciplines, or underrepresented in public life, the claim of the humanities to be a modern institutionalized 'gadfly to the *polis*' will be at its strongest.

- none of these arguments is sufficient without a supporting claim that the value of the objects and cultural practices the humanities study and the kinds of scholarship they cultivate have value 'for their own sake'—that they are good in themselves. We can reject the misleading purity of a claim to intrinsic value (understood as the possession of value by virtue of intrinsic properties alone). The ostensibly less technical claim to value 'for its own sake' is stronger, because it admits that some objects and activities can have value 'as an end', independent of the means by which we individually arrive at agreement or disagreement with the valuation.

The 'for its own sake' claim is not a final answer or a complete defence. There are, and there will remain deep, disagreements about whether knowledge is an end in itself, or whether objects should be evaluated in terms of their instrumental value, or desire-satisfaction, or the contribution higher-level study of them can make to the quality of the democratic culture. But pursuing serious and informed reflection on these matters is in itself one of the definitional purposes of the humanities, and the preservation of that cultural good is among the reasons for valuing them.

These are the arguments that this book has sought to test. Each of them emerges as legitimate though not without bounds on their legitimacy. Together they comprise the ground for a pluralistic defence of the value of the humanities. They are all reasons that apply to how we may want to think about the value of studying the humanities ourselves. Casting them into the ring of debate about the public value of the humanities, however, requires something more to be said.

Advocating for the public value of the humanities constrains the nature of the debate in certain ways. It does not prohibit discussion of how (for example) they 'bring deep fulfilment to us personally' and 'often give meaning and shape to our lives',[1] but it does require such statements to be supported by some sense of how these potential benefits to the individual contribute to public life. As pressingly, thinking about the public value of higher scholarship in the humanities requires one to be able to distinguish different aspects to the idea of a public good. The kinds of good represented by the study of the humanities are not all expressible as 'economic goods' (at least one political theorist has argued that they are much better expressed as 'human goods'— counting among 'the "things" that contribute either directly or indirectly to human being', and that are of course 'richly diverse and heterogeneous in character'[2]). They rarely if ever have the status of

---

[1] David Willetts (Minister for Higher Education), 'The Arts, Humanities and Social Sciences in the Modern University', address to the British Academy, *British Academy Review*, issue 17 (March 2011), 54–8 (54–5, 57).

[2] Russell Keat, 'Market Boundaries and Human Goods', in John Haldane (ed.), *Philosophy and Public Affairs* (Cambridge: Cambridge University Press, 2000), 23–36 (27).

necessities. That is, it is hard to imagine circumstances under which they will meet the standard of basic requirement or 'vital interest' entailed in the word 'need'.[3] Few things do. We have an absolute need of something when we can accurately say that to be deprived of that thing will be to experience harm, or some serious impairment to our capacity to flourish: air, food, peace, a roof over our heads, basic health care, education in our formative years. On the other hand, it is a sign of being a prosperous, stable, educationally and culturally rich society that we can come to experience as 'needs' things whose absence or diminishment would be, strictly speaking, a relative rather than an absolute impoverishment. What would be meant, in such circumstances, by claiming that public support for scholarship in the humanities is 'necessary' is that it is 'strongly desired': for such support to be withdrawn would seem, to those many people who care deeply about the humanities, an impoverishment of their lives not to be silently tolerated (though it would be, in the unlikely *Raft of Medusa* situation, strictly tolerable).

Some people will want to say at this point that the language of need rightly expands its range in keeping with advancements in the wealth and complexity of the society concerned—that it comes to encompass the wish for prosperity. Given that absolute needs still exist, even in highly advanced societies, it seems to me better to retain the clarity of the language, and to talk rather of our desires and interests and cultural attachments as having a different priority from our needs, and requiring a different order of justification. In short, there is a rudimentary distinction to be made between needs (or vital interests) and desires or interests or cultural attachments (which may be strong, but not absolutely vital).[4]

Recognizing that these distinctions apply is only the first stage in comparative deliberation about public goods. The hard part of the problem is finding justifications for those non-necessary desirables that will enable meaningful comparison with other non-necessary desirables in a situation of practical deliberation. The necessities take themselves out of debate by virtue of being necessities. They are priorities

---

[3] See David Wiggins, *Needs, Values, Truth: Essays in the Philosophy of Value*, 3rd edn. (Oxford: Clarendon Press, 1998), 17.
[4] Needs claims are best understood as elliptical (I need X *for* Y), which suggests need-satisfaction is instrumental or at least non-ultimate.

that have to be met (though there will be debates about how to meet them most efficiently, and about which are the legitimate priorities and which the marginal, negotiable, or spurious ones). What one is left with, after that initial step, are problems of judgement: of arbitration between the claims of what will often be seen as incommensurable goods. These judgements of value are not, themselves, economic in kind, though they may well be the means to deciding the allocation of finite economic resources. They will require debate about the relative importance, in a given context, of different values and commitments, many of which will not obviously be rankable on the same scale.

There is a particular form of indignation, familiar within discussions of the value of the humanities, which produces or accompanies an outright refusal to engage with comparisons between incommensurables. The gist of the indignation is that the good of the humanities (for example) cannot be weighed in the balance against most other kinds of public good, because the goods entailed are not only incommensurable but incomparable. So, within the framework of university budgeting, the 'indignant response' would say that we cannot measure the value of the humanities against the value of the sciences or social sciences, because the kinds of work they do are fundamentally unalike; or—within the more complex frameworks required to decide government budgets—we cannot weigh the claims of university research in the humanities against investment in new forms of energy, or new hospitals, or additional resources for the armed forces, because educating the nation, improving its health, increasing its capacity to defend itself and its allies, are fundamentally non-comparable aims.

Whether and in what ways some values are indeed incommensurable and (for some) also incomparable is the subject of a now large literature within the philosophy of value and within economics. Given that my concern is with justifications, or reasons for claiming public value, I restrict my comments here to the philosophical debate, since I take the economic debate to follow from it, and to be a secondary interpretation of fundamentally philosophical issues. I take the term 'incommensurable' to mean 'lacking a common measure' (in Ruth Chang's definition), and to apply most appropriately to abstract values. 'Incomparable' I take to mean 'unable to be compared with respect to some specific covering consideration'; so, to borrow her example, 'two paintings may be incomparable with respect to beauty but comparable with respect to market value; two careers may be incomparable with respect to well-being but comparable with respect to economic-security'.[5]

The view that some values are so distinct as to be incommensurable and (in any generalizable, or theorizable way) incomparable has found eloquent expression from a number of philosophers, starting with Isaiah Berlin.[6] I shall focus on two more recent exponents of that view—David Wiggins and Joseph Raz—whose versions of incommensurability seem to me most pertinent to discussions about a public commitment to funding scholarship in the humanities as it may appear to be in competition with other public commitments. David Wiggins expresses the difficulty in this way:

Incommensurability…reflects the separateness and mutual irreducibility of the standing concerns that make up our orientation towards the distinct values and commitments (and whatever else) that impinge upon us in different sorts of situations. It reflects the fact that these concerns are not all variations upon a common theme.

…How then can the incommensurabilist who stresses the practical aspect of choice, and insists upon the unlimitedness, distinctness and separateness of the various values, concerns, commitments that we care about, best mark or signal all these things and relate them more precisely to the springs of action?

For Wiggins, there can be no satisfactory general answer to that question:

Where A and B are mutually incommensurable, the attempt to extrapolate from the actual choices [an agent makes] between them under such and such circumstances (and under this or that constraint) and the effort this entails on the theorist's part to surmount the relativity of these choices to those circumstances (and constraints) will not succeed in establishing any determinate and projectible ratio of substitution between them.

In less agonistic prose: no formula is possible, and decision theory will not be able to help us much. (That's what 'incommensurable' means, in this interpretation.) We will at best have to rest on a phenomenological account of action and choice—one attentive to the lived situation of

---

[5] See Ruth Chang, 'Incommensurability (and Incomparability)', in *The International Encyclopaedia of Ethics*, ed. Hugh Lafollette (forthcoming); accessed via <http://fas-philosophy.rutgers.edu/chang/Selected%20Publications.html> (28 February 2012).

[6] *Four Essays on Liberty* (Oxford: Oxford University Press, 1969), 49–54.

the choice—supported by 'philosophical analysis of the language' (starting with the distinction between needs and desires).

Joseph Raz offers a further objection to commensuration and comparison of values—arguably a special case objection, but one with large reverberations. He claims that incomparability can be a constitutive, almost a definitive, feature of certain goods. There are some situations, he observes, in which the judgement that two things are incommensurable has 'symbolic significance' for us—one partly determined by social conventions.[7] For example, the idea that one would not trade friendship, or the love of one's child or one's spouse, for any amount of money finds from most of us emphatic approval (and invitations to do otherwise meet with strong resistance, or indeed revulsion). Such judgements may well prove, upon close inspection, not to be absolute: there will be circumstances in which one might act, directly or (more often) indirectly, in such a way as to give the acquisition of money apparent priority over the claims of friendship or family. Raz concludes that 'Certain judgments about the non-comparability of certain options and certain attitudes to the exchangeability of options are *constitutive of* relations with friends, spouses, parents, etc. Only those who hold the view that friendship is neither better nor worse than money, but is simply not comparable to money or other commodities are capable of having friends' (352; my emphasis). So, with regard to the problem under discussion here, we might take the view that only those who hold that higher scholarship in the humanities is neither better nor worse than the pursuit of economic or commercial gain (is simply not comparable to such ends driven activity) are capable of producing humane scholarship.

Such objections to comparisons between some abstract values are, I suspect, likely to appeal to many scholars of the humanities as they contemplate the problem of securing public goods claims on behalf of their work. They are certainly implicit in much casual talk on the subject. But in the years since Wiggins's and Raz's arguments first came to attention, they have met with strong disagreement not only from decision theorists (who could be expected to dispute a fundamental assault on their bases) but also from other, broadly sympathetic, philosophers of value. One critical response is succinctly made by Ruth Chang when she notes that evaluative comparisons

---

[7] *The Morality of Freedom* (Oxford: Clarendon Press, 1986), 345–53 (349–50).

become much more sensible if we 'reject the assumption that evaluative comparisons are modeled on the relations among real numbers': once that error is out of the way, it becomes possible to think of one value as being not just greater than, less than, or equal to another, but 'on a par'—i.e. comparable.[8] (The nature of the comparison will, I take it, be descriptive in the first instance; economic interpretations of that comparison will, again, be secondary and will reflect the particular aims and constraints under which it takes place. Another kind of objection is well expressed by Elijah Millgram, who starts from the observation that we can all think of 'convincing examples of agents faced with considerations that do not contain within them the means of commensuration', but we nevertheless know that many people do regularly reach 'successful decisions' in such difficult circumstances for deliberation, and 'are subsequently prepared to pronounce on the relative importance of the considerations that entered into their decision'.[9] From this perspective, both Wiggins and Raz are, in different ways, mounting metaphysical objections, of an unhelpful purity, to value comparisons, requiring us (in the second case at least) to defer deliberative reasoning indefinitely. (Wiggins allows for case-by-case reasoning, but not for any general theory of such reasoning.)

Millgram's defence of practical reasoning is not only pragmatic, though it may sound like it in my summary: it also involves an appeal to 'eudaemonia', or the idea of the overall happiness of a life, in ways that reflect the fact that many of our values are 'bequeathed to us', without being unchallengeable 'dicta' (166). We may tell our children 'to do and value [certain] things that belong to our own picture of the well-lived life' (166), but we also expect them to form their own judgements, and quite possibly to change those judgements in the course of their lives—not least because their cultural experience, and the contexts in which their society deliberates about public goods, will be different from ours. At a higher level, Millgram's defence relies, indeed,

---

[8] Chang, 'Incommensurability (and Incomparability)', [7].

[9] 'Incommensurability and Practical Reasoning', in Ruth Chang (ed.), *Incommensurability, Incomparability, and Practical Reason* (Cambridge, Mass.: Harvard University Press, 1997), 151–69 (157). See also Douglas Maclean, 'The Ethics of Cost-Benefit Analysis: Incommensurable, Incompatible, and Incomparable Values', in Milton M. Carrow, Robert Paul Churchill, and Joseph J. Cordes (eds.), *Democracy, Social Values, and Public Policy* (Westport, Conn.: Praeger, 1998), 107–22 (111, 116).

on the idea of utility as a final arbiter between values, in a way that takes much (though not all) of the pressure off the idea of value conflict and allows for rational resolutions to situations of choice that (as described by Raz and Wiggins) might otherwise issue in a certain amount of disillusionment about the process of reasoning or, worse, despair about the possibility of reasoning at all.

The appeal to a framing idea about what makes for a fulfilling life seems likely to be disputed in the case of the value of the humanities. There is, indeed, good cause to observe that the implied analogy between how governments or societies reach decisions about allocating finite public resources, and how individuals prioritize different values and commitments that have importance for them, is helpful only up to a point. Beyond that point, we need rather to be able to draw on impersonal justifications that describe what goods we, collectively, think a complex society and culture should continue to support. On the other hand, as Bernard Williams observed at an early stage in the debate about pluralism and incommensurability, we will find ourselves in trouble, as a society, if the ways in which we 'express and encourage important values' 'drift too far' from our private sentiments and intuitions about values:

private understanding...can live with a good deal of 'intuition' and unresolved conflict[;] public order,...unless we are to give up the ethical ambition that it be answerable, can only live with less. At the same time, the public order, if it is to carry conviction, and also not to flatten human experience, has to find ways in which it can be adequately related to private sentiment, which remains more 'intuitive' and open to conflict than public rules can be.[10]

Not the least contribution the humanities can make to the public good is that (as this book has tried to show) they offer long considered and finely developed ways of thinking about what the nature of that relation should be.

I cannot go further than this here. To fabricate a hypothetical scenario in which the humanities' claim to public money would be tested against claims from the NHS, the army, and so forth would be spurious. In practice, in the UK, distributions at this level of comparison are decided largely on the basis of past allocations; the more relevant

---

[10] 'Conflicts of Values', in *Moral Luck: Philosophical Papers 1973–1980* (Cambridge: Cambridge University Press, 1981), 71–82 (82).

comparisons are between claims nearer in kind: say, doctoral research vs. public subsidy for the arts; or funding for certain humanities projects vs. others in the social sciences or sciences. These are, finally, matters for debate and judgement around a table with detailed and current contextual data at hand. In practice and in principle, what matters if the debate and the judgement are to command respect is that those participating have a sufficiently plural and internally refined or refinable understanding of the modes of justification and valuation that support each rival claimant for funding. If the taxonomy worked out here, and the refinements supplied in support of each claim, can make it easier to see what those supports are for the humanities, it will have done enough.

Bibliography

References to the *Oxford English Dictionary* are to *OED Online* (Oxford: Oxford University Press, 2012). <http://www.oed.com>.

References to the *New Dictionary of National Biography* are to *Oxford Dictionary of National Biography* (Oxford: Oxford University Press, 2004); online edn., January 2009 <http://www.oxforddnb.com>.

Abbott, Andrew. *Chaos of Disciplines* (Chicago: University of Chicago Press, 2001).

—— *The System of Professions: An Essay on the Division of Expert Labor* (Chicago: University of Chicago Press, 1988).

Acland, A. H. D. 'The Education of Co-Operators and Citizens', in *The Co-Operative Wholesale Society Ltd. Annual Diary 1885* (Manchester: Co-operative Wholesale Society, 1885).

Adamson, John William. *English Education, 1789–1902* (Cambridge: Cambridge University Press, 1930).

Amsler, Sarah. 'Beyond All Reason: Spaces of Hope in the Struggle for England's Universities', *Representations* 116 (Fall 2011), 62–87.

Anderson, Amanda. 'Character and Ideology: The Case of Cold War Liberalism', *New Literary History* 42/2 (2011), 209–29.

—— *The Way We Argue Now: A Study in the Cultures of Theory* (Princeton: Princeton University Press, 2006).

Arac, Jonathan. 'Peculiarities of (the) English in the Metanarrative(s) of Knowledge and Power', in Bruce Robbins (ed.), *Intellectuals: Aesthetics, Politics, Academics* (Minneapolis: University of Minnesota Press, 1990), 189–99.

Armstrong, Isobel. *The Radical Aesthetic* (Oxford: Blackwell Publishers, 2000).

Arnold, Matthew. *Culture and Anarchy, with Friendship's Garland and Some Literary Essays*, ed. R. H. Super, *The Complete Prose Works of Matthew Arnold* (hereafter *CPW*), v (Ann Arbor: University of Michigan Press, 1965).

—— *Democratic Education*, ed. R. H. Super, *CPW* ii (Ann Arbor: University of Michigan Press, 1962).

—— *Lectures and Essays in Criticism*, ed. R. H. Super, *CPW* iii (Ann Arbor: University of Michigan Press, 1962).

—— *The Letters of Matthew Arnold*, ed. Cecil Y. Lang, 6 vols. (Charlottesville, Va.: University Press of Virginia, 1996–2001).

—— 'Literature and Science', in *Philistinism in England and America, CPW* x, ed. R. H. Super (Ann Arbor: University of Michigan Press, 1974), 53–73.

—— *The Note-Books of Matthew Arnold*, ed. Howard Foster Lowry, Karl Young, and Waldo Hilary Dunn (Oxford: Oxford University Press, 1952).

—— *Philistinism in England and America*, ed. R. H. Super, *CPW* x (Ann Arbor: University of Michigan Press, 1974).

—— *Schools and Universities on the Continent*, *CPW* iv, ed. R. H. Super (Ann Arbor: University of Michigan Press, 1964).

Arts Council England. *Achieving Great Art for Everyone: A Strategic Framework for the Arts* (London: Arts Council England, 2011).

Arts and Humanities Research Council (AHRC). 'Measuring Cultural Value'. <http://www.ahrc.ac.uk/Funding-Opportunities/Documents/DCM-Splacementnotes.pdf>.

Baier, Annette. 'Some Thoughts on the Way We Moral Philosophers Live Now', *Monist* 67/4 (1984), 490–7.

Baldick, Chris. *The Social Mission of English Criticism, 1848–1932* (Oxford: Clarendon Press, 1983).

Bate, Jonathan. 'The Costly New Idea of a University', *Standpoint Magazine* December 2010. <http://www.standpointmag.co.uk/node/3577/full>.

—— (ed.). *The Public Value of the Humanities* (London: Bloomsbury, 2011).

Beckerman, Wilfred. *Economics as Applied Ethics: Value Judgements in Welfare Economics* (London: Palgrave Macmillan, 2010).

Becher, Tony. 'The Significance of Disciplinary Differences', *Studies in Higher Education* 19/2 (1994), 151–61.

—— and Paul Trowler, *Academic Tribes*, 2nd edn (Milton Keynes: Society for Research into Higher Education & Open University Press, 2001).

Beer, Gillian. *Darwin's Plots: Evolutionary Narrative in Darwin, George Eliot and Nineteenth-Century Fiction* (London: Routledge and Kegan Paul, 1983).

Bentham, Jeremy. *Introduction to the Principles of Morals and Legislation* (1789). An authoritative edition by J. H. Burns and H. L. A. Hart, with a new introduction by F. Rosen and an interpretative essay by H. L. A. Hart (Oxford: Clarendon Press, 1996).

—— *The Rationale of Reward* (London: Robert Heward, 1830).

Berlin, Isaiah. *Concepts and Categories*, ed. Henry Hardy, with an introduction by Bernard Williams (London: Hogarth Press, 1978).

—— *Four Essays on Liberty* (Oxford: Oxford University Press, 1969).

Bérubé, Michael. Blog. <http://www.michaelberube.com>.

—— 'Breaking News: Humanities in Decline! Film at 11', <http://crookedtimber.org/2010/11/16/breaking-news-humanities-in-decline-film-at-11/>.

—— *Employment of English: Theory, Jobs, and the Future of Literary Studies* (New York: New York University Press, 1996).

—— *Rhetorical Occasions: Essays on Humans and the Humanities* (Chapel Hill, NC: University of North Carolina Press, 2006).

Birch, Dinah. *Our Victorian Education* (Oxford: Blackwell, 2008).

'Blair's University Targets Spelt Out', BBC News, 30 January 2002, <http://news.bbc.co.uk/1/hi/education/1789500.stm>.

Bledstein, Burton. *The Culture of Professionalism: The Middle Class and the Development of Higher Education in America* (New York: W. W. Norton & Co. Inc., 1976).

Bowie, Andrew. *Aesthetics and Subjectivity: From Kant to Nietzsche* (Manchester: Manchester University Press, 1990).

——'Confessions of a "New Aesthete": A Response to the "New Philistines"', *New Left Review* 1/225 (1997), 105–26.

Brenkman, John, Elizabeth Lloyd, and David Albert (eds.). *The Sokal Hoax: The Sham that Shook the Academy* (Lincoln, Nebr.: University of Nebraska Press, 2000).

British Academy. *'That Full Complement of Riches': The Contributions of the Arts, Humanities and Social Sciences to the Nation's Wealth* (London: The British Academy, 2004).

Brown, Wendy. 'Neoliberalism and the End of Liberal Democracy', in *Edgework* (Princeton: Princeton University Press, 2005), 37–60.

[Browning, Oscar.] Review of *Schools and Universities on the Continent*, *Quarterly Review* 125 (October 1868), 473–90.

Burnyeat, M. F. 'What was the "Common Arrangement"? An Inquiry into John Stuart Mill's Boyhood Reading of Plato', *Utilitas* 13/1 (2001), 1–32.

Burrow, John. 'The English Tradition of Liberal Education' (review of Sheldon Rothblatt, *Tradition and Change in English Liberal Education* (1976)), *History of Education Quarterly* 20/2 (1980), 247–53.

Butler, Judith. 'Critique, Dissent, Disciplinarity', *Critical Inquiry* 35 (2009), 773–95.

——'What is Critique? An Essay on Foucault's Virtue', in David Ingram (ed.), *The Political: Readings in Continental Philosophy* (London: Basil Blackwell, 2002), 212–28.

Cameron, Deborah. 'Feminist Linguistic Theories', in Stevie Jackson and Jackie Jones (eds.), *Contemporary Feminist Theories* (Edinburgh: Edinburgh University Press, 1998), 147–61.

Castle, Terry. *The Professor and Other Writings* (New York: HarperCollins, 2011).

Castree, Noel. 'Neoliberal Environments: A Framework for Analysis', *Manchester Papers in Political Economy*, Working Paper no. 04/07, 10 December 2007.

Champlin, T. S. 'Doing Something for its Own Sake', *Philosophy* 63/239 (1987), 31–47.

Chang, Ruth. 'Incommensurability (and Incomparability)', in *The International Encyclopaedia of Ethics*, ed. Hugh Lafollette (forthcoming); accessed via <http://fas-philosophy.rutgers.edu/chang/Selected%20Publications.html>, 28 February 2012.

Chace, William M. 'The Decline of the English Department: How It Happened and What Could Be Done to Reverse It', <http://www.theamericanscholar.org/the-decline-of-the-english-department/>.

Christie, John and Sally Shuttleworth (eds.). *Nature Transfigured: Science and Literature, 1700–1900* (Manchester: Manchester University Press, 1989).

Coleman, Stephen. 'William Morris and "Education towards Revolution": "Making Socialists" versus "Putting them in their Place" ', <http://www.morrissociety.org/JWMS/AU94.11.1.Coleman.pdf>.

Coleridge, Samuel Taylor. *Poetical Works*, 3 vols. (London: Pickering, 1828).

—— *Sibylline Leaves* (London: Rest Fenner, 1817).

Collini, Stefan. 'Against Prodspeak: "Research" in the Humanities', in *English Pasts: Essays in History and Culture* (Oxford: Oxford University Press, 1999), 233–51.

—— *Arnold* (Oxford: Oxford University Press, 1988).

—— 'Impact on the Humanities', *Times Literary Supplement* 13 November 2009, 18–19.

—— *What Are Universities For?* (London: Penguin, 2012).

Commager, Steele. *The Odes of Horace: A Critical Study*, foreword by David Armstrong (London: University of Oklahoma Press, 1995).

Connell, W. F. *The Educational Thought and Influence of Matthew Arnold* (London: Routledge and Kegan Paul, 1950), reissued with an introduction by Sir Fred Clarke (1990).

Corbyn, Zoë. 'Thousands of Academics Call for Impact to Be Axed', *Times Higher Education Supplement* 3 December 2009. <http://www.timeshighereducation.co.uk/story.asp?storycode=409395>.

Council for Science and Technology, *Imagination and Understanding: A Report on the Arts and Humanities in Relation to Science and Technology* (July 2001). <http://www.bis.gov.uk/assets/cst/docs/files/whats-new/01-1051-imagination-understanding>.

Court, Franklin E. *Institutionalizing English Literature: The Culture and Politics of Literary Study, 1750–1900* (Stanford, Calif.: Stanford University Press, 1992).

Crisp, Roger. *Routledge Philosophy Guidebook to Mill on Utilitarianism* (London: Routledge, 1997).

'Crooked Timber' [blog]. <http://crookedtimber.org/>.

Culler, Jonathan. 'In Need of a Name: A Response to Geoffrey Harpham', *New Literary History* 36/1 (2005), 37–42.

Dahl, Robert. *Democracy and its Critics* (New Haven: Yale University Press, 1998).

Dames, Nicholas. 'Why Bother?', *n + 1*, issue 11, *Dual Power* (Spring 2011). <http://nplusonemag.com/why-bother>.

Delbanco, Andrew. 'The Decline and Fall of English Studies', *New York Review of Books* 4 November 1999. <http://www.nybooks.com/articles/archives/1999/nov/04/the-decline-and-fall-of-literature/>.

Derrida, Jacques. 'In Praise of Philosophy', interview by *Libération*, in *Eyes of the University: Right to Philosophy 2*, trans. Jan Plug et al. (Stanford, Calif.: Stanford University Press, 2004).

—— 'Mochlos, or The Conflict of the Faculties', in *Eyes of the University: Right to Philosophy 2*, trans. Jan Plug et al. (Stanford, Calif.: Stanford University Press, 2004), 83–112.

Derrida, Jacques. *On the Name*, ed. Thomas Dutoit, trans. David Wood, John P. Leavey Jr, and Ian McLeod (Stanford, Calif: Stanford University Press, 1995).

——'The Right to Philosophy from the Cosmopolitan Point of View (the Example an International Institution)', in *Negotiations: Interventions and Interviews, 1971–2001*, ed., trans., and with an introduction by Elizabeth Rottenberg (Stanford, Calif.: Stanford University Press, 2002), 329–42.

Dewey, John. *Theory of Valuation*, in Dewey, *The Later Works, 1925–1953*, Collected Works of John Dewey, vol. xiii: 1938–1939, *Experience and Education, Freedom and Culture, Theory of Valuation, and Essays*, ed. Jo Ann Boydston, with an introduction by Steven M. Cahn (Carbondale, Ill.: Southern Illinois University Press, 1988), 189–251.

Docherty, Thomas. *For the University: Democracy and the Future of the Institution* (London: Bloomsbury Academic, 2011).

Dorsey, Dale. 'Can Instrumental Value be Intrinsic?', *Pacific Philosophical Quarterly* 93 (2012), 137–57.

Eagleton, Terry. 'Ideology and Literary Form', *New Left Review* 1/90 (1975), <http://www.newleftreview.org/?page=artivle&view=403>.

—— *The Ideology of the Aesthetic* (Oxford: Basil Blackwell, 1990).

Edgerton, David. 'C. P. Snow as Anti-Historian of British Science: Revisiting the Technocratic Moment, 1959–1964', *History of Science* 43 (2005), 187–208.

Eliot, T. S. *Selected Essays*, 3rd enlarged edn. (London: Faber and Faber Ltd, 1951).

Feldman, Fred. *What Is This Thing Called Happiness?* (Oxford: Oxford University Press, 2007).

Fish, Stanley Eugene. *Doing What Comes Naturally: Change, Rhetoric and the Practice of Theory in Literary and Legal Studies* (Oxford: Clarendon Press, 1989).

Fletcher, Guy. 'Mill, Moore, and Intrinsic Value', *Social Theory and Practice* 34/4 (2008), 517–32.

——Review of Ben Eggleston, Dale Miller, and David Weinstein (eds.), *John Stuart Mill and the Art of Life*, *Notre Dame Philosophical Reviews* (16 April 2011), <http://ndpr.nd.edu/review.cfm?id=23469>.

Flyvbjerg, Bent. *Making Social Science Matter: Why Social Inquiry Fails and How it Can Succeed Again* (Cambridge: Cambridge University Press, 2001).

Foucault, Michel. '*Qu'est ce que la critique? Critique et* Aufklärung', *Bulletin de la Société française de philosophie* 84/2 (1990), 35–63.

——'What is Critique?', in David Ingram (ed.), *The Political: Readings in Continental Philosophy* (London: Basil Blackwell, 2002), 191–211.

Gagnier, Regenia. 'Operationalizing Hope: The Neoliberalization of British Universities in Historico-Philosophical Perspective', forthcoming in *Occasion: Interdisciplinary Studies in the Humanities* 5 (2013) <http://arcade.stanford.edu/journals/occasion/>.

Goldman, Lawrence. 'Education as Politics: University Adult Education in England since 1870', *Oxford Review of Education* 25/1–2 (1999), 89–101.

Goldsworth, Amnon. 'Bentham's Concept of Pleasure: Its Relation to Fictitious Terms', *Ethics* 82/4 (1972), 334–43.

Gosling, J. C. B. and C. C. W. Taylor, *The Greeks on Pleasure* (Oxford: Clarendon Press, 1982).

Grote, John. *An Examination of Utilitarian Philosophy*, ed. Joseph Bickersteth Mayor (London: Bell and Daldy, 1870).

Guillory, John. 'Critical Response II: The Name of Science, the Name of Politics', *Critical Inquiry* 29/3 (2003), 526–41.

—— *Cultural Capital: The Problem of Literary Canon Formation* (Chicago: University of Chicago Press, 1993).

——'Preprofessionalism: What Graduate Students Want', *Profession* (1996), 91–9.

——'The Sokal Affair and the History of Criticism', *Critical Inquiry* 28/2 (2002), 470–508.

——'The System of Graduate Education', *PMLA* 11 (2000), 1154–63.

Halévy, Élie. *The Growth of Philosophic Radicalism*, trans. Mary Morris (1928), new edn. with preface by John Plamenatz (London: Faber, 1972).

Harpham, Geoffrey Galt. 'Beneath and Beyond the "Crisis in the Humanities"', *New Literary History* 36/1 (2005), 21–36.

—— *The Humanities and the Dream of America* (Chicago: University of Chicago Press, 2011).

Harvard Committee on the Objectives of a General Education in a Free Society. *General Education in a Free Society*, with an introduction by James Bryant Conant (Cambridge, Mass.: Harvard University Press, 1945).

Higher Education Statistics Agency, Statistical First Release 130, 26 January 2009, <http://www.hesa.ac.uk/dox/pressOffice/sfr130/sfr130r_table7.pdf>.

Hill, Geoffrey. *Collected Critical Writings*, ed. Kenneth Haynes (Oxford: Oxford University Press, 2008).

——'Confessio Amantis', *The Record* (Keble College Oxford, 2009), 45–52, <http://www.keble.ox.ac.uk/alumni/publications-2/Record09.pdf>.

——'Strongholds of the Imagination' (interview with Alexandra Bell, Rebecca Rosen, and Edmund White), *The Oxonian Review* 9/4 8 May 2009, <http://www.oxonianreview.org/wp/geoffrey-hill/>.

—— *A Treatise of Civil Power* (London: Penguin, 2007).

——Video interview with *The Economist*, <http://www.economist.com/blogs/prospero/2011/12/economist-books-year-festival-geoffrey-hill?fsrc=rss>.

Hirsch, E. D., Jr. 'Rorty and the Priority of Democracy to Philosophy', *New Literary History* 39/1 (2008), 35–52.

Holub, Miroslav. 'Rampage, or Science in Poetry', in Robert Crawford (ed.), *Contemporary Poetry and Contemporary Science* (Oxford: Oxford University Press, 2006), 11–24.

Hollinger, David A. 'Science as a Weapon in *Kulturkämpfe* in the United States during and after World War II', *Isis* 86 (1995), 440–54.

Honan, Park. *Matthew Arnold: A Life* (London: Weidenfeld and Nicolson, 1981).

Howell, James. *Instructions for Forrein Travell* (London, 1642).

Hume, David. 'Of the Standard of Taste', in Hume, *Essays Moral, Political, and Literary*, ed. Eugene F. Miller, rev. edn. (Indianapolis: Liberty Classics, 1987).

Hunter, Ian. 'Literary Theory in Civil Life', *South Atlantic Quarterly* 95/4 (1996), 1099–134.

Hurka, Thomas. 'Two Kinds of Organic Unity', *Journal of Ethics* 2 (1998), 299–320.

Huxley, Thomas Henry. 'Science and Culture', in *Science and Education: Essays* (London: Macmillan and Co., 1893), 134–59.

Jameson, Fredric. *Late Marxism: Adorno, or, the Persistence of the Dialectic* (London: Verso, 1990).

Jones, H. S. *Intellect and Character in Victorian England: Mark Pattison and the Invention of the Don* (Cambridge: Cambridge University Press, 2007).

Jordanova, L. J. (ed.). *Languages of Nature: Critical Essays on Science and Literature* (New Brunswick, NJ: Rutgers University Press, 1986).

Kagan, Jerome. *The Three Cultures: Natural Sciences, Social Sciences, and the Humanities in the 21st Century* (Cambridge: Cambridge University Press 2009).

Kagan, Shelly. 'Rethinking Intrinsic Value', *Journal of Ethics* 2 (1998), 277–97.

Kaldor, Mary. 'Democracy and Globalisation', Working paper series, WP 03/2008. Centre for the Study of Global Governance, London School of Economics and Political Science, London. <http://www.lse.ac.uk/Depts/global/PDFs/0708ch2mkaldor.pdf>.

Kant, Immanuel. *Groundwork of the Metaphysics of Morals*, ed. Mary Gregor, introduction by Christine M. Korsgaard, Cambridge Texts in the History of Philosophy (Cambridge: Cambridge University Press, 1997).

Keat, Russell. 'Market Boundaries and Human Goods', in John Haldane (ed.), *Philosophy and Public Affairs* (Cambridge: Cambridge University Press, 2000), 23–36.

Kermode, Frank. 'Changing Epochs', in Alvin Kernan (ed.), *What's Happened to the Humanities?* (Princeton: Princeton University Press, 1997), 162–78.

Kernan, Alvin (ed.), *What's Happened to the Humanities?* (Princeton: Princeton University Press, 1997).

Korsgaard, Christine M. 'Two Distinctions in Goodness', *Philosophical Review* 92/2 (1983), 169–95.

—— with G. A. Cohen, Raymond Guess, Thomas Nagel, and Bernard Williams. *The Sources of Normativity*, ed. Onora O'Neill (Cambridge: Cambridge University Press, 1996).

Kronman, Anthony. *Education's End: Why our Colleges and Universities Have Given Up on the Meaning of Life* (New Haven: Yale University Press, 2004).

Leavis, F. R. 'Two Cultures? The Significance of C. P. Snow', *Spectator* 9 March 1962, rpt as 'Two Cultures? The Significance of Lord Snow', in his *Nor Shall my Sword: Discourses on Pluralism, Compassion and Social Hope* (London: Chatto and Windus, 1972), 41–74.

—— *Thought, Words and Creativity: Art and Thought in Lawrence* (London: Chatto and Windus, 1976).

Leighton, Angela. *On Form: Poetry, Aestheticism, and the Legacy of a Word* (Oxford: Oxford University Press, 2007).

Lepenies, Wolf. *Die drei Kulturen: Soziologie zwischen Literatur und Wissenschaft* (1985), trans. R. J. Hollingdale, *Between Literature and Science: The Rise of Sociology* (Cambridge: Cambridge University Press, 1988).

Levidow, Les. 'Marketizing Higher Education: Neoliberal Strategies and Counter-Strategies', in Kevin Robins and Frank Webster (eds.), *The Virtual University? Knowledge, Markets, and Management* (Oxford: Oxford University Press, 2002), 227–48.

Levine, George (ed.). *One Culture: Essays in Science and Literature* (Madison: University of Wisconsin Press, 1987).

McDonald, Peter v. Peter Atkins. 'Poetry is Beautiful, but Science is What Matters?'<http://www.ox.ac.uk/oxford_debates/past_debates/hilary_2009_poetry_and_science/>.

McKie, Michael. 'In Defence of Poetry', (review of David-Antoine Williams, *Defending Poetry* (2010)), *Essays in Criticism* 61/4 (2011), 421–31.

Maclean, Douglas. 'The Ethics of Cost-Benefit Analysis: Incommensurable, Incompatible, and Incomparable Values', in Milton M. Carrow, Robert Paul Churchill, and Joseph J. Cordes (eds.), *Democracy, Social Values, and Public Policy* (Westport, Conn.: Praeger, 1998), 107–22.

Mahmood, Saba. *Politics of Piety* (Princeton: Princeton University Press, 2004).

Marmontel, Jean-François. *Memoirs of Marmontel*, trans. anon., 4 vols. (London: Longman, Hurst, Rees, and Orme, 1805).

Martin, Randy. 'Taking an Administrative Turn: Derivative Logics for a Recharged Humanities', *Representations* 116/1, Special issue on The Humanities and the Crisis of the Public University (2011), 156–76.

Mazlish, Bruce. *James and John Stuart Mill: Father and Son in the Nineteenth Century* (New York: Basic Books, Inc., 1975).

—— 'The Three and a Half Cultures', *Leonardo* 18/4 (1985), 233–6.

Menand, Louis. *The Marketplace of Ideas: Reform and Resistance in the American University* (New York: W. W. Norton, 2010).

Mill, J. S. *Autobiography and Literary Essays*, ed. John M. Robson and Jack Stillinger, in *Collected Works* 33 vols., ed. John M. Robson (Toronto: University of Toronto Press, London: Routledge and Kegan Paul, 1963–91) (hereafter *CW*), i (Toronto: University of Toronto Press, 1981).

—— 'Bentham' (1838), in *CW* x, *Essays on Ethics, Religion and Society*, ed. John M. Robson, introduction by F. E. L. Priestley, *CW* x (Toronto: University of Toronto Press, 1985).

Mill, J. S. *Considerations on Representative Government* (1861), in *Essays on Politics and Society* ii, *CW* xix (Toronto: University of Toronto Press, 1977).

—— 'Inaugural Address Delivered to the University of St. Andrews 1867', in *Essays on Equality, Law, and Education*, *CW* xxi, introduction by Stefan Collini (Toronto: University of Toronto Press, 1981), 215–57.

—— *The Later Letters of John Stuart Mill, 1849–1873*, ed. Francis E. Mineka and Dwight N. Lindley, 4 vols., *CW* xiv–xvii (Toronto: University of Toronto Press, 1972).

—— *Notes on Some of the More Popular Dialogues of Plato* (1834–5), in *Essays on Philosophy and the Classics*, *CW* xi (Toronto: University of Toronto Press, 1978).

—— *A System of Logic Ratiocinative and Inductive: Being a Connected View of the Principles of Evidence and the Methods of Investigation*, 2 vols., ed. John M. Robson, introduction by R. F. McRae, *CW* vii–viii (Toronto: University of Toronto Press, 1973–4).

—— *Utilitarianism*, with an introductory essay by D. P. Dryer, in Mill, *Essays on Ethics, Religion and Society*, ed. John M. Robson, introduction by F. E. L. Priestley, *CW* x (Toronto: University of Toronto Press, 1985).

Mill, James. *Analysis of the Phenomena of the Human Mind* (1829), ed. John Stuart Mill (London: Longmans, 1869).

Miller, Dale E. *J. S Mill: Moral, Social and Political Thought* (Cambridge: Polity Press, 2010).

Millgram, Elijah. 'Incommensurability and Practical Reasoning', in Ruth Chang (ed.), *Incommensurability, Incomparability, and Practical Reason* (Cambridge, Mass.: Harvard University Press, 1997), 151–69.

—— 'Mill's Incubus', in Ben Eggleston, Dale Miller, and David Weinstein (eds.), *John Stuart Mill and the Art of Life* (Oxford: Oxford University Press, 2010), 169–91.

Milner, Andrew. *Literature, Culture and Society* (London: UCL Press, 1996).

Mulhern, Francis. *Culture/Metaculture* (London: Routledge, 2000).

—— 'Humanities and University Corporatism', paper delivered at the 'Why Humanities?' conference, Birkbeck College, University of London, 5 November 10; podcast at <http://backdoorbroadcasting.net/2010/11/francis-mulhern-humanities-and-university-corporatism/>.

Nairn, Tom. 'Make for the Boondocks', *London Review of Books* 27/9 5 May 2005, <http://www.lrb.co.uk/v27/no9/tom-nairn/make-for-the-boondocks>.

Newfield, Christopher. 'Critical Response I: The Value of Nonscience', *Critical Inquiry* 29/3 (2003), 508–25.

—— *Unmaking the Public University: The Forty Year Assault on the Middle Class* (Cambridge, Mass.: Harvard University Press, 2008).

Newman, John Henry. *The Idea of a University*, ed. I. T. Ker (Oxford: Clarendon Press, 1976).

Nussbaum, Martha. 'Being Human', *New Statesman* 1 June 2010. <http://www.newstatesman.com/ideas/2010/05/liberal-education-arts-mill>.

—— *Not for Profit: Why Democracy Needs the Humanities* (Princeton: Princeton University Press, 2010).

—— *Upheavals of Thought: The Intelligence of Emotions* (Chicago: University of Chicago Press, 2001).

O'Gorman, Francis. 'Ruskin's Science of the 1870s: Science, Education, and the Nation', in Dinah Birch (ed.), *Ruskin and the Dawn of the Modern* (Oxford: Oxford University Press, 1999), 35–55.

OECD. *Education at a Glance: OECD Indicators* (Paris: OECD, 2011).

—— *Improving Health and Social Cohesion through Education* (Paris: OECD, 2010).

—— *Social Capital, Human Capital and Health: What is the Evidence?* (Paris: OECD, 2010).

—— *Understanding the Social Outcomes of Learning* (Paris: OECD, 2007).

Ortolano, Guy. 'The Literature and the Science of "Two Cultures" Historiography', *Studies in History and Philosophy of Science* 39 (2008), 143–50.

Packe, Michael St John. *The Life of John Stuart Mill*, with a preface by F. A. Hayek (London: Secker and Warburg, 1954).

Parfit, Derek. *On What Matters*, ed. and introd. Samuel Scheffler, 2 vols. (Oxford: Oxford University Press, 2011).

Plato. *The Dialogues of Plato*, trans. with analyses and introduction by Benjamin Jowett (Oxford: Clarendon Press, 1875).

Rabinowicz, Wlodek and Toni Rønnow-Rasmussen. 'A Distinction in Value: Intrinsic and For its Own Sake', *Proceedings of the Aristotelian Society* ns 100 (2000), 33–51.

Raz, Joseph. *The Morality of Freedom* (Oxford: Clarendon Press, 1986).

Readings, Bill. *The University in Ruins* (Cambridge, Mass.: Harvard University Press, 1996).

Ree, J. 'Socialism and the Educated Working Class', in C. Levy (ed.), *Socialism and the Intelligentsia 1880–1914* (London, Routledge & Kegan Paul, 1985), 211–18.

Reeves, Richard. *John Stuart Mill: Victorian Firebrand* (London: Atlantic Books, 2007).

Riley, Jonathan. 'Interpreting Mill's Qualitative Hedonism', *Philosophical Quarterly* 53/212 (2003), 410–18.

Ringer, Fritz. *The Decline of the German Mandarins: The German Academic Community, 1890–1933* (1969; rpt Hanover, NH: University Press of New England, 1990).

Robbins, Bruce. 'Cut to Controversy', *Chronicle of Higher Education* 6 May 2012, <http://chronicle.com/article/Cut-to-Controversy/131765/>.

—— 'Less Disciplinary than Thou: Criticism and the Conflict of the Faculties', *Minnesota Review* ns 45–6 (1995–6), <www.theminnesotareview.org/journal/ns45/robbins.htm>.

—— *Secular Vocations: Intellectuals, Professionalism, Culture* (London: Verso, 1993).

Robinson, Peter. 'Contemporary Poetry and Value', in Robinson (ed.), *The Oxford Handbook of Contemporary British and Irish Poetry* (Oxford: Oxford University Press, forthcoming 2013).

Roos, David A. 'Matthew Arnold and Thomas Henry Huxley: Two Speeches at the Royal Academy, 1881 and 1883', *Modern Philology* 74/3 (1977), 316–24.

Rorty, Richard. 'The Priority of Democracy to Philosophy', in *The Rorty Reader*, ed. Christopher J. Voparil and Richard Bernstein (Chichester: Wiley-Blackwell, 2010), 239–58.

——'Reply to Andrew Ross', *Dissent* (Spring 1992), 263–7.

——'A Talent for Bricolage: An Interview with Richard Rorty', Interviewer Joshua Knobe, *The Dualist: Undergraduate Magazine* 2 (1995), 56–71.

—— *Truth and Progress* (Cambridge: Cambridge University Press, 1998).

Rothblatt, Sheldon. 'The Limbs of Osiris: Liberal Education in the English-Speaking World', in Rothblatt and Björn Wittrock (eds.), *The European and American University since 1800: Historical and Sociological Essays* (Cambridge: Cambridge University Press, 1993), 19–73.

—— *The Modern University and its Discontents: The Fate of Newman's Legacies in Britain and America* (Cambridge: Cambridge University Press, 1997).

—— *The Revolution of the Dons: Cambridge and Society in Victorian England* (Cambridge: Cambridge University Press, 1968).

—— *Tradition and Change in English Liberal Education: An Essay in History and Culture* (London: Faber and Faber, 1976).

Ruskin, John. *The Works of John Ruskin*, ed. E. T. Cook and Alexander Wedderburn, 39 vols. (London: George Allen, 1903–12), xi. 258–63.

Ryan, Alan. *Liberal Anxieties and Liberal Education* (New York: Hill and Wang, 1998).

——Introduction to J. S. Mill and Jeremy Bentham, *Utilitarianism and Other Essays* (London: Penguin, 1987).

Said, Edward W. *Humanism and Democratic Criticism* (New York: Columbia University Press, 2004).

Sandel, Michael J. *What Money Can't Buy: The Moral Limits of Markets* (New York: Farrar, Straus, and Giroux, 2012).

Scarry, Elaine. *On Beauty and Being Just* (Princeton: Princeton University Press, 1999).

Schmidt-Petri, Christoph. 'Mill on Quality and Quantity', *Philosophical Quarterly* 53 (2003), 102–4.

Schofield, Malcolm. 'Plato', in E. Craig (gen. ed.), *Routledge Encyclopedia of Philosophy Online*, version 2.0 <http://www.rep.routledge.com/article/A088SECT17>.

—— *Plato: Political Philosophy* (Oxford: Oxford University Press, 2006).

Scott, Peter. 'What Kind of University?', *Oxford Magazine* 320 (2nd week, Hilary Term, 2012), 5–7.

Sedgwick, Eve Kosofsky. 'Paranoid Reading and Reparative Reading; or, You're So Paranoid, You Probably Think this Introduction Is about You', in Sedgwick and Adam Frank, *Touching Feeling: Affect, Pedagogy, Performativity* (Durham, NC: Duke University Press, 2003), 123–52.

Small, Helen. 'Caprice: On Aesthetic Subjectivism', in Ronan McDonald (ed.), *The Values of Literary Studies* (Cambridge: Cambridge University Press, forthcoming).

——'The Function of Antagonism: Miroslav Holub and Roald Hoffmann', in John Holmes (ed.), *Science in Modern Poetry: New Directions* (Liverpool: Liverpool University Press, 2012), 19–37.

—— *The Long Life* (Oxford: Oxford University Press, 2007).

Smith, Adam. *An Inquiry into the Nature and Causes of the Wealth of Nations*, gen. eds. R. H. Campbell and A. S. Skinner, textual editor W. B. Todd, 2 vols. (Oxford: Clarendon Press, 1976).

Smith, Barbara Hernstein. *Contingencies of Value: Alternative Perspectives for Critical Theory* (Cambridge, Mass.: Harvard University Press, 1988).

Snow, C. P. *The Two Cultures*, introduction by Stefan Collini (Cambridge: Cambridge University Press, 1993).

Soper, Kate. Review of Terry Eagleton, *Ideology of the Aesthetic*, *New Left Review* 1/192 (March–April 1992), 120–32.

Southern, R. W. 'From Schools to University', in *The History of the University of Oxford*, gen. ed. T. H. Aston, vol. i: *The Early Oxford Schools*, ed. J. I. Catto (Oxford: Clarendon Press, 1984), 1–36.

Sparrow, John. *Mark Pattison and the Idea of a University* (London: Cambridge University Press, 1967).

Spivak, Gayatri Chakravorty. 'Speaking for the Humanities', *Occasion: Interdisciplinary Studies in the Humanities* 1/1 (15 October 2009), <http://occasion.stanford.edu/node/19>.

Stewart, Susan. *Poetry and the Fate of the Senses* (Chicago: Chicago University Press, 2002).

Tate, Rosemary. 'The Aesthetics of Sugar: Concepts of Sweetness in the Nineteenth Century' (Oxford D.Phil. thesis, University of Oxford, 2011).

Trevelyan, George Otto. *The Life and Letters of Lord Macaulay*, 2 vols. (London: Longmans, Green, and Co., 1876).

Trilling, Lionel. 'Science, Literature, and Culture: A Comment on the Leavis–Snow Controversy', *Commentary* (1962), reprinted in his *Beyond Culture: Essays on Literature and Learning* (New York: Viking Press, 1965), 133–58.

—— *Matthew Arnold* (London: George Allen and Unwin Ltd, 1939).

Turner, David. 'Call for Review of 50% Target', *Financial Times* 30 March 2010. <http://www.ft.com/cms/s/0/d5e1bfc8-3b3a-11df-a1e7-00144feabdc0.html#axzz1E2rdtrG9>.

US Department of Commerce, *United States Census* (October 2009). Table 1, 'Enrollment Status of the Population 3 Years Old and Over, by Sex, Age,

Race...', <http://www.census.gov/population/www/socdemo/school/cps2009.html>.

Warner, Michael. 'Uncritical Reading', in Jane Gallop (ed.), *Polemic: Critical or Uncritical* (London: Routledge, 2004), 13–38.

Warner, Rex. *The Professor* (London: Penguin Books, 1945).

Wiggins, David. *Needs, Values, Truth: Essays in the Philosophy of Value*, 3rd edn. (Oxford: Clarendon Press, 1998).

Willetts, David. 'The Arts, Humanities and Social Sciences in the Modern University', *British Academy Review*, issue 17 (March 2011), 54–8.

Williams, Bernard. 'Conflicts of Values', in *Moral Luck: Philosophical Papers 1973–1980* (Cambridge: Cambridge University Press, 1981), 71–82.

Williams, David-Antoine. *Defending Poetry: Art and Ethics in Joseph Brodsky, Seamus Heaney, and Geoffrey Hill* (Oxford: Oxford University Press, 2010).

Wilson, Fred. 'Mill on Psychology and the Moral Senses', in John Skorupski (ed.), *The Cambridge Companion to Mill* (Cambridge: Cambridge University Press, 1998), 203–54.

Young, Robert J. C. 'The Idea of a Chrestomathic University' (1992), in *Torn Halves: Political Conflict in Literary and Cultural Theory* (Manchester: Manchester University Press, 1996), 290–351.

Young, Robert M. *Darwin's Metaphor: Does Nature Select?* (San Jose, Calif.: San Jose College, 1971).

Zhang, Donghui. '*Tongshi* Education Reform in a Chinese University: Knowledge, Values, and Organizational Changes', *Comparative Education Review* 56/3 (2012), 394–420.

Index

Made in the USA
Columbia, SC
03 June 2021